FRANCIS JOSEPH

PROFILES IN POWER
General Editor: Keith Robbins

ELIZABETH I
Christopher Haigh

RICHELIEU
R. J. Knecht

GUSTAVUS ADOLPHUS (2nd Edn)
Michael Roberts

OLIVER CROMWELL
Barry Coward

PETER THE GREAT (2nd Edn)
M. S. Anderson

JOSEPH II
T. C. W. Blanning

ALEXANDER I
Janet M. Hartley

DISRAELI
Ian Machin

JUÁREZ
Brian Hamnett

CAVOUR
Harry Hearder

NAPOLEON III
James McMillan

FRANCIS JOSEPH
Steven Beller

ATATÜRK
A. L. Macfie

LLOYD GEORGE
Martin Pugh

HITLER
Ian Kershaw

CHURCHILL
Keith Robbins

NASSER
Peter Woodward

DE GAULLE
Andrew Shennan

FRANCO
Sheelagh Ellwood

MACMILLAN
John Turner

CASTRO (2nd Edn)
Sebastian Balfour

FRANCIS JOSEPH

Steven Beller

LONGMAN
London and New York

Addison Wesley Longman
Edinburgh Gate
Harlow, Essex CM20 2JE, England
and Associated Companies throughout the world.

*Published in the United States of America
by Addison Wesley Longman Publishing Inc., New York*

First published 1996

ISBN 0 582 060907 CSD
ISBN 0 582 060893 PPR

British Library Cataloguing in Publication Data

A catalogue record for this book is available from the British Library

Library of Congress Cataloging-in-Publication Data

Beller, Steven, 1958–
    Francis Joseph / Steven Beller.
        p. cm. — (Profiles in power)
    Includes bibliographical references and index.
    ISBN 0–582–06090–7 (csd). — ISBN 0–582–06089–3 (ppr)
    1. Franz Joseph I, Emperor of Austria, 1830–1916. 2. Austria–
–Kings and rulers—Biography. 3. Austria—History—Francis Joseph,
1848–1916. I. Title. II. Series: Profiles in power (London,
England)
DB87.B45   1996
943.6'04'092—dc20
[B]
                                                              96–19897
                                                                   CIP

Set by 5 in 10½/12pt Baskerville
Produced by Longman Singapore Publishers (Pte) Ltd.
Printed in Singapore

CONTENTS

ACKNOWLEDGEMENTS

To write a short book on the sixty-eight-year long career of the ruler of a multi-national empire requires some inspiration, a great deal of encouragement and help, and not a little patience on the part of others. For my initial interest in the history of Central Europe, and the Habsburg Monarchy in particular, the figure of my maternal step-grandfather, Peter Hailböck, must be given pride of place. My earliest recollection of a personal connection to the Habsburg past is his recounting how he got the scar on his face – from fighting against the Serbs in the First World War as a soldier of Francis Joseph. Jan and Herta Palme have shown me why the Austrian past was worthy of study, and Norman Stone provided the inspiration and the wherewithal to engage in that pursuit. I am most grateful to Keith Robbins and Longman for the opportunity of writing on this particular aspect of that past.

In Austria, Gerald Stourzh and Waltraud Heindl were of particular help in shaping my ideas on the subject. Although I fear they will not agree with my conclusions, I also am grateful to Elisabeth de Gelsey and Erich Feigl for their generous help. Gabriele Praschl-Bichler, Klaus Koch, and Lothar Höbelt were also most helpful, as was Emil Brix, who, with Jacek Purchla and Barbara Szyper, enabled me to try out the themes of this book, at the College for New Europe in Cracow.

In Britain, I profited greatly from the advice of Tim Blanning, Derek Beales, Peter Pulzer, Alan Sked, John Röhl, Laszlo Péter, Roy Bridge and Chris Clark. In the United States, I am very grateful to James Shedel and Aviel Roshwald for their help and advice. The Lauinger Library at Georgetown is to be commended for its collection on Central European history. At the Library of Congress, Mr Martin has been most considerate and helpful, as was Denise Reijc-Quistorp, who provided me the first opportunity to talk on the theme of this book.

Two scholars, Solomon Wank and Robert Evans, deserve special thanks on my part, for their detailed and thorough reading of the manuscript at various stages, and their judicious and well-informed criticism of it. They have saved me from many pitfalls; I fear that I alone, however, am responsible for those which remain.

I also wish to thank the National Endowment for the Humanities and the Institute for Advanced Study, Princeton for supporting my research into the problem of ethnicity in Central Europe. A special mention is due to those at Longman for their work on the book, and for making its final production as painless as possible from my perspective.

On a more personal note, I would like to thank: Christl Fabrizii; Alan and Bea Corgan; and the Haiböck family. I also owe a great deal to Andrew and Doris Brimmer. To their beautiful daughter, Esther, I owe more than words can express. When it comes to inspiration, encouragement, help and patience as regards myself, she has but two rivals: my parents. It is to them that I dedicate this book.

Steven Beller,
Alexandria, Virginia.
1996

Chapter 1

INTRODUCTION

. . .

THE GOOD OLD EMPEROR

There are two images which dominate our understanding of Francis Joseph. The prevailing image is that which appears on a certain type of postcard sold to tourists and nostalgia seekers in Vienna and other former Habsburg capitals. On the right half, in whichever language is spoken in that particular part of the former empire, sometimes in more than one language, are printed the opening lines of the Imperial Hymn, 'Gott erhalte, Gott beschütze, Unser'n Kaiser, Unser'n Land' (God preserve, God protect, Our Emperor, Our Country). The left half is taken up by a portrait of the emperor himself, or rather the 'good old emperor', an ancient patriarch in his uniform, smiling benignly on his peoples. It is an image of benevolence and security, the emperor as symbol and guarantor of the 'good old times', when Austria meant something, and when Central Europe enjoyed peace, security and prosperity, relatively good government, a relatively free and tolerant political and cultural atmosphere, before the lights went out.

The other image, not as fashionable today as it once was, is of the 'abstract monarch' , also of an old emperor, but without the benevolence.[1] This is Francis Joseph as the first bureaucrat, cold-hearted, correctly but mechanically running the state as he had for decades, while modernity passed him – and his Monarchy – by. It is of a man surrounded by paperwork, with hardly any contact with society at large, running the state and its foreign policy according to principles already old-fashioned in his youth, but now completely anachronistic. The symbolic moment for this view of the emperor is Francis Joseph's signing of the declaration of war in 1914, a death sentence of the fathers on the sons.

What these images share is that they are both images of Francis Joseph as an old man, near to death. They both, implicitly,

1

are images of loss and decline. They both assume the dominant fact of Central European historiography, the collapse of the Habsburg Monarchy and its disastrous consequences, with Francis Joseph as a symbol of the region's tragedy and its nostalgia-tinged past.

Yet there are other images of Francis Joseph which show the emperor-king in a different light. There is an older, now less fashionable image of him as 'criminal' and 'tyrant' for denying the nations of Central Europe their freedom, and for leading his subjects into the bloodbath of the First World War simply for the sake of his dynasty's honour and prestige. There is also the image of him as the 'German prince', who maintained the German hegemony in Central Europe, primarily at the expense of the Slavs, and stayed wedded to the Dual Alliance with Prussia–Germany long after it had become more of a hindrance to his Monarchy's survival than a help. And then there is the image of the young Francis Joseph, resplendent in his full dress Austrian officer's uniform, the absolute monarch of a unified empire, ruling by Divine Right and the bayonets of his loyal troops, the embodiment of the 'imperial idea' of the most prestigious ruling house of European history.

Francis Joseph was not just the old man of nostalgic memory, he was also the eighteen-year-old who thought he could run a multi-national empire. He was the monarch who reneged on constitutional government, only to have it forced back on him. He was the monarch who tried to completely subjugate Hungary, only to be forced to become Hungary's constitutional monarch. He was also the monarch who lost the Habsburgs' position in both Italy and Germany, and whose one acquisition for the family domain happened to be – Bosnia–Herzegovina. He was the man who married one of the great royal beauties of the age, only to have his private family history become one of almost unremitting tragedy. He was a staunch Catholic, who signed a Concordat with the Papacy, yet was forced to accept essentially anti-clerical legislation, and became almost a symbol of religious toleration and pluralism even before his death. He was a man with absolutist convictions and aristocratic preferences, who nevertheless became a supporter of universal male suffrage. Above all, after the calamity of 1866–67, he came to pride himself as the 'peace emperor', only to go down in history as the man who started the First World War.

The chocolate-box images of the ancient Franz Joseph mask,

as it is the function of nostalgia to do, the immense complexities and tensions in the long career of this ruling monarch. His reign spanned the aftermath of one of Europe's great upheavals, the revolutions of 1848, to the horrors and disasters of an even greater one, the First World War. He ruled over the transition from a largely feudal and traditional society, to an increasingly urban, modern one, which saw mass industrialisation and mass politics, and which produced Sigmund Freud, Ludwig Wittgenstein, Franz Kafka, George Lukács and Adolf Hitler. His reign also saw the further development of mass nationalism, with all its pressures and problems, especially for a dynastic, multi-national state such as the Habsburg Monarchy. He presided over the decline of that Monarchy from one of the leading great powers of Europe to, by his death, a clearly subordinate status to its ally, in many ways its nemesis, the German Empire. His legacy, both in what he left behind, and did not, still shapes the character of Central Europe to this day.

Francis Joseph is a crucial figure not only in the history of the Monarchy which he ruled for over half a century, but also for modern Central European and European history in general. Indeed it is nigh impossible to separate an assessment of Francis Joseph as political actor from the whole panoply of Habsburg and Central European history in the nineteenth and early twentieth centuries. Francis Joseph is in many ways more interesting for the context in which he acted than for himself. It is as a chief player in the question which dominates modern Central European historiography, of the survivability of the Habsburg Empire, that Francis Joseph is of most significance for historians.

. . .

THE 'INEVITABILITY' DEBATE

The debate has been going on more or less since the Monarchy's collapse, if not before it. It has often receded from the forefront of historical discussion, as has the fate of Central Europe generally, especially when it was regarded in Neville Chamberlain's inimitable phrase as a 'far away country' inhabited by 'people of whom we know nothing', or when it was folded into the concept of Eastern Europe in the Cold War. Yet, whenever Central Europe has approached the centre stage of world affairs, the debate over the collapse of the Monarchy has revived, so that today there is probably more interest among historians and the public in the question than there has since the immediate aftermath in the 1920s.

In that post-war period debate was focused on explaining the most salient fact of the time, the Monarchy's demise. In the English-speaking world the dominant tone was set by such figures as, in England Henry Wickham Steed and R. W. Seton-Watson, in the United States Oskar Jászi, and in translation from Austria Joseph Redlich. While Steed and Seton-Watson had been critical before the war of many Habsburg policies, especially of Habsburg refusal to intervene in the Hungarian persecution of minorities, they had not been entirely unsympathetic to the Monarchy's problems, nor totally pessimistic about its ability to overcome them.[2] During the war their attitudes hardened until after the war there was a strong element of 'I told you so' in their analyses of the Monarchy's disappearance. The title of Steed's talk of 1936, 'The doom of the Habsburgs' needs little further comment. The dynasty's selfishness had obstructed national emancipation on the one hand, but broken up any coherence in the governing classes on the other. The 'immorality of the dynastic principle' in an age marching towards democratic nation-states had determined the fate of the anachronistic Monarchy.[3]

Oskar Jászi's diagnosis was not that much different. In one of the classic analyses of the subject, *The Dissolution of the Habsburg Monarchy*, first published in 1929, Jászi, an Hungarian Jewish emigré from a left-liberal background, described the centripetal and centrifugal forces, which in his estimation had determined the Monarchy's history and fate. Although he thought that some sort of Danubian federation was very desirable, even necessary for the prosperity and security of the region, Jászi also thought that the *Monarchy* itself, that is to say the dynastic and quasi-constitutional institutions which had ruled the empire, had ultimately been disastrous, because they had taught the worst sort of 'civic education' (the ostensible topic of his book): that power was something that came from above, or at least from the back-room deals cut with the corrupt and corrupting bureaucracy. It was a zero-sum game, in which one nationality's victory was another's defeat. In Jászi's estimation, therefore, not only had the Monarchy collapsed under its own internal contradictions, but it had left a very dangerous legacy of over-dependence on bureaucracy and fierce national rivalries.[4] Redlich, primarily in his classic biography of Francis Joseph, presented a similar argument, arguing that from 1897 the empire was doomed, and largely, in Redlich's view, because of the inability of the 'dynastic power, incorporated in Francis Joseph' to see the necessity of yielding gracefully to the new, nationalist forces in the empire.[5]

The prevailing consensus of the 1920s, at least in the English-speaking world, was therefore a negative one, that the Monarchy was doomed to fail, and deserved to do so. After all, why bewail its fate when one had in its place model liberal democratic states such as Czechoslovakia, run by that heroic figure, the philosopher-president, Thomas Masaryk? Even monarchists and those sympathetic to the dynasty, such as Alexander Margutti, a former aide-de-camp of Francis Joseph, could offer little more than declamations of the essential decency of the Habsburg dynasty and administration, and could say little against the inevitability of the empire's demise.[6]

As the bright hopes in Central European democracy dimmed in the 1930s, and as the power vacuum formed by the empire's collapse began to be filled by a resurgent Germany under National Socialist rule, perspectives began to change. In foreign policy terms, the concept of the 'necessity' of Austria as a collective balancing force in the region between Germany and Russia began to have some impact on Western policymakers. Even so, when the 'Central European' governments in exile tried to reach some collaborative agreements while the region was under Nazi occupation, it was the idea of regional co-operation, and not the Monarchy as such, which was seen as missing.[7]

The leading historical interpretations of the post-Second World War period, those of Robert Kann in the United States and A. J. P. Taylor in Britain continued and developed these themes. Both interpretations sympathised with the idea of Central European regional co-operation, but both were agreed that the Habsburg Monarchy had not been the way to provide it. Kann, attempting to be as judicious as possible, could see both sides of the question of whether the dissolution of the empire was due to internal or external forces, but ultimately came down on the side of internal sources of collapse, primarily the Habsburg establishment's inability to deal effectively with the nationalities problem, Kann's most famous subject.[8]

Taylor, as always, was rather blunter: 'To place hope in any Habsburg was to fail to understand the nature of the Habsburg Monarchy. Kossuth atoned for all his shortcomings by recognising that the overthrow of the Habsburg dynasty was the first condition for a reconstruction of central Europe.'[9] For both Kann and

Taylor the Habsburgs stood in the way of real national co-operation, Kann regarding as tragic the dynasty's initial rejection of constitutional government in 1849, while Taylor, like Jászi and Steed before him, held to the liberal and democratic line that the refusal of the dynastic authorities to give real responsibility to the population was at the root of the Monarchy's problems.[10] Both saw the Monarchy as in poor shape by 1914, yet both were also agreed that it was only the decision to go to war in that year which sealed the fate of the Monarchy, either in victory or defeat.[11] Their answer to those who blamed external forces, that is to say the impact of the First World War and the Allies' ultimate decision to back the break-up of the Monarchy, for the collapse, was to point out that it had been the Monarchy which had started the war, due to internal pressures, and that much of the pressure to take apart the empire came from *emigré* national leaders, that is to say inside forces.

Since the 1950s, however, as Soviet occupation of Central Europe turned it into Eastern Europe, the tendency to dismiss the Monarchy as an anachronistic and 'doomed' force, has diminished in favour of a nostalgia-tinged sense that the Monarchy cannot have been that bad, for after all it must have been better than what replaced it. There was already a groundswell of such opinion, of the essentially beneficial and viable nature of the Monarchy, so unluckily destroyed at the whim of the ignorant Western powers in 1918, when Kann was writing his long-considered opinion in the 1970s. The revisionist school of Habsburg historiography has not been a particularly coherent body, but it has over the last few decades gradually eroded the previous consensus on the fate of the Habsburg Monarchy, and replaced it with a far more sympathetic, even positive, one.

One of the prominent earlier efforts at an at least partial rehabilitation of the Monarchy in the English-speaking world (in Austria there had always been a more vocal pro-Habsburg lobby) was Edward Crankshaw's *The Fall of the House of Habsburg* (1963). A 'popular' work in relatively large circulation, this has probably had more impact on views of the Monarchy than most books. Crankshaw took the view that Francis Joseph's government had actually not been that bad, that the emperor was really more of a constitutional president by the last decade of the Monarchy, and that, if only the Monarchy had been left alone to solve its own problems in peace, it was well on the way to being a constitutional monarchy in the Western sense. The general tenor of his arguments is summed up in the assertion that: 'Outside Hungary things were going very well.'[12] Crankshaw also pointed out, as have many subsequent defenders of Francis Joseph and his Monarchy, that 'compared with what happened next, the age of Franz Josef was an age of enlightenment.'[13] The war which Crankshaw saw as the cause of the Monarchy's destruction was not Austria's fault, but rather that of 'a deep-seated moral sickness' which pervaded all of Europe.[14]

On the other side of the Atlantic, historians such as Arthur J. May also tended to see the Monarchy in a much more positive light. While not denying its immense problems, the strengths – Jászi's centripetal forces – were emphasised, and the loss caused by the Monarchy's disappearance bewailed.[15] Fritz Fischer's 'revelation' of the German responsibility for starting the First World War, put Austria's role in a far different light, as at most a dupe rather than an instigator of its own destruction.[16] An increasingly pluralistic society in the United States and Western Europe also began to undermine confidence in the principle of the nation-state, which had justified the break-up of the Monarchy. Indeed American historians increasingly saw the empire as a testing ground for multi-national and pluralist solutions for a 'United States' of Europe.

The growth of the supra-national institutions of the European Common Market naturally encouraged this perspective on the Monarchy, while disillusionment with 'socialist' rule in Eastern Europe also worked to give the history of the Monarchy a rosier aspect. If the alternatives to Habsburg 'oppression' were either Nazi rule or a fake national independence under ideological, communist domination, then it was understandable that a certain nostalgic admiration for the Monarchy should surface in the successor 'People's Republics', and among their *emigré* historians, ensconced in Western universities.

One other development, the emergence of a much stronger and more self-confident West Germany, also influenced the debate over the Habsburg Monarchy. In the *Historikerstreit* (historians' debate) of the 1980s the assumptions which had underpinned Western historiography on Germany, that ever since Bismarck it had 'gone wrong', that is left the path of liberal, democratic modernity and taken a 'special path' (*Sonderweg*) which ended in the Holocaust and the 'Zero Hour', were brought into question by a combination of conservative German historians and left-leaning English historians, albeit from quite differing perspectives.[17] From this debate it seemed that Germany was not in fact that different from other capitalist Western states, and that its role as arch-fiend in the historiography of the twentieth century was the result more of accident than some all-embracing inevitable fate. But if Germany had not been that different from its Western neighbours, nor doomed to its fate, could not the same be argued for the rest of Central Europe, Austria–Hungary? While Fritz Fischer's accusation against Germany for starting the First World War had taken the pressure off the Habsburg Monarchy, the questioning of the underlying *Sonderweg* thesis had the effect of further improving the Monarchy's standing. Not only was Austria–Hungary no longer guilty, it had not even been doomed to collapse.

While many historians, such as Solomon Wank, have continued to stress the traditional, negative picture of a politically very sick, if not necessarily doomed, Monarchy, brought down by its own internal contradictions,[18] they are now confronted by a field of various approaches which see the Monarchy as a much more viable and even positive force, whose disappearance was, in varying degrees, an unfortunate accident. The benefits of the economic union provided by the Monarchy are now stressed, most effectively by David Good.[19] Austria's declaration of war in 1914 is seen as more due to diplomatic clumsiness and German pressure than as due to internal contradictions. Indeed one prominent historian of international relations, Paul Schroeder, has blamed Austria's declaration of war not even on Germany, but on Great Britain, whom he sees as not acting responsibly as guarantor of the peace.[20]

With the decline and break-up of the Soviet Empire in the 1980s, and the re-emergence of the nation-states of Eastern (Central) Europe since 1989, historians such as Istvan Deák have suggested that the Monarchy, rather than being a warning of what not to do, should be looked to for a 'positive lesson' of supra-national co-operation.[21] Among the most fervent admirers of the former empire are now, irony of ironies, Hungarian historians. Instead of the dynasty getting in the way of the nationalities, it is now almost as if it is the nationalities who got in the way of the one thing that could have saved them – and by implication the rest of us – from the terrors of the twentieth century, the institutions of the Habsburg Monarchy.

One of the latest attempts at the theme of the *Decline and Fall of the Habsburg Empire* (1989) has even concluded that there was no decline, that the Monarchy was perfectly viable in 1914, doing pretty well in fact. Yet here we reach a rich paradox, for the author of this latest approach, Alan Sked, instead explains the Monarchy's precipitate fall not by nationality conflicts, but by the continued existence at the centres of power in Austria–Hungary of feudal values of honour and prestige, which forced Francis Joseph to go to war against Serbia, not in pursuit of *raison d'état*, but rather to protect the honour and standing of the Habsburg dynasty.[22]

. . .

THE ROLE OF PERSONALITY

Alan Sked's paradoxical conclusion brings us back to where we came in. As will be evident, in all this back and forth between viability and inevitable collapse, 'bad luck' and guilty connivance in the fall of the old order, the role of the monarch of the Habsburg Monarchy is never far from the centre of the action, if only as an absence. All the great decisions of the Monarchy were ostensibly taken – or not taken – by one man, Francis Joseph, whether it be the attempt at absolutism in 1851, the turn to liberalism in 1867, the refusal to intervene against Magyarisation in Hungary, the occupation and later annexation of Bosnia, and most notoriously the decision to go to war in 1914. He was the 'first bureaucrat' to whom the vast Habsburg officialdom reported, he was the man who reigned over a Monarchy which was either doing quite nicely, or heading to its doom, depending on one's historiographical allegiance.

Yet how central was Francis Joseph actually in deciding policy in the Habsburg Monarchy? While all large policy decisions were officially taken by the emperor-king until his death in 1916, both halves of the Monarchy, after 1867, had constitutional, or at least quasi-constitutional structures, in which Francis Joseph was not alone in making decisions. Furthermore, even under an absolutist regime, the role of bureaucracy takes on a life of its own, which it is often difficult for a monarch, no matter what his powers on paper, to control. And if bureaucracies are hard to control, then the larger social and economic forces by which historians so often explain events, must surely be beyond any individual's reach. As none other than Karl Marx put it: 'Men make their own history, but they do not make it just as they please.'[23] Or, to cite another

contemporary of the emperor, no matter how much one criti-
cises Tolstoy's amateur attempts at a philosophy of history, the
idea that Napoleon – and by analogy Francis Joseph – were not
fully in control of their own fate, let alone that of the empires
they ruled, still carries a great deal of cogency.[24]

Closely parallel, and often connected, to the debate between
the 'viability' or 'inevitable collapse' Schools of Habsburg history, is that between those who emphasise the significance of
individual choice, and those who tend to ignore or even rule out
such influences over events in favour of all-embracing historical
forces, whether they be those of 'modernisation', 'nationalism',
or the 'class struggle of the proletariat'. The question of Francis
Joseph's role in the fate of the Habsburg Monarchy is thus a
modern-day version of the old theological debate between free
will and predestination, with, perhaps not surprisingly, the 'Calvinist' camp seeing Francis Joseph as powerless to stop his Monarchy's
inevitable demise.

The predestinarian school of history, under the influence of
Marxian models of explanation, long held the advantage in post-
Second World War scholarship, which looked to large-scale social
and economic factors to explain events in the new, modern mass
society. One talked of social classes, elites and economic sectors
as the leading agents of history, not of the 'Romantic' notion of
individual choice and action. Recently, however, the individual
has made a comeback, as the series in which this book appears
attests. The reasons for this shift are unclear, perhaps having to
do with post-modern scepticism about the efficacy of wide-
ranging social theories, or the collapse of the greatest theology
of inevitability, Marxism-Leninism. Whatever the explanation,
attempts to create comprehensive socio-economic models to
account for historical change have become unfashionable,
pushed aside by two more old-fashioned explanations, luck and
individual character.

The trend is explicit in recent work on two of Francis Joseph's
most important contemporary monarchs, Nicholas II of Russia
and William II of Prussia–Germany.[25] In both cases the importance
of the monarch's own personality – and furthermore the power
of each in actually deciding policy and shaping their government's
character – has been emphasised, in stark contrast to the much
more deterministic accounts given by previous historians.
Monarchy in both Russia and Germany really meant rule by the
monarch, to a much greater extent than was previously thought.

Personality, profiles of individuals in power, are thus of much more consequence in turn-of-the-century Europe than the conventional view until now held. The same is claimed for Francis Joseph by his most recent biographers, and Sked's paradox only lends credence to this voluntaristic view.[26]

Even in the freest of circumstances, though, choice can only be free within limits, and if Francis Joseph did have freedom to choose as an historical actor, the complex context of the Habsburg Monarchy, Central Europe and the European great power system, nevertheless set similarly complex limits on how he exercised that freedom. That is to say that a profile of Francis Joseph's power is inevitably also the history of the power structure of the Habsburg Monarchy in the nineteenth and early twentieth centuries, of the power relationships in Central Europe and of the balance of power in the 'great game' of international great-power relations. To an extent which may well surprise, Francis Joseph played a large personal role in shaping this power structure from his accession in 1848 till his death. At the same time, however, his decisions were so shaped by the circumstances in which he found himself, that one can well argue that the occasions were rare when his choice was anything approaching what we would think of as free. His freest choices were almost all among his most fateful.

It was in the dialectic between free choice and predestination that Francis Joseph operated, exercising, as we shall see, real power, but often in ways which were the outcome of his background, were forced on him or were the result of a lack of the presentation of other options. Moreover, he was a man dogged by the fact that his choices, once made, so often resulted in consequences the reverse of what he would have expected or wished. In his extraordinarily long encounter with the historical, structural, social and national complexities of his realm, Francis Joseph shaped that Monarchy's fate, and was shaped by it.

. . .

A PROFILE IN POWER

The question of free choice or predestination, as well as the question of the Habsburg Monarchy's 'doom' or essential viability, resolve themselves into a set of questions on one subject, the nature of power in nineteenth and early- twentieth-century Central

Europe, more specifically here the nature of Francis Joseph's power within this context.

The first question which needs to be addressed is what power did Francis Joseph actually have, how much and of what kind? The more actual power he had, the more freedom he had in his choice, and the more his own personality and choices mattered in the shaping of the events in his reign and after. The quality of power also mattered, for although in later years it is arguable that Francis Joseph's political power, his ability to get things done within the complex and gridlocked structures of his empire, was severely compromised, his presence has often been seen as a vital source of moral power, which kept together an otherwise rickety edifice.

Assumed here is also a supplementary question: power on what level? For although, as we shall see, Francis Joseph had a great deal of power within his Monarchy, even after he had given up his pretensions to absolute power, power within the formal governmental structure turned out to be a secondary consideration when faced with the realities of great-power relations on the one hand, and social and national aspirations on the other.

The second main question is what Francis Joseph did with the power he had. If he had the power to choose his fate, what choices did he make, why did he make them, and how did they in turn affect his power to make further choices? As will soon be clear, whatever freedom of choice Francis Joseph had, his range of options was severely self-limited, both by his upbringing and a character which was normally loath to go beyond what he already knew, and what he felt he must preserve, namely the heritage of his family, the Habsburg dynasty. Whatever freedom to choose in the emperor's possession was sharply limited by the preferences and prejudices which he, and his advisers, brought to the problems and issues before them. Whatever the pros and cons of the various plans to reform the Monarchy, for instance, they were all moot, given the government's reluctance, that is Francis Joseph and his ministers' reluctance, to consider them.

Finally, the third question looks to what the effects of this use of power were on Francis Joseph's successors, within the dynasty and without. If Francis Joseph's use of power affected his own status and power within the Central European context, it also had very long-range effects on those who came after. What was his legacy to his immediate successor, Charles? How much can

Francis Joseph be held directly responsible for the collapse of the Monarchy two years after his death? What direct and indirect responsibility did he have for the condition of the inter-war states which succeeded the Habsburg Monarchy? In the shadow of what happened after 1933, both under National Socialism and the Soviet Empire, what was Francis Joseph's contribution to the large part of Central Europe he had ruled? Was it to have given the region a half a century of peace before an inevitable deluge? Or was it Francis Joseph's use of the substantial power at his disposal which made sure not only that his Monarchy collapsed, but that it took down the best of Central European civilisation with it?

A profile of the power of Francis Joseph is a profile of the power of dynastic monarchy in an age of social, economic and political modernisation. It is thus a study of the nature of monarchy in the modern age, when it still seemed a viable form of government. It is also a study, therefore, of the strength of traditional sources and institutions of power at the dawn of the twentieth century.

A study of Francis Joseph will always have an additional aspect to address: longevity. Francis Joseph experienced immense changes in almost all aspects, whether political, social, economic or cultural, over the sixty-eight years of his reign. The political system went from constitutionalism to neo-Absolutism, to dualist constitutionalism, to quasi-constitutional bureaucratism with universal male suffrage; society was partially transformed from being feudal, agrarian, traditional to being modern, industrial and urban. The economy went from being overwhelmingly agrarian and backward, to having some parts at the forefront of economic, capitalist development. Culturally, Vienna by 1914 was the heart of some of the more influential and radical intellectual and cultural trends of the age, with Freud's psychoanalytic movement at their head. The same man who had ruled before Sigmund Freud had even been born still was there when Freud the patriarch was ejecting Adler and Jung from his following. The man who had asked Nicholas I for help against the Hungarians in 1849 was the same man who in 1914 started the war which brought down both Habsburg and Romanov dynasties.

The sheer breadth of this timespan means that any attempt to deal with the questions of Francis Joseph's power raised above in a static, purely analytic way is unrealistic. That is why in what follows the thematic of Francis Joseph's power is dealt with in a series of chronological steps. So much changed over the almost three-quarters of a century of Francis Joseph's reign that it is only through charting the stages of that change that we can fully comprehend Francis Joseph's part in it, and realise just how much Francis Joseph himself was shaped by his lifelong career in the business of monarchy, or conversely how much he shaped the events around him. By looking at his life in this way, we can also get a better insight into the question of how much the monarch was responsible for the ultimate collapse of his Monarchy, and its terrible aftermath.

. . .

NOTES AND REFERENCES

1. H. Broch, *Hugo von Hofmannsthal and his Time: The European Imagination 1860–1920,* trans. ed. M.P. Steinberg, University of Chicago 1984, pp. 72–4.
2. H.W. Steed, *The Habsburg Monarchy,* Fertig, New York, reprint 2nd edn 1914, pp. 294–5; H. & C. Seton-Watson, *The Making of a New Europe: R. W. Seton-Watson and the Last Years of Austria–Hungary,* University of Washington, Seattle 1981, pp. 96, 101.
3. H.W. Steed, *The Doom of the Habsburgs,* Arrowsmith, London 1937, p. 95.
4. O. Jászi, *The Dissolution of the Habsburg Monarchy,* Chicago 1929 (Studies in the Making of Citizens).
5. J. Redlich, *Emperor Francis Joseph of Austria: A Biography,* Macmillan, New York 1929, pp. 448, 509.
6. A. Margutti, *The Emperor Francis Joseph and His Times,* Hutchinson, London 1921, pp. 55, 205–6.
7. J. Havránek, 'Central Europe, East Central Europe and the Historians 1940–1948'. In E. Somogyi (ed.), *Verbürgerlichung in Mitteleuropa,* Budapest 1991, pp. 299–308.
8. R.A. Kann, *A History of the Habsburg Empire, 1526–1918,* University of California, Berkeley 1977, pp. 517–20.
9. A.J.P. Taylor, *The Habsburg Monarchy 1809–1918,* Penguin, Harmondsworth 1948 (1964), p. 243.
10. Kann, *History of the Habsburg Empire,* pp. 310–12; Taylor, *The Habsburg Monarchy,* pp. 241–4.
11. Kann, *History of the Habsburg Empire,* p. 519; Taylor, *The Habsburg Monarchy,* pp. 245–50.
12. E. Crankshaw, *The Fall of the House of Habsburg,* Viking Penguin, New York 1963, p. 305.

13. Ibid., p. 312.
14. Ibid., p. 304. A more reliable work in a similar direction is C.A. Macartney, *The Habsburg Empire 1790–1918*, Macmillan, London 1969.
15. A.J. May, *The Habsburg Monarchy, 1867–1914*, Harvard, Cambridge, Mass. 1951, p. 489.
16. R.J.W. Evans, 'The Habsburg Monarchy and the Coming of War'. In R.J.W. Evans, H. Pogge von Strandmann (eds), *The Coming of the First World War*, Clarendon, Oxford 1988, p. 34; cf. Fritz Fischer, *Germany's Aims in the First World War*, London 1967.
17. Cf. C.S. Maier, *The Unmasterable Past: History, Holocaust and German National Identity*, Harvard, Cambridge, Mass. 1988; D. Blackbourn, G. Eley, *The Peculiarities of German History: Bourgeois Society and Politics in Nineteenth-Century Germany*, Oxford 1984.
18. S. Wank, 'The Nationalities Question in the Habsburg Monarchy: Reflections on the Historical Record'. *Working Papers in Austrian Studies*, vol. 93 (3), 1933.
19. D.F. Good, *The Economic Rise of the Habsburg Empire, 1750–1914*, University of California, Berkeley 1984.
20. P.W. Schroeder, 'Munich and the British Tradition', *The Historical Journal* vol. 19; (1976) pp. 225–37; cf. Alan Sked's discussion, A. Sked, *The Decline and Fall of the Habsburg Empire 1815–1918*, Longman, London 1989, pp. 246–7.
21. I. Deák, *Beyond Nationalism: A Social and Political History of the Habsburg Officer Corps 1848–1918*, Oxford 1990, p. 9.
22. A. Sked, *Decline and Fall of the Habsburg Empire*, pp. 230–4, 256–8.
23. K. Marx, 'The Eighteenth Brumaire of Louis Bonaparte'. In R.C. Tucker (ed.), *The Marx-Engels Reader*, 2nd edn, Norton, New York 1978, p. 595.
24. L.N. Tolstoy, *War and Peace*, revised edn (2 vols), trans. R. Edmonds, Penguin, Harmondsworth, vol. 2, pp. 1, 168ff.
25. D. Lieven, *Nicholas II, Emperor of all the Russias*, Pimlico, London 1993; J.C.G. Röhl, *Kaiser, Hof und Staat: Wilhelm II und die deutsche Politik*, Beck, Munich 1987.
26. For example, J.-P. Bled, *Franz Joseph*, trans. T. Bridgeman, Blackwell, Oxford 1992.

Chapter 2

TRADITION

. . .

HISTORY AS GENEALOGY

Francis Joseph became the ruler of a vast Central European empire in 1848 as the result of an accident of birth. There were other significant circumstantial reasons, as we shall see, but his main claim to the right to be emperor was a simple one: he was by birth heir to the House of Austria, the Habsburgs. This dynasty had perhaps the most stupendous career of all European ruling houses. Over more than half a millennium it evolved, adapting to the changes in the nature of authority and power in Europe, but with one constant, paramount aim, to maintain and enhance the power and prestige of itself. In this it was to prove the most dynastic European dynasty of all.

Starting not in present-day Austria but in what is now south-western Germany and northern Switzerland, the Habsburgs had taken over the lands of the defunct Babenberg dynasty in the south-eastern borders of the Holy Roman Empire in the thirteenth century. From there they gradually built up their feudal power and influence. Rudolph, the acquirer of the Austrian lands for the Habsburgs, had been elected German king in 1273, but it was from 1452 on, when Frederick III was elected Holy Roman Emperor, that they achieved the ultimate goal for a medieval dynasty in Central Europe of being virtually hereditary holders of the imperial office. The Habsburgs now turned their attention from martial to marital conquests. As the oft-repeated phrase states: 'Bella gerant alii, tu felix Austria nube.' (Let the others wage war, you, faithful Austria, marry.) By an astute dynastic marriage policy and genealogical luck, the Habsburg family came by 1526 to possess not only the 'hereditary lands' of Austria, but also most of the lands of the Burgundian kingdom (including the rich Netherlands) and the lands of the Spanish kingdom, including a large part of Italy, and the potentially immense empire of the New World. Furthermore, the death of the Jagellonian Louis II at the Battle of Mohacs in that year meant the succession of the Habsburgs to the prosperous territories of the Bohemian crown, and, if they could win it back from the Turks, the potentially rich lands of the Hungarian Crown of St Stephen.

Given its dazzling success, it is hardly surprising that the dynasty at this point in its career acquired immense, truly imperial pretensions, seeing itself as chosen by divine providence for a leading role in world affairs. Elaborate efforts were made to identify the dynasty as the 'last descendants of Aeneas', and thus the authentic heirs to Rome and Roman world rule.[1] The acronym adopted by the family was equally ambitious: A.E.I.O.U. This either meant: 'Austriae est imperare orbi universo' (It is for Austria to rule the entire world); or 'Austria erit in orbe ultima' (Austria will outlast the others). Neither bespoke particular modesty.

In all of the dazzling array of Habsburg lands, the original Austrian territories in Central Europe had become of only secondary importance. When Charles V ascended to the Habsburg legacy in 1519 and decided to divide his unmanageably large patrimony in half, he handed over control of his Austrian (and Bohemian and Hungarian) lands to his younger brother Ferdinand. It was thus to the *junior* branch of the *casa Austria* that the original Austrian territories went. For the next almost two centuries the senior branch of the family was based in Spain, not Central Europe.

Habsburg pre-eminence did not go unchallenged. There was almost continuous warfare with France; puny England successfully resisted the Great, Habsburg Armada; in Italy the larger states, especially Venice, disputed imperial pretensions. In the east the Turks still threatened the Central European Habsburg lands, and occupied most of the Hungarian heritage. It was, however, in the religious realm that Habsburg power and authority was most threatened. The Reformation inspired by Martin Luther not only undermined Habsburg imperial authority through the latter's close association with the established Catholic Church, it also offered a convenient rallying point for second tier powers, such as the German princes in the Holy Roman Empire, to resist Habsburg attempts to realise the potential power of the imperial office.

At the same time, the crisis of religious authority caused by the Reformation provided the Habsburgs with the main role in European affairs which they were to retain to their demise in

1918, as the upholders and defenders of the Counter-Reformation Catholic Church. The Austrian branch was much slower than the Spanish branch to counter effectively the spread of Protestantism in its lands, but, when it did, the resulting Austrian Counter Reformation and the Thirty Years War which accompanied it had profound consequences, both for the dynasty and for the lands it ruled. The war proved disastrous for the international position of the Habsburgs, both as rulers of Spain and as Holy Roman Emperors (since 1558 in the Austrian line); but it established the absolute rule of the Austrian Habsburgs within their Central European lands. This was especially so in Bohemia, where the defeat of the rebel nobility at the Battle of the White Mountain of 1620 created large opportunities for Habsburg power-building. Habsburg supporters – and the Counter-Reformation Church – were rewarded with vast tracts of expropriated noble lands. The resulting alliance of dynasty, Church and aristocracy developed by the late seventeenth century into an interlocking system of absolutism, feudalism and Counter-Reformation which was held together by and expressed in the ideology and culture of the Baroque. While Habsburg pretensions were now more limited, their dynastic power within their own lands was amplified by their new mission as the Counter-Reformation dynasty *par excellence*.[2]

Already by the late seventeenth century, however, this new Baroque settlement was becoming anachronistic as a basis for Austrian Habsburg authority. Religion was ceasing to be the main motor to international politics. Thus even a religious zealot such as Leopold I, who had expelled the Jews from Vienna in 1670, nevertheless became a close ally of the leading Protestant prince, William of Orange, against the very Catholic Louis XIV of France. Domestically as well, notions of the secular state were beginning to undermine the sort of religiously based authority which had justified Habsburg rule. Unfortunately for the Habsburgs, a set of purely dynastic, even genealogical, problems were severely to handicap and complicate the Habsburgs' adjustment to this new, secularising world.

The problem, in both branches of the family, was the lack of a direct male heir. The failure of the Spanish branch to produce a male heir led in 1700 to the War of the Spanish Succession, which resulted in large acquisitions for the Austrian branch in Italy and the Netherlands, but the loss of the still vast Spanish Empire to a Bourbon. The dynastic embarrassment in the Austrian branch,

Charles VI's lack of a male heir, was even more critical, threatening to end the illustrious career of the dynasty altogether. To prevent this awful prospect Charles VI started a campaign to have what came to be known as the Pragmatic Sanction agreed to by all the other interested parties, both without and within the Habsburg territories. This document, drawn up in 1713, confirmed two main points. First, that the territories now under the rule of the Habsburgs must remain intact, under one ruler. Second, that this ruler was after Charles' death to be, in the first instance, his daughter Maria Theresa, and in subsequent instances her descendants.[3] Whereas in Britain the succession was decided by act of parliament, in Austria it was decided by a set of bargains between Charles, his fellow monarchs, and the various representative institutions, estates, still left in Austria, to which Charles was forced to make various concessions to secure agreement. Having been built up brilliantly by the skilful playing of the dynastic game, the Habsburg power found itself in 1740 the hostage of the quirks of dynastic, genealogical fate.

. . .

THE AUSTRIAN STATE IDEA

The Austrian succession as laid down in the Pragmatic Sanction was not left uncontested. In 1740 Frederick II of Prussia invaded Silesia, one of the Habsburgs' most prosperous (and German) territories, and, despite Maria Theresa's strenuous efforts and two major wars (the War of the Austrian Succession (1740–48) and the Seven Years War (1756–63)), Prussia held on to all but a tiny sliver of it. The loss of Silesia made obvious what Austrian defeats by the French and the Turks were already making clear in the 1730s: the inadequacy of the Baroque settlement for maintaining the Habsburg Monarchy as one of Europe's leading great powers.[4] The Pragmatic Sanction itself, in its proclamation of the indivisibility of the Habsburg lands, had been part recognition of the need to move from treating the Habsburg territories purely dynastically, as a collection of *estates*, to viewing them rather together as one *state*. Now the humiliation suffered at the hands of small, but well-organised Prussia necessitated a further, more profound rethinking by the Habsburg power.

The Austrian response to the loss of Silesia was to adopt, as well as the empress's advisers could, and to the extent that the dynasty's Catholic principles allowed, the weapons of their successful rivals. What this amounted to, as Blanning describes, was a shift both from the 'imperial idea' to the 'state idea', and from an emphasis on the periphery to the centre.[5] The key model for Austria was, not surprisingly, Prussia. The small Prussian state, at first a ragbag of territories scattered over the North German Plain, had developed since the seventeenth century into a centralised state, with a mercantilist attitude to the economy, a relatively tolerant attitude to religious minorities, and a huge standing army out of all proportion to the size of its population or economy. If Britain, with its large navy, ability to raise large revenues and buy allies, represented the power of money in international relations, Prussia showed, with brutal frankness when used by Frederick II, the advantages of superior military might, no matter the resources which underpinned it.

The lesson drawn from the nadir of mid-century by Maria Theresa and her circle of advisers, most notably Prince Wenzel Kaunitz and Count Friedrich Haugwitz, was that in order for Austria to maintain its position in the new European order, it would have to concentrate on being a state, rather than being the imperial dynasty. Moreover, it would have to be a state on the most modern lines, to be able to compete in Frederick II's Europe. This entailed concentrating on the Habsburgs' own territories rather than on their position within the Empire, and it meant attempting to run those Habsburg territories as a unitary state, with direct control by the sovereign. As history seemed to have shown, only states with contiguous territories could do this effectively, so much more emphasis was now placed on making the core lands of the Habsburgs, in Central Europe, function effectively, at the expense of attention to the lands on the Habsburg periphery in the Netherlands, south-western Germany, Italy – and Hungary.[6]

The reforms enacted by Maria Theresa and her advisers were far-reaching. At the core of the Habsburg territories, the Austrian and Bohemian chancelleries were combined, forming the basis for a new, modernised bureaucracy; the power of the monarch and central government over the localities was greatly enhanced, dramatically increasing revenues and with it the ability to support a much expanded standing army. Industry and trade were given much more encouragement. The embarrassing and crippling backwardness of Jesuit-led education in the Habsburg heartlands was partially remedied by large-scale expropriation of many religious institutions and a transfer of the proceeds towards more 'useful' pursuits such as schools and the secular clergy. Catholic reformers were brought in to remake the Baroque Catholicism of Habsburg Central Europe in the image of a latter day Jansenism, or 'Catholic Enlightenment'.[7]

Maria Theresa herself remained a devout, and in many respects superstitious, Catholic. In the interests of rescuing and reasserting the position of the dynasty, however, she was prepared to follow the advice of her inner circle, which saw the reform programme as the only way to counteract the trends of the day embodied in Frederick's Prussia. Reforms on Enlightened lines were necessary because of their 'utility' in creating the building blocks of state, and hence dynastic, power: education to provide a set of efficient administrators; religion to provide obedient, productive subjects; prosperity to provide resources; a rational bureaucracy to collect those resources and turn them into a fighting force to beat the Prussians. This was Enlightened Absolutism, the establishment of a unitary Austrian state, but still in pursuit of dynastic ends.

With the reign of Maria Theresa's son, Joseph II, reform came to be fully in the Enlightenment's spirit. Joseph II was co-regent from his father's death in 1765, but was only allowed full rein after his mother's death in 1780.* He then unleashed a whole array of radical reforms which were intended to haul Austria into the nineteenth century, and went much further, much faster, than his mother had ever envisaged. In religious affairs there was a much more radical attack on church privileges, in order partly to bring (Enlightened) religion closer to the people. To increase the utility of his subjects, Joseph also decreed toleration for Protestants and Jews. In the cultural sphere, he relaxed censorship of the press, at least until it became too critical of his reforms. There was also a radical reorganisation of government, on the most modern principles. Vastly expanding the nascent state bureaucracy, Joseph extended it to other parts of his realm which Maria Theresa had left untouched.[8] Most notorious was his attempt to replace the local, feudal administration in Hungary, conducted in Latin, with a new, centralised German-speaking

---

*Formally, the Habsburg dynasty died out with Maria Theresa; her successors were of the House of Habsburg-Lorraine.

bureaucracy, in the interests of greater administrative efficiency (not German national sentiment).[9]

The aim of the project of Enlightened Absolutism which Joseph II undertook was to create a state of uniformity and equality, in which, to borrow a phrase from Frederick II, the monarch as first servant of the state ruled over a population equally subject to him. Joseph was an ardent admirer of humanity, *Menschheit*, if only in the abstract. His attempts to liberate his state's peasantry from some of its more onerous restrictions, such as formal serfdom, derived at least partially from this sort of enlightened idealism. Ultimately, though, such measures had more to do with his love of an equal, uniform and strong state than with his philanthropy, for it was thought that by freeing the peasantry this would improve the economic performance of the state, and hence contribute to that beneficial spiral outlined above which led to large armies and thus an effective foreign policy.

Joseph II's intervention on behalf of the peasantry was also part of his plan to replace the remaining feudal power structures by a comprehensive administration of all his subjects, whether noble, bourgeois or peasants, by the state and for the state. Under Joseph the Austrian bureaucracy became the vanguard of modernisation and reform, the tutelary state which was to act to develop the raw human material of the Austrian population into the humanity of Enlightened ideals. Not surprisingly, this attempt to subvert the existing order in a much more radical fashion than his mother left Joseph facing immense and unyielding opposition from a whole host of sources within the unwieldy amalgam of disparate authorities which was the reality of his realm.[10]

Moreover the attempt to rationalise and make uniform Austrian administration throughout his realms, not only in Austria-Bohemia but also in Hungary, Belgium and newly acquired Galicia, pointed up the immense difficulties inherent in the Habsburg project of converting their power from a purely dynastic one, in which the imperial title could rest more or less comfortably next to other titles and deeds of various lands, to one in which the dynasty was identified with a modern state, characterised by absolute power and the elimination of difference, whether social, constitutional or geographical – or even national. This was a problem which Joseph's campaign for Austrian statehood, in exacerbating particularist and socially privileged interests, failed to solve, and was a lasting legacy for his successors, as we shall see.

The clearest dilemma raised by the transformation of the Habsburg territories into a modern state was the relationship of this state with the Holy Roman Empire, that is to say the institutional framework of the German lands. While Joseph at first made some attempt to reform the Empire from within, he clearly put Austrian state interests first. One of the typical projects of Enlightened Absolutism was Joseph's attempt to follow through on the theory of the need of a state's territories for contiguity by proposing the exchange of the Austrian Netherlands (present-day Belgium) for contiguous Bavaria. On a map this made perfect sense for the power and strategic position of the Habsburg state, but it undermined all the fine balancing mechanisms within the framework of the Empire, and as a result Austrian prestige and popularity among the other German princes. An attempt to strengthen the Austrian state in its rivalry with Prussia ended up playing into Frederick II's hands, as the League of Princes of 1785 proved.[11] Joseph's cavalier attitude to his imperial position was another legacy of great consequence in the emerging split between Habsburg German and Austrian interests.[12]

The purpose of Joseph's state was ultimately to enhance its power and territory. Whether for itself or for its ruling family was an unimportant question; the Austrian interest, under Joseph as well, was 'more land'. Joseph may have been an admirer of humanity, but he was also a keen student of military affairs. He saw in his army the ultimate expression of his state, for without an effective armed force Austria could not be a great power and all his efforts would be in vain. The test of a state's viability was seen to be its ability to expand its borders, and it is no accident that the massive crisis in which Joseph's reign ended took place in the shadow of his war against the Turks. It was initial failures on that front which unleashed much of the resistance to his other reforms, so that by his death in 1790 his empire was in turmoil, the Austrian Netherlands in open revolt. The first attempt to turn Austria into a modern, powerful state through a centralised absolutism, was thus defeated by the combination of military difficulties and domestic particularist resistance.[13]

. . .

LEGITIMACY

If Joseph's attempts to modernise the Habsburg state were heading for failure on his death, events surrounding his sister, Marie

Antoinette, Queen of France, ensured that his successor, his brother Leopold II (1790–92), would have to continue the retreat that he himself had already started. The French Revolution, far from setting off the trend to modernisation in Europe, stopped reform attempts already under way in most continental states in their tracks.[14] This was certainly the case in Austria, where all thoughts of reform were swept aside by the critical threat to the Habsburg position posed by the revolutionary French state.

In the crisis which was to plunge Europe into another even more devastating quarter century of war, in the French Revolutionary and then Napoleonic Wars, Austria was involved from almost beginning to end, again with profound consequences. Under the rule of Francis II (1792–1835), Leopold's son, the Austrian armies went from major disaster to major disaster. The advent of Napoleon made things worse. His proclaiming himself as Emperor of France in 1804 led to Francis scrambling to adopt a similarly hereditary imperial title, Emperor of Austria, as opposed to the 'elected' office of Holy Roman Emperor. The devastating defeat of Austerlitz a year later led to a settlement which virtually dismembered Austria. The creation of the Confederation of the Rhine in 1806 led Francis to abdicate as Holy Roman Emperor, and dissolve an empire which Napoleon had effectively wiped off the map of Europe. (Hence he went from being Francis II of the Holy Roman Empire to Francis I of Austria.) Further military defeat in 1809 led to Austria becoming a mere satellite state and Napoleon taking as his bride Francis's daughter, the great-niece of Marie Antoinette, Marie Louise. The Habsburgs had never been so low.

Within five years, however, Austria had become the doyen of great powers again, the linchpin of a new, anti-revolutionary international order. The architect of this remarkable turnaround – abetted by Napoleon's own foolhardiness – was Clemens Prince Metternich, who became Austrian Chancellor in 1810 and remained in the post until 1848. The lessons he drew from the Habsburg state's dramatic turns of fate during the crisis of revolution were largely to determine the shape of post-Napoleonic Austria, and Europe. While a full restoration of the *ancien régime* was deemed impossible at the Congress of Vienna in 1815, Metternich had come to the conclusion that the best way to preserve the newly won status of Austria as again a decisive player on the European scene was to make Austria the standard bearer of the principle of legitimacy, and convince the other powers, but at least Russia, that legitimacy, the preservation of traditional authority and the restored status quo, was the way to keep Europe peaceful and its monarchs on their thrones.[15]

In many ways, therefore, Francis I's Austria reverted under Metternich from the Enlightened étatisme of Joseph II to a much more conservative reliance on Austrian, dynastic rights, as laid down in the Vienna settlement. From having essentially abandoned the imperial status quo in the 1780s, Austria under Metternich's guidance went to being the leader of the conservative drive to make sure every surviving monarch's rights, above all those of the Habsburgs, were maintained against the pressures of a modernising society. The Habsburgs could reasonably adopt this stance, as they had come out of the crisis with not only the restoration of their Central European territories, but also with the renewed seniority within the German Confederation (the Vienna Congress's surrogate for the extinct Holy Roman Empire), a very large part of prosperous northern Italy, and junior Habsburg branches placed in much of the rest of central Italy. Habsburg politics in Europe and the Monarchy once more became a matter of arbitrating between claims, and defending the rights – of monarchs and the ruling elites.

Joseph's shift from a dynastic to a state focus proved short-lived, with the result that any development of an identification with the Austrian state beyond that of an identification with the dynastic house itself, was strangled at birth. The abandonment by the Habsburg authorities of Andreas Hofer's 'patriotic' rebellion in the Tyrol was only the most obvious sign that the Habsburgs were no longer interested in creating a state patriotism beyond loyalty to themselves. It might well be apocryphal, but Francis I's question when told that a man seeking audience was a patriot: 'But is he a patriot for me?', sums up the return to a traditional, dynastically based understanding of the Monarchy.[16]

Yet this return could not in any way be a complete one. The supposed legitimacy which Metternich sought to defend at home and abroad was not built on the firmest of foundations. The imperial title was no longer that of the time-honoured Holy Roman Empire, but an artificial title of questionable legality adopted in imitation of a parvenu (now failed) Corsican. The German Confederation was a new body pretending to be heir to the Empire, but obviously quite different and without traditional authority. Austria still had her share of the partition of Poland, which itself had been a blatant breach of the principle of legitimacy.

Even within the Monarchy, the system of administration bore little resemblance to traditional forms. Austria in the early nineteenth century became the home of many of the more conservative German Romantics, and they rallied around an image of the Habsburg state as the bastion of Catholic organicism. Yet it was the Josephist bureaucracy, developed under Maria Theresa and Joseph II to turn Austria into a modern, Enlightened state, which was now made to serve as an instrument of reaction against radical change, or even much change at all. Even the censorship and police intelligence system which became so notorious a part of Metternich's 'System' had been introduced by Joseph.[17] What efforts at change Metternich and Francis I's other advisers did make, in the form of a revival of the provincial estates, merely tried to provide a mask of legitimacy to what remained a system run by bureaucratic regulation and military main force.[18] Nor could the defence of the status quo, to which the policy of legitimacy amounted, prevent the Josephist state machine running out of steam quite quickly after 1815. Much as in the late seventeenth century a highpoint of Habsburg brilliance rapidly gave way to inefficiency and backwardness.[19]

Part of this was undoubtedly due to the inadequacies of the ruler, who, despite Metternich's reputation and immense influence, remained the key figure in the Austrian power structure. Francis offered a picture of *petit bourgeois* respectability and homeliness, which made him popular with the Viennese, and he also appeared as a conscientious bureaucrat, pushing paper whenever he could. The problem was that his role in the administration of his state was as often as not to push the paper back in the direction whence it had come, or to the back of a drawer in his desk. The reason why hardly any major reforms were undertaken during Francis's reign was that he kept sending anything which required decisive action back for further consideration. He made sure by his procrastination that nothing was done.[20] He also ensured that his more talented brothers were excluded from positions of any power. After what he had gone through, Francis's tenacity in keeping things as they were, is understandable. Yet the impact on the efficiency of the Habsburg bureaucracy was pernicious.

His attitude to the educated classes in his realm had an equally baneful effect. His stated preference for blind obedience over any independence of thought, which he deemed unnecessary for running his state, lent credence to the image of Austria as a benighted land, a 'prison of the peoples'.[21] The educational deficit with northern Germany, which had been clear since Maria Theresa's time, and which Joseph had tried so hard to close, opened up once more, giving Prussia above all the advantage in the race for cultural prestige within the German orbit.[22]

In economic terms as well, Francis's reign, while showing a recovery from the awful dislocations of the era of wars, was a period when Austria began to slip behind those countries to the north and west of her which were experiencing the onset of the spurt of economic growth and technological change known as the industrial revolution. Metternich might have been keen to encourage such economic growth, but his emperor, the inefficient bureaucracy, educational backwardness and political oppression, as well as a chronic fiscal situation, made such a goal difficult or impossible to achieve. Austria's economic weakness in turn made her financially unable to sustain the role Metternich had given her of guarantor of the conservative settlement of 1815.[23]

Metternich's policy of a return to legitimacy, buttressed by the role of Francis, ended up exacerbating the problems of Austria by clinging to its dynastic character. By the 1830s there were other forms of legitimacy emerging which were pushing aside the sort of dynastic and religious claims to authority on which the Franciscan version of the Habsburg state rested. Liberalism, nationalism, theories of progress generally, threatened the very foundation of the Habsburg position as restored by Metternich.

Liberalism, with its ideas of popular sovereignty and citizenship, as well as individual freedom, was clearly anathema to a dynastic establishment that claimed to rule by divine right. Nationalism, which derived its legitimacy from the authority of a particular community of people, however connected, was equally threatening, even more so in the Habsburg case than in others due to the neglect of the Habsburgs to build a specifically Austrian state identity separate from themselves. The centres of national identification were thus not state based, but provincially and – even worse – ethnically determined. Austria, even in its core territories, was to prove to be a nationalities-state and not a nation-state. The ambivalence of the dynasty in this respect, neither purely a-national, nor convincingly German, was to prove a key factor in its nineteenth-century fate.

Yet in a sense it was the idea of Progress itself which was to prove for Austria the most destructive of all modern sources of legitimacy, for it betokened in international terms a return to the principles which had led to the invasion of Silesia, the partition of Poland, and the disappearance of the Holy Roman Empire. The Hegelian concept of history as the world's court of judgement was the death-knell of an international settlement based on legitimacy, on the status quo, for it discarded the claims of tradition and of ancient right (even if not so ancient) for what worked, what succeeded. Given that 'progress', in political, educational and economic terms, became the principal ideological commitment of the leading Western powers and of much of the German educated classes, that 'utility' and 'freedom' came to dominate the political discourse of the leading economic and financial power of the age, England, Metternich's positioning of Austria as the upholder of tradition, of legitimacy, of the divine right of dynasties to rule their subjects no matter the changes going on in the world, came to look of more and more dubious wisdom.

By the death of Francis in 1835, Austria's star had already dimmed considerably. In foreign policy, Metternich had been unable to prevent the spread of both liberalism and nationalism wherever British ships could intervene effectively, as in Belgium and the Iberian peninsula, or where Russian sentiment and self-interest overcame arguments of imperial solidarity as in Greece.[24] At home concessions had been forced from the absolutist regime in Hungary, where the diet was allowed to meet for the first time in many years in 1825.[25] The finances remained in a parlous state, inadequate for Metternich's commitment to keep the peace – and the revolution down – in the Austrian spheres of interest in Germany and Italy. Austria, having set herself up as the 'European' protector of legitimacy, the status quo and Reaction, had made herself the primary target of reformers, revolutionaries, liberals and nationalists all over Europe, both within the Monarchy's borders and beyond, especially in the Habsburg spheres of Germany and Italy. The accession to the throne, in strict dynastic succession, of Ferdinand, an amiable but epileptic half-wit, yet another unfortunate Habsburg dynastic accident, did not bode well for the future.

. | . .

NOTES AND REFERENCES

1. M. Tanner, *The Last Descendant of Aeneas: The Habsburgs and the Mythic Image of the Emperor*, Yale, New Haven 1993.
2. R.J.W. Evans, *The Making of the Habsburg Monarchy, 1550–1700: An Interpretation*, Clarendon, Oxford 1979.
3. C. Ingrao, *The Habsburg Monarchy 1618–1815*, Cambridge 1994, p. 129 (New Approaches to European History).
4. T.C.W. Blanning, *Joseph II*, Longman, London 1994, pp. 21–9 (Profiles in Power).
5. Ibid., pp. 27–39.
6. Ibid., p. 38.
7. Ibid., pp. 40–4.
8. W. Heindl, *Gehorsame Rebellen: Bürokratie und Beamte in Österreich, 1780–1848*, Böhlau, Vienna 1991, pp. 21–34 (Studien zu Politik und Verwaltung).
9. Blanning, *Joseph II*, pp. 70–2.
10. Ibid., pp. 92–119.
11. Ibid., pp. 132–3, 143–50.
12. J. Whaley, 'Austria, "Germany", and the Dissolution of the Holy Roman Empire'. In R. Robertson, E. Timms (eds), *The Habsburg Legacy: National Identity in Historical Perspective* (*Austrian Studies* vol. 5), Edinburgh 1994, p. 9.
13. Blanning, *Joseph II*, pp. 176–89.
14. T.C.W. Blanning, 'The French Revolution and the Modernization of Germany', *Central European History*, vol. 22 (2) (1989): pp. 122–4.
15. F.R. Bridge, *The Habsburg Monarchy among the Great Powers, 1815–1918*, Berg, Oxford 1990, pp. 26ff.; A. Sked, *The Decline and Fall of the Habsburg Empire 1815–1918*, Longman, London 1989, pp. 8–25.
16. A.J.P. Taylor, *The Habsburg Monarchy 1809–1918*, Penguin, Harmondsworth 1948 (1964), p. 25; O. Jászi, *The Dissolution of the Habsburg Monarchy*, Chicago 1929, p. 83 (Studies in the Making of Citizens).
17. J.-P. Bled, *Franz Joseph*, trans. T. Bridgeman, Blackwell, Oxford 1992, pp. 11–12.
18. Sked, *Decline and Fall of the Habsburg Empire*, p. 27.
19. Heindl, *Gehorsame Rebellen*, pp. 329–30.
20. Ibid., p. 74; Sked, 1989, *Decline and Fall of the Habsburg Empire*, p. 28.

21. Sked, *Decline and Fall of the Habsburg Empire*, p. 48; Jászi, *Dissolution of the Habsburg Monarchy*, p. 78.
22. Heindl, *Gehorsame Rebellen*, pp. 112ff.; H. Lentze, *Die Universitätsreform des Ministers Graf Leo Thun-Hohenstein*, Akademie der Wissenschaften, Vienna 1962, pp. 25–8.
23. Sked, *Decline and Fall of the Habsburg Empire*, pp. 69–70; N.T. Gross, 'The Habsburg Monarchy'. In C.M. Cipolla (ed.), *The Fontana Economic History of Europe* (5 vols), Fontana, Glasgow 1973, vol. 4, pt. 1, p. 248; Bridge, *The Habsburg Monarchy*, p. 27.
24. Bridge, *The Habsburg Monarchy*, pp. 33ff.
25. Sked, *Decline and Fall of the Habsburg Empire*, p. 35.

Chapter 3

ABSOLUTISM, 1830–59

. . .

AN EMPEROR IN THE MAKING

Francis Joseph was born on 18 August 1830 into a Habsburg family whose regime was stable, if showing signs of stagnation, and alarm at the revolutions of that year. The new-born's grandfather, Francis I, still ruled and presided over a court which was staunchly conservative, even if the presence of the Duke of Reichstadt, the son of Napoleon Bonaparte's marriage with Francis's daughter, Marie Louise, was a reminder of other times. Then, Francis had been prepared to play the dynastic game to save his position, but now in his old age, another aspect of dynasticism, the problem of succession, loomed ever larger.

Francis's eldest son, Ferdinand, was the legitimate, and Francis's chosen, heir, but his medical and mental condition made him only dubiously fit to succeed to the demanding position of absolute ruler of the Monarchy. It was also unlikely that he would ever himself have offspring, and although he was to marry in 1831 his wife remained childless. Next in succession was Francis's second eldest son, Francis Charles, not much cleverer than Ferdinand, but at least sound in body and mind. For the Habsburg (-Lorraine) line to continue in a more or less uncomplicated manner thus required that his marriage to the Bavarian princess Sophie (sister of Francis I's fourth wife) should produce a male heir. The arrival of Francis Joseph, their first child, was thus very welcome, as it secured the succession.

To no one was the birth of Francis Joseph more welcome than the mother herself. Sophie of Bavaria was from the beginning very ambitious for her son, pouring into him all the hopes for future greatness and power which she, as a Bavarian female outsider at an Austrian court obsessed with preserving the male line, could never realise for herself. Sophie combined this ambition with a powerful intelligence, a strong Catholic piety and a conservative cast of German Romanticism. She devoted herself to her son, over whom she was to have a very strong, lifelong influence, at times of critical importance to Francis Joseph's policies as emperor.[1]

After the initial scare of Ferdinand's marriage in 1831, it soon became clear that no children were to be expected, and that Francis Joseph, healthy and at least of average intelligence, could be brought up as prospective emperor, in accord with Sophie's plans. The education of 'Franzi', as Francis Joseph was called as a child, was conducted according to Habsburg court tradition, with Sophie retaining an active interest. (She often attended the lessons herself.[2]) At age six he passed from the supervision of his 'aja' (nanny) to that of his 'primo ajo', Count Heinrich Bombelles, and his formal education began. Bombelles, the descendant of an aristocratic emigré from revolutionary France and Metternich's personal choice for this important job, devised an elaborate educational plan for the future ruler.[3]

Under his supervision and that of the 'secundo ajo', Count Alexander Coronini-Cronberg, Franzi started with a thirteen-hour week of lessons at age six, going to a thirty-two-hour week at age seven. At that point his lessons already included German, writing, geography, religion, drawing, dancing, gymnastics, fencing, swimming and military drilling, as well as French, Hungarian and Czech.[4] Other subjects added subsequently were history, riding and music, as well as another language, Italian. By his twelfth year, Francis Joseph was having fifty hours of lessons a week. The very conscientious and punctual pupil did his best to keep up with all this, even though he tended to be outshone by his livelier younger brother, Ferdinand Max, and was not a great reader, preferring drawing and the military arts. Yet the burden eventually became too much. By age thirteen the extent to which he was being overworked had led to stress-induced illness.[5] After some respite he was then submitted to more subjects. Abbot Othmar von Rauscher taught him philosophy from 1844, by age sixteen Francis Joseph was also learning law, diplomacy, astronomy, technology and Polish. His lessons began at 6 a.m. and lasted until 9 p.m.[6]

This heavy regimen, with its special emphasis on languages was clearly intended for the ruler of a dynastic, multi-national state which was also one of Europe's great powers. Not only would a ruler have to speak his subjects' languages (or at least those that

counted), but he would also need to be able to converse in
international circles, in French. (He was never taught English.)
As a prospective absolute ruler, it was never envisaged that he
would have to abase himself by appealing to the people or their
representatives, so in the midst of all his lessons in practical rul-
ership (fencing, dancing, etc.) he was never taught the art of public
speaking.[7]

What he was taught were the manly, and above all the martial,
arts. As a youth, at his father's side, he developed a passion for
hunting which remained with him his whole life. Yet the shooting of game was only a pastime. His great love, from a very early
age, was one of the prime fields of an absolute ruler's duties in
the post-Napoleonic age, the army. He was given his first uniform
when he was three, and his first regiment at age thirteen.[8] He
came to revel in all aspects of military life, from the drilling of
the imperial guards outside his window when he was very small,
to the lessons under his military tutor, Franz von Hauslab when
he was a teenager. The family encouraged this love of things
military, plying him with military gifts at Christmas time. It was
at Christmas 1835 that the five-year-old Francis Joseph declared:
'What is military is what I like best.'[9] His identification with the
military, as with his penchant for wearing military uniform, was
something which stayed with him his whole life.

One major reason for Francis Joseph's particular love of the
army was that its way of life clearly appealed to his character. There
was always a large streak of obstinacy, which did not fit the model
of blind obedience favoured in the army, but was quite befitting
a commander-in-chief. Apart from that, the qualities of punctual-
ity, punctiliousness, conscientiousness, sense of duty, and above
all a sense of the need to maintain order, which Francis Joseph
showed in abundance as a child, were all virtues prized in military
life. Furthermore, his tendency to see issues empirically, his preference for practical, often expedient, solutions based on the
common-sense lessons of experience, rather than for complex
policies based on high theoretical considerations, also made the
Habsburg army culture well suited to him. He was never a great
thinker, and that did not put him at odds with the *esprit de corps*
of the Austrian army.[10]

He did have his principles, however: those imbibed from the
Metternichian educators. If Rauscher taught him 'philosophy'
from the perspective of a hyper-conservative Catholicism, Joseph
Fielo taught him history in such a way that it was drummed into

33

Francis Joseph that 'liberalism' and 'constitution' were two things which a self-respecting Habsburg such as himself, a ruler-to-be by Divine Right, should avoid at all costs.[11] This conservative, absolutist worldview was buttressed by the equally reactionary vision of his mother, who in 1830 had prayed for the divine destruction of revolutionary Paris, spoke of William IV's 'liberal stupidities' and could never stomach the 'illegitimate' Orleanist regime in France.[12] His education in the theory and practice of absolutism was capped by a series of Sunday afternoon lessons which the teenager started with Metternich himself in November 1847 on the subject of statecraft. Not surprisingly the lessons emphasised the need of the ruler of the Habsburg lands to put foreign policy before domestic affairs.[13]

By early 1848, therefore, Francis Joseph was being groomed to become, at some indeterminate time, a worthy successor to his namesake, Francis I. At this point, 'Franzi' was still known only by his first name, in conscious deference to his grandfather's memory and tradition. The reason why he was to become emperor so much sooner than expected, was also the reason why he was to be known not as Francis II, but as Francis Joseph I. The additional name was in deference to Joseph II, the radical lover of humanity and hero of Austrian liberals. That it had to be added bespoke the depth of the crisis that brought Francis Joseph to the throne as saviour of a shaken dynasty.

·   ·   ·

BEFORE MARCH

The problems developing within the Habsburg central administration at the end of Francis I's reign were not made any easier by the succession of the heavily incapacitated Ferdinand. Part of the problem had to do with Ferdinand himself. As Francis Joseph's mother, Sophie herself put it, it was difficult to look up to one's 'commander', when he had the scrawny physical presence of Ferdinand.[14] The major part of the problem, however, was that the *de facto* governing body, the State Council, consisting of Metternich, Franz Anton Count Kolowrat, Archduke Louis and Francis Joseph's father Francis Charles, never was able to fill the vacuum left by Ferdinand's problems. Metternich and Kolowrat continued to squabble over who should run which part of the domestic administration, while Archduke Louis proved an even greater procrastinator than Francis I.[15]

Metternich continued to press for tighter control of the provinces, especially in Italy and Hungary, and more money for the army and the police, while Kolowrat resisted any further drain on the Monarchy's finances, which were usually in a parlous state. Louis tended to take the line of least resistance, which meant backing Kolowrat and doing not very much.[16] While central policy drifted, the Josephist bureaucracy became worse and worse paid and, partly in consequence, more and more demoralised. The government, run on a threadbare budget, now itself became a hive of criticism, in the form of frustrated officials calling for a reform of government to suit their modern, and increasingly liberal, ideals. The Habsburg state, having produced an educated class of officials, now became a target of their sometimes intellectual, but often all too material, dissatisfactions. Austrian liberalism, as often as not, came from within the Austrian state apparatus.[17]

The main problem of the Habsburg Monarchy in the *Vormärz* (the period before March 1848) was that there was never enough money or resources for Austria either to fulfil its foreign policy responsibilities, or invest in building an effective domestic regime. Metternich's policies had meant expensive military interventions, or at least preparations – such as the army stationed in Italy to counter the French threat – which the finances of the Monarchy could never match. Partly this was due to the Habsburg Monarchy's relative economic backwardness, which meant that there were not the resources to exploit that there were, for example, in England. But the other problem was that even those resources that were there were left largely untaxed because of the ambivalences of the imperfect absolute state which it had become.[18]

The retreat from Joseph II's policies had left the Habsburgs with only partially absolute control of their state. Hungary, above all, retained a great many privileges and institutions, such as the county system of local government, which went against absolutist Habsburg claims.[19] Habsburg budgetary austerity was at least partially due to the fact that every time they needed money from Hungary they had to call the Diet, which pressed for – and often got – more concessions every time it met from 1825 until 1848.[20] In those parts where it did have practical absolute control, vested interests in the localities were sufficiently feared by the centre not to push them too much. The result was a lack of ready money, which in turn limited the ability of the Habsburgs to pay the soldiers and officials needed to confirm and expand the power of the centre in places such as Hungary, which could thus resist paying more taxes . . ..

In the 1840s Metternich tried to impose a more stringent, if largely covert, central control on the provinces, especially in Italy and Hungary. Yet this in itself led to even greater resistance there, necessitating larger expenditures on troops and police to check unrest, and thus making the crackdown largely futile in its main purpose: to make the Monarchy's central authorities richer and thus more powerful.[21] The struggle between centre and periphery was heading for a showdown in which it was not at all clear that the centre held the advantage.

. . .

THE NATIONALISM PROBLEM

The provincial resistance to the extension or realisation of Habsburg power was intimately connected by the 1840s with the large growth of nationalism among Europe's educated elites. As adumbrated earlier, nationalism had become fashionable as a largely liberal ideology, which opposed the Metternichian defence of the historic rights of legitimate dynastic rulers with the rights of historic peoples to determine their own, national government. Whatever their inspiration, and the sources were many, educated and politically conscious elites all over early nineteenth-century Europe – in other words the part of the populace that mattered – were full of vocal demands for the changing of the map of Europe so that borders fitted, with each nation having its own self-determining state.

Not every nation without a state was in the same predicament in mid-nineteenth-century Europe. There were some large, 'historic' nations, such as the Germans and the Italians, spread out over several states. There were also middling 'historic' nations, whose established historical territories now existed within larger imperial borders, as did those of the Magyars, or were split between empires, as were those of historic but now partitioned Poland. There were also smaller 'nations without history', otherwise known as nationalities, which either had little historical tradition as independent political units (the main test of the all-important 'historical' status) as in the Slovene case, or had had their 'history' crushed out of them by conquest, as in the case of the Czechs at the notorious Battle of the White Mountain of 1620.[22]

The fact that the relegation of the Czechs from the premier league of 'historical' nations could be so easily pinpointed was of course a problem in keeping the Czechs in the non-historical category of nineteenth-century national taxonomy, but the decimation of the Czech political nation (nobility) at that point, and the caesura in Czech cultural development were nevertheless powerful arguments against the Czechs in the struggle for historical ranking. The importance of history, even the 'manufacturing' or 'invention' of history in Central Europe, stemmed from the fact that a nation's status was greatly influenced by how it fared in the 'historic'/'non-historic' ranking.[23] The Czechs' ability to remake, and reclaim their history so that they became a 'historic' nation was thus not only a sign of the growth in their power, but also a substantial cause of it.

While some of the 'nationalities' had not fully 'awoken' from their 'history-less' slumbers by mid-century, all the 'historic' nations had, and many of the others had too, especially the Czechs. That is to say that, whatever the bulk of the populations of each nation might think – or most likely not think – about their national plight and or rights, each nation had acquired leaderships, usually self-selected, which demanded recognition, autonomy, ultimately independence for their nation, or at least a fair part in, and of, state affairs. That they did not have this in so many instances in early nineteenth-century Europe was the cause of the various nationalist movements pressuring the status quo.

The problem posed by nationalism to the Habsburg Monarchy can be appreciated by the fact that all the above national examples were of peoples either wholly or partially inside its borders. As touched on above, because of the dynastic character of the state no dominant *state* nationality had been formed, therefore no *Austrian* identity achieved parity with more ethnically or linguistically based identities, let alone with the identities of locality and province.[24] At the centre there was an Austrian patriotism among the more enlightened parts of the bureaucracy, but even here this was overshadowed by a legitimist identification of the state with the Habsburgs themselves.[25]

In other circumstances, this might not have been such a problem: all one needed was one dominant national group to lord it over the others. Every 'nation-state' in Europe had, and most still have, minority nations within their borders who, if not oppressed, still pose a problem to claims to complete national uniformity. Britain (that is to say the English) had the Welsh, the Scottish, and above all the Irish. Yet the dominant nation, if there are enough of them, can usually keep such groups in order and inside the polity. This was not the case with the Habsburg Monarchy. As Rudolf Kjellén put it: 'A Great Power can endure without difficulty one Ireland, as England did, even three, as imperial Germany did (Poland, Alsace, Schleswig). Different is the case when a Great Power is composed of nothing else but Irelands, as was almost the history of Austro-Hungary.'[26]

As luck would have it, the demography of Central Europe and the accidents of dynastic acquisition and loss conspired to make the Habsburg Monarchy a state without a demographically dominant national linguistic or ethnic group. If Silesia had not been lost, if Bavaria had been gained instead of Galicia, if Eugene's gains against the Turks had not been quite so large, if Joseph II had been able to impose German as the language of administration throughout his realm, the German position might have been a much more viable basis on which to build a unitary Austrian identity. As things stood, however, the Germans were not a dominant percentage of the population, even if they were clearly hegemonic in most other respects.

That the counter-factual arguments begin so early in this account tells us something about the character of the Habsburg Monarchy and its historiography; one can equally say that, if the Germans had been more dominant, then the Monarchy would not have been the same in any case. One can go further: the polyglot nature of the state was not purely the result of fortune or geography, but of the attitude of the dynasty, which had never restricted itself to any national, or proto-national identity, and rarely to that of any particular state, even its own. It had picked up talent wherever it could find it, whether the Savoyard Eugene, the Dutchman Gottfried Van Swieten, the originally Irish Taaffe family, or the Germans Beethoven and Mozart. As we have seen, it had also picked up territory wherever it could, regardless of nationality, contiguity, or the interests of state integration.

One can even argue, with Ernest Gellner, that in the pre-modern era, when mass communication was not a key requirement of economic or political success, it was indeed in the dynasty's interests to rule over a set of peoples separated by language, and hence less likely to unite against the common denominator of the central power.[27] But what worked in a pre-modern dynastic state did not do so well in a modern state reliant on ease of communication; in fact it blocked any such project, as Joseph II had all too well discovered. The separation of peoples through language remained, however, of some value to the dynastic power, as we shall see.

The Habsburg Monarchy in 1848 was indeed a multitude of Irelands (see Map 2). The Germans within the Austrian Empire were concentrated in the western territories, and in the northwestern borderland with the rest of the German Confederation, as well as having settlements scattered throughout the empire. As outlined above, they were clearly the closest to fulfilling the role of dominant nation, and in many ways acted and were seen as the *Staatsvolk*, state people of the Monarchy.[28] The central administration spoke German, and the dynasty was of German origin, indeed prided itself on being the chief German princely family. Francis Joseph was to call himself 'a German prince' and by descent he was largely right. He was, after all, on his mother's side Bavarian, and he himself married another Bavarian. Germans were also the dominant presence in the cities of mid-nineteenth-century Central Europe, with, apart from their dominance in Vienna itself, majorities in Prague, Pressburg (now Bratislava), and Buda/Pest, as well as many lesser centres, such as Budweis (České Budejovice) and Brünn (Brno).[29]

Part of this German urban dominance was deceptive, as many 'Germans' were of non-German background, but had adopted German because it was the language of commerce and administration in most of the empire. Many of these 'Germans' were more loyal to the Habsburgs than they were to any German nationality, as were most of the German-speaking aristocracy. Their loyalties tended to be to pre-modern institutions, such as the dynasty or their own estate, rather than to modern concepts such as the nation. Other Germans, however, precisely because they were the most prosperous and best educated group in the Monarchy (excluding Lombardy–Venetia), were at the vanguard of modern change. The German educated middle classes included in their ranks the leaders of the cause of Austrian liberalism against Metternichian (Habsburg) 'tyranny'. That this leadership also identified this liberal cause with that of the German national cause was to lead very quickly to huge complications.[30]

The Italians in the Monarchy were actually more prosperous

and educated than the Germans, but the bulk of Habsburg Italians in Lombardy–Venetia (as opposed to the much older Habsburg Italian populations in the Tyrol and along the Adriatic's littoral) were not integrated into the rest of the empire beyond the Alps, and were in no way as closely identified with the Monarchy as the Germans. Power resided in Vienna, not Milan or Venice, and the Milanese and Venetian elites increasingly resented this fact, as well as the high-handed if relatively efficient Austrian bureaucracy. That their sons found little chance of easy career advancement within that bureaucracy did not help endear the Austrians to the Italian nobility. Their exclusion from the Habsburg court only made things worse. By 1848 the Italian provinces were highly restless at Habsburg rule, open to nationalist propaganda and the blandishments of the Piedmontese. Thus they presented a huge problem, while at the same time being vital for shoring up Habsburg finances and providing a key asset against French interests in Italy.[31]

The Magyars, or rather the Magyar political elite of the nobility and gentry, were also dissatisfied with their lot, but unlike the Italians they had far more institutional room in which to express and act on it. Hungary had always been a challenge for the Habsburgs. With most of the kingdom's territories only reconquered from the Turks at the turn of the seventeenth and eighteenth centuries, the dynasty had never been able to impose its absolute will on the traditional Hungarian administration, based on the *Comitati*, counties, governed by the *Congregationes*, assemblies of local noblemen. Joseph II had made the most radical attempt, in the process trying to replace the traditional Latin with German as the language of administration. The Magyar nobility and lesser nobility, or gentry, had successfully defended the historically based rights of the Hungarian estates, and the feudal privileges which supported them. [32]

By the early nineteenth century the Habsburgs had been forced to recognise the Hungarian Estates or Diet as the legal provider of taxation in St Stephen's kingdom. Although Francis and Metternich might have persuaded themselves that this was only window-dressing, the Magyar leadership had skilfully played up the theoretical 'constitutional' powers of the Diet, so that by 1848 it had established itself as a major centre of power in – and major thorn in the side of – the Habsburg Monarchy. The development of a modern constitutional theory based on the medieval rights of the Magyar 'nation' (the nobility and gentry), and the replacement of Latin not by German but by a modernised and rejuvenated Magyar language, were already encouraging both voluble Magyar nationalism, and claims to increased constitutional rights, if not autonomy for the lands of the crown of St Stephen.[33]

The Poles also figured in the ranks of the 'historic nations' and had been the favourite political cause of early nineteenth-century liberalism. The Polish elite in Galicia had been part of the periodically active movement to rescue the Polish kingdom from Russian, Prussian and Austrian captivity. Their latest attempt to shake off Austrian shackles, in 1846, had ended in complete catastrophe, however, as their nationalist revolt had been met not by the Austrian authorities so much as by a revolt by the peasantry oppressed by them, whether of Polish or Ukrainian stock. At this point national causes did not necessarily dominate social ones, and could in fact be destroyed by them, as the Habsburg authorities noted. In 1848 Galicia was relatively peaceful.[34]

Still in the process of battling out of the 'non-historic' division after their dramatic demotion in 1620, the Czechs, concentrated in the Bohemian crownlands in the north-west quadrant of the Monarchy, were by 1848 in the midst of a very strong national revival. At first evident in the cultural sphere, Czech nationalism had begun to politicise, with its largely educated-middle-class leadership allying with members of the Bohemian nobility, many of whose ancestors had been the main beneficiaries of Habsburg largesse during the Counter-Reformation assault on Bohemian society. Still lagging behind the Magyars, the Czech nationalists were also beginning to demand the recognition of the 'state right' of the lands of the crown of St Wenceslas, that is to use 'historic' rights based on provincial boundaries for nationalist ends.[35]

On the southern flank of the Monarchy, the various South Slav peoples, Slovenes, Croats and Serbs, did not appear a threat to the integrity of the Habsburg state. Far from it; there were, it is true, some who dreamt of a restoration of the Napoleonic kingdom of Illyria, which had given a short-lived independence to large parts of the South Slav territories, but any such trend was more than counter-balanced by a very strong pro-Habsburg tradition, especially among the Croats, and particularly in the territories on the Monarchy's Southern border known as the Military Frontier, where Croat and Serb had been resettled with their families as defenders against the Turkish threat. (The large number of Serbs who were to be found before the recent breakup of Yugoslavia living far to the west of Serbia is partially the result of Habsburg imperial policy.) Croatian loyalty to the Habsburgs was greatly strengthened by their animosity against the neighbouring Magyars.[36]

This last example shows that there were still large compensations to be had from having a state with such a number of diverse populations. While the diversity made any coherent action as a state very difficult, if one was content to operate as a dynastic power, à la Gellner, then diversity left a large amount of room open to practise that most traditional imperial policy: divide and rule. The Habsburg authorities were to profit from this in the next years, if often only unintentionally.

The largest point of division was one which was close to, but not identical with, the 'historic'–'non-historic' split, and that was the fact that though the Magyars and the Germans were the leading groups within the state (north of the Alps), Slavs when counted all together were almost half of the population. If and when these populations developed economically and culturally, as the Czechs were already doing, then both German and Magyar hegemony was going to be in serious trouble. The Czechs were already a concern for the Germans, the Croats of concern to the Magyars. At this point the Slovaks and Rumanians were largely quiescent, at the bottom of the 'non-historic' division, but the potential was there to complicate – and exacerbate – the ethnic and national situation in the Habsburg Monarchy even more.

If the problem of nationalism within the Monarchy was bad, it was even worse in the two major Habsburg spheres of interest in Metternichian Europe, Italy and Germany. In Germany Austria was the senior partner in the German Confederation to Prussia and more than thirty other states. The Vienna settlement, of a crisis caused by the French Revolution, had made the Austrian monarch, as a quasi-Holy Roman Emperor, the leader of the German states against any recurrence of the French threat, and against any revolution from within Germany itself. It had similarly made the Habsburgs the main guarantor of stability in Italy, not only building up Austrian territories in the Lombard Plain to protect against France's southern flank, but also putting other branches of the dynasty in power in Tuscany, Parma and Modena. An alliance with the Kingdom of Naples, and as the main defender of Catholic tradition a position of informal protector of the Papacy, meant that Italy was almost entirely under Habsburg control, except for Piedmont.[37]

These were, given Metternich's westward orientation, the main areas of interest for Habsburg foreign policy until 1848. Germany was a traditional Habsburg interest, and politically the Habsburg position in the two 'geographical expressions' gave Austria the diplomatic *raison d'être* as guarantor of the European order (against France) which had been the goal of Metternich's stratagems. In addition, Austria's Italian possessions were fiscally profitable for the constantly strapped state finances. Economically and culturally, Germany and Italy were certainly on a far higher level than the other potential Austrian sphere of interest, the Balkans. This region was a backwater for Habsburg interests before 1848. Metternich's main policy here was to hold the line, when possible. Over Greece he had of necessity given in to Russian and Western Pan-Hellenism, but generally he tried, as diplomatically as possible, to hinder Russian attempts to drive back the Turks, and instead allied with Britain, otherwise the bane of his policies, to support Turkey's position. The Balkans were a sideline for him; Metternich operated not on a Balkan, but on a European stage.[38]

Metternich was a 'European' to the extent that he cast Austria in the role of protector of legitimacy and the established order in Europe, as laid down in the Vienna settlement. Ironically, the concentration on Germany and Italy not only led Metternich into the two main lions' dens of liberal nationalism in mid-nineteenth-century Europe, but the very Vienna settlement which had given Austria the considerable burden of defending order in both these areas had also built up the two nuclei around which national hopes were soon to coalesce.

In Germany, in their wish to counter the danger of another expansionary French war, the signatories of Vienna had not only put Austria back in charge of 'Germany', but also given large swathes of territory to Prussia, so that the 'junior' partner, the traditional rival, was only junior on paper, and had a dominant position in northern Germany. Subsequent developments, crucially the expansion of the commercial *Zollverein* (tariff union), had not only integrated Prussian territories with each other, but also in practice with the surrounding states. While the Prussian king, Frederick William IV had a Romantic notion of fealty to the imperial Habsburgs, many sectors of Prussian opinion, in and outside the government, were already looking to nationalism as a lever for increased Prussian power.

In Italy, the Vienna settlement had similarly hedged against the French threat by not only putting Austria in charge, but also building up the one remaining independent Italian power, Piedmont–Sardinia. As in the example of Prussia a centre had thus been provided around which nationalist ambitions could rally, and a potential rival to the Austrians created for hegemony in one of their major spheres of interest. Not for the first time, the wish to stop the last war happening again ended up providing the balance of forces and circumstances for a new and different war.

The Vienna settlement was not wholly to blame. What provided the lighter fuel of the revolutions of 1848 was the steady spread of those ideas of freedom and national unity mentioned above. It may well be true that economic and social change was by no means well advanced in most of Central and Southern Europe by 1848, but there had been a great growth of urban populations, a relatively large expansion of officialdoms and hence of educated middle classes. Above all improvements in communication, the spread of a mass press, meant that even the notorious attempts at censorship in Metternich's system could not prevent the politically conscious elites learning of what was happening in the West, especially of the dramatic changes in England's economy, society and political structure, and the ideas associated with them.

The ideas leapt to the East much more quickly than any economic or social change. One sign of this was that the leading circles of liberalism and liberal nationalism in the 'Austrian area' contained, apart from the expected educated middle classes, a very large proportion of noblemen, especially in Hungary and Italy.[39] Another sign of the extent to which the Habsburg position had deteriorated relative to the new ideologically driven movements, was that when Louis Philippe had ascended the French throne in 1830 he had been despised and given the cold shoulder by the Habsburg court and Sophie. When he abdicated in February 1848, his disappearance was felt as a great loss by the same court.[40] They were right to be concerned. When the 'illegitimate' Orleans dynasty fell, the dreaded return of apparently real French revolution found a whole apparatus of territories, alliances, police forces and bureaucracies, designed to counter this very threat, to be hardly more than a house of cards. Austria, put there by Metternich's policies, found itself at the centre of revolts against foreign-backed anti-national regimes (in Germany and Italy), and revolts at home against Habsburg absolutist rule from Vienna. Metternich's 'System' blew up in his face. It seems only fitting that the spark that lit the lighter fuel, apart from the fall of the House of Orleans, was a fiscal crisis at home in Vienna.

. . .

MARCH AND AFTER MARCH

On 13 March 1848, after turmoil in the streets of Vienna and in the inner circles of the Habsburg court, Metternich was dismissed, and the whole of Central Europe plunged into revolution. Francis Joseph's enthronement the following December was a direct result of, and response to, the events which together make up the revolution of 1848, the 'Springtime of the Peoples'.[41]

Behind the events which shook the European establishments to their core in 1848 lay a whole panoply of factors. Looming large in the background was a severe crisis of food production in a still overwhelmingly agricultural economy. A string of harvest failures combined with population growth, led to destitution, unrest and eventually large-scale peasant revolts.[42] At the same time, the non-agricultural sector in Central Europe was growing, benefiting from the delayed impact of the industrial developments in the West.[43] The onset of industrialisation had been accompanied, however, due to the rapid growth of population, by an explosion in population of cities, such as Vienna, which were ill-prepared to deal with the influx from the countryside. It was precisely those regions suffering from only incipient and hence *inadequate* industrialisation, which were most vulnerable to revolution in 1848.[44]

These elements of economic and social unrest, when combined with the ideological and material dissatisfactions of the educated middle classes and nobilities discussed above, led to there being pockets of unrest all over Western and Central Europe in the winter of 1847–48. They were not restricted to Habsburg territories or even Habsburg spheres of interest, as the revolution in France in February attests, but because of the central position of Metternich's policies in *Vormärz* Europe, it was the Habsburg Monarchy which became the centre of the whirlwind.

It was a concatenation of revolts which produced 1848, and even then it was more the collapse of the old regime than the strength of the revolution which created such a huge upheaval. There was already large-scale unrest within the Monarchy. In Italy, the Tobacco Riots in Milan in January 1848 and unrest elsewhere had led to the imposition of martial law there by February.[45] In

45

Hungary the meeting of the Diet saw a majority of deputies supporting further reforms against Habsburg wishes. In Vienna the troubles in Lombardy–Venetia and the revolt in Sicily,[46] within the Habsburgs' Italian sphere of interest, had already led to a financial crisis of confidence, the 'Bank Hullabaloo', as it was clear that the Metternichian government could not afford more large expenditures without risking bankruptcy.[47] Louis Philippe's abdication, and the prospect of a newly revolutionary France, communicated now rapidly to the rest of Europe with the latest technologies, not only led to even greater nervousness among the Monarchy's financial creditors, but was also the signal for liberals everywhere to pressure their governments for constitutions and reforms.

One chain reaction set off revolutions in the more western German states. Another chain reaction saw Louis Kossuth's speech to the Hungarian Diet demanding constitutional government for the whole empire setting off demands within the Bohemian and Lower Austrian Estates for reforms from a Metternichian regime virtually bankrupt and thus unable to pay for the additional forces necessary to beat back the – until now relatively polite – insurgency. In the ensuing excitement, a crowd of demonstrators, calling on the Lower Austrian Diet to demand reform, was fired on by troops in the Herrengasse, unleashing chaos, which led to the municipal guard going over to the 'revolutionaries'.[48] With a regimen that was clearly not functioning well, the Habsburgs now deserted their erstwhile 'saviour' and caved before the pressure of events. Metternich's subsequent sacking truly opened the floodgates of revolution. On 15 March, Ferdinand promised to give his realm a constitution. On the 17th a separate Hungarian ministry was set up under Count Batthyány.[49] On the 18th there was revolution in Berlin. Milan had exploded in open, nationalist revolt on the same day, forcing Radetzky to withdraw on the 22nd, and causing Piedmont to declare war on Austria.[50] In the space of a few days the whole structure of Central Europe, and hence of Europe generally, had been radically changed. The way seemed clear for fundamental change along liberal and nationalist lines.

What was quite unclear was what the character and substance of that change should be. In the months after March, the forces which had together produced the revolution proved themselves unable to coalesce to maintain it. Although social unrest in the lower orders, in the peasantry and the urban masses, had been a vital ingredient of many of the revolts, also in Vienna, the bulk of the revolutionary leadership was far more interested in questions of liberal reform and national unification than social issues. Little was done to relieve urban distress until the radicalisation of the revolution in October. The one major reform passed in the Habsburg Monarchy which addressed social issues, the emancipation of the peasantry, had the net effect of satisfying the peasants, who then lapsed back into very non-revolutionary political apathy.[51]

This left the liberals, radicals and nationalists of various stripes to argue over what should be done with the Habsburg Monarchy, now that the dynastic authorities seemed to be receptive to demands which before 13 March had been unthinkable. Over the summer of 1848 the internal contradictions within the revolution became increasingly evident. What had started out in Vienna as a combination of social revolt and liberal demands for reform increasingly took on the form of a movement for national union with the rest of the German lands. At one point the black–red–gold flag of German nationalism flew not only from St Stephen's Cathedral, but from the Hofburg itself.[52] The centre of action shifted from Vienna to Frankfurt-am-Main, where the assembly in Paul's Church debated the lineaments of a new, national German state. Such a body would necessitate a radical change in the character of the Habsburg Monarchy, even its disappearance as such. Almost immediately, however, the Czechs called a Slav Congress in Prague, precisely to illustrate that the Bohemian crownlands, seen by Germans as an integral part of the historically German territories, would not be so easily included in the envisaged greater Germany.[53] In Hungary in the meantime the revolutionary government, led in effect by its Minister of Finance, Kossuth, was blending into its mostly liberal programme a considerable admixture of Magyar chauvinism, an unwise move in a kingdom where non-Magyars amounted to over half the population.[54]

Having been presented the spoils of revolution virtually without a fight, the revolutionary leaders fell out over how, or even whether, to divide them. While some in Vienna wanted to dissolve the Monarchy and join Germany, others wanted to preserve it as a means of bringing German civilisation to the Slavs, while still others wanted to make Austria a viable, liberal multi-national state. (That all this was far from being necessarily anti-Habsburg is shown by the occupant at Frankfurt of the office of *Reichsverweser*, 'imperial vicar' or 'regent', being Archduke John.) How the other nationalities of the Monarchy should be handled was also a problem, with the Hungarians getting a more sympathetic hearing than the troublesome Czechs in the august debates at Frankfurt and Vienna.[55] Meanwhile the Habsburg government remained in charge in Vienna, still under the titular leadership of Ferdinand, but with generals increasingly calling the tune.

In retrospect, it is clear that the reason why the revolution of 1848 was so quickly defeated was that the revolutionaries in Vienna never wrested control of the army from the Habsburg dynasty, or, failing that, established an effective fighting force of their own. At the time, this naïvety was understandable, considering that the ease of revolutionary victory had seemed to show that the power of ideas and the 'people's will' could overcome even Metternich's system, which seemed to almost all involved, also in the Habsburg administration, as dead and buried. What 1848 was to show, however, was the opposite: that ideas were not enough, that what really counted was the loyalty of the army, and the ability to use it. One can criticise the revolutionaries for petty arguments over unimportant issues, and their failure to address effectively their mutual concerns on social and national issues, but in the end the revolution was defeated, and the Habsburg Monarchy saved, by main force.

'In deinem Lager ist Österreich.' In your camp is Austria. As with many clichés, Franz Grillparzer's over-used adage about the Habsburg army in 1848 is over-used because it is so accurate. The key to the restoration of Habsburg power was a string of military victories over the summer and autumn of 1848. Count Joseph Radetzky's victory over the Piedmontese and Italian forces at Custozza was the critical if improbable success which, with Prince Alfred Windischgrätz's crushing of unrest in Prague and Josip Jellačić's invasion of Hungary from Croatia, turned the tide of revolution. When Jellačić and Windischgrätz joined forces to put down the radical revolt in Vienna in October, in the process scaring off an attempt by the Magyar army to come to the Viennese revolutionaries' aid, the stage was set for a restoration of 'order' on Habsburg terms.[56]

The imperial family had been forced to flee their capital not once but twice, first to Innsbruck, then, after a return to Vienna, to Olmütz. Now, while not yet returning to a subjugated Vienna, they and their entourage were back in charge. This need not have meant a return to Habsburg absolutism. The Magyar forces were still undefeated, Germany was still in the process of national unification, and there was an Austrian parliament, sitting at Kremsier to draw up a workable Austrian constitution. Moreover, this parliament, with its members elected by near universal suffrage and consisting largely of moderate liberals and nationalists, had in its majority been in favour of the army's efforts to restore order.[57] Throughout the events of 1848 there had remained a strong moral support among most of the populace, including its educated classes, for the dynasty. The problems of *Vormärz* had been blamed on Metternich alone, subsequent problems on bad advisers. A majority of public opinion had been against the radical revolt in October, in favour of the army assault, if aghast at the 'clumsiness' of its execution and aftermath.[58]

When, therefore, following the plan of their new 'dictator', Windischgrätz, and the advice of the new prime minister, Windischgrätz's brother-in-law, Prince Felix Schwarzenberg, the imperial family decided that Ferdinand should abdicate, that his brother Francis Charles be passed over as not up to the task, and that his young, elegant eldest son be made emperor, there was a great deal of hope and optimism on all sides that this youth would be able to recreate the dynastic state in a way befitting the new times.[59] The very name chosen as his official appellation, Francis Joseph, was an effort to appeal not only to the legitimacy of his grandfather, Francis I, but also to the 'liberalism' of his radical ancestor, Joseph II.[60]

Schwarzenberg and Windischgrätz might assume that the young man would slavishly follow their 'advice', but the situation was very open to what the new monarch would decide. During the ceremony of abdication on 2 December, Ferdinand said to the new emperor Francis Joseph: 'God bless you! Be good and God will protect you.'[61] Francis Joseph had been '*brav*' (good) all his life, but as the student of an absolutist education. The consequences were soon clear to all.

. . .

THE VERY MODEL OF A MODERN ABSOLUTIST

In the first, crucial years of his reign, Francis Joseph remained the obedient pupil he had been before his accession, but now his teacher was neither Bombelles nor Metternich, but the new prime minister, Schwarzenberg. In some ways he was an unlikely saviour of the Habsburgs. A soldier and diplomat, he had led a

Byronic career of scandal and broken hearts, with the pessimistic affectations to match. His world-weary cynicism and often
anti-traditional scepticism were to have a decided impact on
subsequent events.[62]

He did have principles, chief among which was loyalty to the
Habsburgs, and the necessity of restoring them to their rightful
place, within and outside the borders of the Monarchy. Although
one of the more illustrious members of the Austrian aristocracy,
he was contemptuous of the aristocracy's traditional rights and
role within society, seeing them as more of a threat to Habsburg
order than a support. Instead he saw the mass of the Monarchy's
peasantry as a far more reliable and effective ally of the dynastic
state, but the support which for him was most reliable, and hence
most to be relied upon, was the army.[63] Unlike Metternich,
Schwarzenberg was far less inclined to let principles of legitimacy
get in the way of the needs of state power. His regime amounted
to a return to the policy of Frederick II of Prussia, on the model
of Louis Napoleon of France. Schwarzenberg held in contempt
the rights of traditional society, except for the right of the Habsburg dynasty, the most traditional of all, to rule Central Europe.
It is thus fitting that the era which he ushered in should be called
neo-absolutism, because it was an attempt not to restore the old
absolutism, but to create a new, modern one.

Schwarzenberg was not at first averse to playing along with the
constitutionalist establishment bequeathed by the revolution. From
his entry into office on 21 November into the early spring he
tolerated and even worked with the parliament at Kremsier. Francis Joseph's accession did not at first change the relations between
the ministry and the parliament. The latter therefore continued
to debate and develop the draft of a constitution which would
resolve within itself all the divisions, especially national ones, which
the revolution had brought to the light of day.[64] The most difficult division was between those (mostly Germanophone) who
wanted a strong central government and those (mostly Slav) who
wanted more autonomy for the provinces and nationalities. The
compromise solution reached envisaged a Monarchy in which
domestic political power was divided between a central parliament, the historic provinces, and 'circles' or counties, divided
along ethnic lines, within those provinces. The equal rights of
every nationality within the empire were guaranteed, as were the
usual liberal rights of citizens. The Roman Catholic Church was
disestablished and the equality of all citizens before the law

proclaimed. By March 1849 it only remained for the ministry to dot the i's and cross the t's.[65]

This did not happen, because key elements within the Habsburg inner circle, chief among them Francis Joseph himself, were not prepared to accept as radical a document as the draft Kremsier constitution. Even though this might have been the one vehicle to provide for a broad, consensual settlement of the nationality problem, the nationalities were far from being the only, or even most important part of the power structure of the Monarchy. The draft was clearly unacceptable to a Habsburg dynasty just back in the saddle of power, and intent on staying there. The disagreement with the original Kremsier draft was as fundamental as could be: the origin of power within the state. One clause stated that: 'All sovereignty proceeds from the people, and is exercised in the manner prescribed in the constitution.' To someone raised on doctrines of Divine Right, such as Francis Joseph, whose office was 'by grace of God', this statement amounted to blasphemy. Francis Joseph never did accept the idea of popular sovereignty in Austria, even after 1867. He certainly did not accept it in 1848, and the parliament was forced to drop this claim.[66]

Even so, the limitations on the emperor's powers, on the latest liberal model, were very irksome for the young emperor and his advisers. Ministers would be responsible to parliament and not to him, he would only have a suspensive veto, his powers of proroguement and dissolution were minimal. The result would be a constitutional, parliamentary regime; despite the formal concession over sovereignty, and a large control over foreign policy, the emperor would hardly be ruler any more. Moreover, the parliament refused to include the rebellious provinces of Lombardy–Venetia and Hungary in their plans, thus threatening the imperial unity which was one of Francis Joseph's main goals. In the interest of dynastic power, therefore, it was decided by Francis Joseph and Schwarzenberg by late January that the Kremsier parliament would have to go, and its draft constitution, seen by many constitutional historians to this day as the last best hope for solving the national crisis, with it.

The Kremsier parliament was informed of the ruler's decision on 6 March, was then dispersed and a number of the deputies were arrested.[67] In place of the Kremsier draft, another constitution, drawn up by Count Franz Stadion, was put in place, or rather given to his peoples by the grace of the emperor. A more centralist and moderate version in many respects of the

Kremsier draft, Stadion's constitution suffered from two large drawbacks. First: it lacked the authority which a Kremsier constitution, decided on and agreed to by an elected parliament, would have had. In Kann's words, Kremsier 'represented the will of the people'.[68] Stadion represented a grudging concession from the group that had the guns. Second: the new, decreed constitution was never put into practice in any case, for by the time the authorities had overcome the crises still outstanding in the Monarchy by force, Stadion's appeared an unnecessarily liberal compromise.

Over the course of 1849 Schwarzenberg's regime put down the remaining insurrections – in Italy and Hungary, but at huge cost to the prestige of the Monarchy. While in late March Radetzky effectively ended the Italian insurrection by his victory again over the Piedmontese at Novara (Venice was eventually to fall that August), what had appeared in late 1848 at first as a cakewalk in defeating the hastily assembled Hungarian national army turned into humiliating retreat by the late spring of 1849. Windischgrätz, the saviour of the dynasty, the stalwart of high conservatism and 'the grace of cannon', was relieved of his command, much to the young emperor's embarrassment. Julius von Haynau was eventually put in charge and, as in Italy, was to prove effective.[69] Before then, however, Schwarzenberg and Francis Joseph had come to the humiliating conclusion that the only way to avert a possible, catastrophic Hungarian victory was to accept the offer of the Russian tsar, Nicholas I, to send a Russian army into Hungary. This was in order to make the world safe for monarchy again, and the Habsburg Monarchy horribly indebted to Russia. It can be argued that this humiliation was not really necessary, that the Austrian army under a competent general like Haynau would have beaten an increasingly ragged Hungarian force anyway, and in fact did.[70] Be that as it may, the invitation was accepted, Prince Ivan Paskievich's army crossed into Hungary, and received the Hungarian general, Arthur Görgei's surrender in August of 1849, to the chagrin of the Austrians, who had done almost all the fighting to bring the Hungarians to this. That the Romanovs had saved the Habsburgs *again* was a dynastic disgrace which was to have long-lasting repercussions.

The immediate response from the Austrian regime was to extract a primitive retribution on the defeated. This should not have been unexpected. After the putting down of the October revolution in Vienna, Windischgrätz had had a fair number of the 'ringleaders' executed, including the Frankfurt deputy Robert Blum, despite his supposed immunity. (The Frankfurt Parliament still appeared at this point the legitimate government of Germany.) Haynau, similarly had been none too subtle in his punitive policies while in Italy, earning the soubriquet 'the Hyena of Brescia'. Even so, the measures taken against the Hungarian insurgents shocked European public opinion, and had a lastingly negative effect on the image of the Habsburgs among the Hungarian populace.

Görgei himself was spared execution. Yet the conditions of honourable surrender which he had negotiated for his generals and men with the Russians were otherwise ignored by the Austrians. At the 'bloody assizes of Arad', thirteen generals were put to death, and in the ensuing weeks a total of 114 'rebels' were executed. Included, most notoriously, was the by then long-retired Hungarian prime minister, Count Lájos Batthyány, whom public opinion held not guilty of the later excesses of the revolution. Others who had escaped into exile, including Count Gyula Andrássy, were executed in effigy.[71]

It is unclear quite who was directly responsible for this judicial bloodbath. That Haynau was an enthusiastic promoter of this policy is clear, that Schwarzenberg decided to let him proceed also seems clear. What is less clear is how hard he had to try to persuade Francis Joseph to accept this policy. Ultimately, though, it was Francis Joseph who bore the responsibility as emperor of allowing the executions, and thus compounding the disgrace of Russian intervention by the disrepute of blood-soaked vindictiveness. As Johann von Wessenberg, the former Austrian foreign minister warned: 'The young emperor is being forced to make his way to power over the scaffold and the bloodbath instead of being given the chance of coming with the olive branch in his hand and so founding a lasting peace in the spirit of conciliation.' [72] Yet it is even unclear that Francis Joseph was 'forced': he might have had his qualms, but once Schwarzenberg, his new mentor, had proposed his policy of 'a little hanging first', he had quickly snapped into line. By October he relented, and ordered the executions stopped, but by then 'Justice' – and the damage – had been done.

From the capitulation of the Hungarians and Venetians in August 1849 there was a steady reassertion of Habsburg power, indeed more of a clampdown, in the Monarchy and its spheres of interest. In the Italian provinces, Radetzky was put in charge and proceeded to punish the rebellious Italian nobility by various harsh measures, including expropriation, which nevertheless were lenient by Hungarian standards.[73] In Germany Schwarzenberg's threats and bluster, coupled with a Prussian King Frederick William IV who was in any case psychologically beholden to the Habsburgs, thwarted an attempt by Prussia to form a 'narrower federation', the Erfurt Union, in place of the by then defunct Frankfurt Parliament.

At the *Punktation* of Olmütz in November 1850 Schwarzenberg reasserted Austrian seniority within the German Confederation, humiliating the Prussians in the process, but the eventual settlement was in effect a stand-off, ominously for Austria. Schwarzenberg, once he had shown Austrian power, thereby created enough resistance among the other German states to make impossible the realisation of his plans for an 'empire of seventy million', with the whole of Austria included in the German Confederation and in the Prussian-led *Zollverein* (customs union). Austrian refusal to share the presidency of the new empire with Prussia (Francis Joseph was loath to accept at this point that the upstart Hohenzollerns could be the Habsburgs' peers) meant that the result of the Dresden Conference of 1851 was no result at all, except for an expression of the support of Prussia's position among a majority of German states. Habsburg power had been reasserted, but Prussia had become the clear hope of German unification.[74]

In Vienna, the gratifying return of dynastic power at home and abroad, with its enemies either repulsed or vanquished, allowed the young emperor, brought to his position by the wave of revolution, to consider how best to respond to the new-old state of affairs. In 1850 Francis Joseph was still only in his twentieth year. He was young, full of energy and military ardour, ceaselessly working at his desk on government matters and learning at the side of Schwarzenberg, but also still under the strong influence of his mother and of his spiritual adviser, Rauscher. He remained absolutely convinced of the Habsburg mission to rule, by Divine Right. From this perspective, a constitution, any constitution, was still an infringement on the ruler's God-given duties to rule as his conscience saw fit. Francis Joseph had been brought up an absolutist, and he remained one in his deepest convictions, despite what Schwarzenberg had persuaded him to say and do from his accession.

Austria had in effect been an absolutist state from the dissolution of the Kremsier parliament in March 1849. Yet Schwarzenberg had felt it served the purposes of the regime to keep at least the forms of constitutional government. Moreover the quasi-fictional discipline of having to justify policy to a future parliament was also an effective protection against any youthful impetuosity on the part of the monarch. Francis Joseph all too soon did away with precisely this annoying figleaf on his power.

It remains unclear whether Francis Joseph or Karl von Kübeck – or a third party – originated the plan to return Austria to a formal absolutism. What is known is that Francis Joseph initiated the process in October 1850 by asking Kübeck, an elderly, Josephist official, to draw up plans for the *Reichsrat*, a part of the Stadion constitution whose nature and powers remained vague. Over the next months Kübeck used his mission to argue to Francis Joseph that the whole system of ministerial responsibility was a charade, indeed dishonest, and that the best way to restore order to the Austrian government was to do away with it. The Ministerial Council would disappear, with ministers reporting directly instead to the *Reichsrat*. This was to be a body of elder statesmen (much like the State Conference of before 1848), who would then advise the monarch, who would rule.[75]

The *Reichsrat* was instituted in March 1851, with Schwarzenberg's grudging acceptance.[76] It was, after all, allowed for in the constitution. By August, things had progressed much further, however, with Francis Joseph by now making no attempt to hide his preference for doing away with the constitution altogether. At one meeting of the still existent Ministerial Council Francis Joseph opened discussion by asserting the 'inapplicability of the English-French constitutional principle to the Austrian imperial state, something recognised by all with insight'.[77] On 20 August he wrote to his mother, triumphantly: 'We have moved a big step forward, we have thrown the constitution overboard and Austria has from now on only one master. Now we must work even harder.'[78]

With this sort of pressure from the ruler himself, the outcome of ensuing events was never in much doubt. August saw the abolition of ministerial responsibility, September the all too indicative return of Metternich to Vienna. December saw the preparations for a complete renunciation of Stadion's March constitution. While Schwarzenberg and Minister of the Interior,

Alexander Bach, struggled against the tide, the eventual declaration of absolutism, embodied in the three rescripts known collectively as the *Sylvesterpatent* (New Year's Eve Edict), amounted to a declaration of full independence from the dashing young man on the imperial throne. Anything smacking of popular sovereignty was to be removed from the Austrian system of government, including the elected local councils envisaged by Stadion. The emancipation of the peasantry was confirmed, as was the legal equality of all subjects. The equality provisions concerning language and nationality were expressly revoked, as was the list of individual rights. Although Kübeck had drawn up a document confirming the emancipation of the Jews, the young Francis Joseph refused to sign it.[79] The new system was a return to a former age in more ways than one.

Schwarzenberg was prepared to function under these new circumstances as well, and it soon became evident that Francis Joseph paid little attention to Kübeck's *Reichsrat*, still relying on Schwarzenberg to advise him and run the government. Yet we will never know whether he would have retained his position of authority, for he died in April 1852.

Francis Joseph had already been asserting his control over the government. The whole move to absolutism showed that, and he thought he had a full sense by then of what he was taking on. When he heard of Louis Napoleon's *coup d'état* in Paris in December 1851, Francis Joseph said: 'He is perfectly right. The man who holds the reins of government in his hands must also be able to take responsibility. Irresponsible sovereignty are, for me, words without meaning; such a thing is a mere printing machine for signatures.'[80] Yet Schwarzenberg's death was still a great shock, for it left Francis Joseph not fully prepared in practice to take over the reins of government. As he had been at the forefront of the drive to give himself absolute power and absolute responsibility, on his own account, he had no one to blame but himself for what was to happen next.

· · ·

THE BACH ERA

After Schwarzenberg's death the leading figure in domestic affairs was the Minister of the Interior, Alexander Bach.[81] It was under Bach that the approach adumbrated by Schwarzenberg found its realisation. The general policy direction, known as neo-Absolutism, was yet another attempt to solve the problems of the Habsburg Monarchy by modernisation, from the top down. In many ways Bach's neo-Absolutism was a rerun of the programme of Joseph II. That Bach should lead this effort, despite having started out as a liberal revolutionary is therefore not all that surprising, despite all the claims of apostasy made by his critics. There was always a tension between the need for 'Progress' and 'Liberty' in nineteenth-century liberal thought, and Bach was not the only one to choose the former over the latter, as the *Kulturkampf* in Germany a couple of decades later attests.[82]

The neo-Absolutist rationale was that the absolute state would make the concession of political rights unnecessary by forcibly providing a modern economy, administration and educational system for all. It was another attempt to realise the Enlightenment ideals of uniformity and equality – under the emperor. The one area in which the Franciscojosephinian version of absolutism radically differed from its Josephist predecessor was in its attitude to religion, specifically its generosity towards the Roman Catholic Church, due to the influence of Sophie, Rauscher and Francis Joseph's own personal convictions.[83] In all other respects, though, neo-Absolutism meant the destruction of traditional institutions, of traditional, time-honoured sources of power and authority, of history.[84]

Instead of the authority of historical right and custom, neo-Absolutism relied on power. It amounted to a power system designed to create more power for the Habsburg state and its ruler, Francis Joseph, so that he could maintain and enhance his, the Habsburgs' dynastic position in Europe. Francis Joseph's projected image could be that of a Prince Charming, in his tight-fitting Austrian officer's uniform, with the 'virgin' white jacket and bright scarlet trousers, surrounded by a glittering court and, from 1854, married to reputedly the most beautiful empress in Europe, Elisabeth of Bavaria (his first cousin);[85] but the reality of the regime by which he chose to govern was one in which the white kid gloves were definitely off.

Francis Joseph's chosen role was to be a real absolutist. In personal terms this meant working all day every day, from dawn till dusk, to keep up with the administrative responsibilities in the army and bureaucracy which fell to the head of government. Kübeck's *Reichsrat* existed, but was rarely consulted. Instead Francis Joseph would tend to go to Bach for advice, although he himself was clearly his own prime minister, his own first adviser.[86] There was no avenue for formal consultation of the populace or the political nation.[87] All representative institutions, even those which Metternich had preserved for cosmetic reasons, were abolished, the claim of historical 'legitimacy' practically abandoned.

This, as Redlich points out, was a dramatic break with the ruling style of his grandfather, Francis I, who, in response to the French Revolution, had retained at least the forms of tradition while ruling in practice absolutely.[88] Now Francis Joseph imposed a naked absolutism, without such figleaves of legitimacy. Historical rights, 'since time immemorial', were ignored or abolished. The change was particularly radical in Hungary, where the constitution was held to be defunct due to the Kossuthian revolution. As a result the whole structure of administration, especially the customary county system, was scrapped.[89]

The customary social and economic structures of Central Europe were also shaken at their roots by the neo-Absolutist regime. The acceptance of the emancipation of the peasantry meant that the whole relationship between peasant and lord had to be regulated anew, by the Bachian bureaucracy. Historical noble tax privileges disappeared, as did the system of feudal dues. In the very highest echelons of Habsburg society, in the high nobility at the Viennese court, these changes in legal status did not lead to any levelling in practice. Because of Francis Joseph's belief that, after the army, the high nobility and magnates (excluding the Hungarians) had been the most loyal support of the Monarchy, and his own preference for persons in the 'cousinage', this small group actually increased their power, Francis Joseph giving its members almost all the top jobs.[90] But further down the social scale the Bach era witnessed the removal of customary and institutional privilege across the board, whether for the middle and lesser nobility, or craft guilds.

Francis Joseph was even prepared to give up one of the Habsburgs' most traditional and powerful sources of authority, their control over the Church within their realms. The 1855 Concordat, signed on Francis Joseph's birthday, returned the bulk of control over the Austrian church to the Pope, and handed primary education and the regulation of marriage over to the church authorities. This completely reversed the Josephist achievement of tight control over the Church and church pulpits, the main vehicle of propaganda before the age of mass literacy. The Papacy was a grateful and enthusiastic ally of Francis Joseph's conservative religious policies (one result of the gratitude being Rauscher's elevation to Cardinal), but this was still a large concession of power on the monarch's – and state's – part.[91]

Having dispensed with historical rights, legitimacy, popular agreement, customary social hierarchy and control of religion as the bases of authority (political, moral or otherwise) for his regime, Francis Joseph, following largely Schwarzenberg's example, relied on dynastic prestige, an effective administration, and the army, to provide him with the authority and power to fulfil his imperial task. It was said at the time, that Francis Joseph ruled with four armies: a standing army (of soldiers), a sitting army (of officials), a kneeling army (of priests) and a crawling army (of informers). It is not a very kind description, but it does sum up the basis of the neo-Absolutist system.

His actions in allowing for the execution of the Viennese and Hungarian revolutionaries had tainted for many the good standing of the dynasty, and their view of Francis Joseph in particular, but the emperor could still rely on the strong feelings of loyalty of a large part of the population, feelings encouraged by the attempt on his life by a Hungarian tailor in 1853.[92] The one aspect of historic right and legitimacy which Francis Joseph was intent on not throwing overboard was that concerning the dynasty and his Divine Right to rule as its representative. In this the Church was expected to act as a close ally and propagandist, despite, or rather because of, the new freedom the Concordat gave it.

If the Church attempted to influence the minds of the populace to act loyally, the expanded bureaucracy attempted to make sure that they did so, and a much larger police force, with a large network of informers, made doubly sure that the officialdom made sure. Francis Joseph was so intent on being in control that he had his own ministers watched, as well as bishops and foreign diplomats.[93]

What Francis Joseph really relied upon to maintain his rule was at base the military, material force. In this he was following in Joseph II's footsteps. Joseph II had always worn a uniform, whereas Francis and Ferdinand had tended to a civilian attire. Francis Joseph – following Schwarzenberg's example – also was almost always to be seen in uniform. (One of the first reforms he ordered at his court was to give the lifeguards newly designed uniforms.)[94] The army had been his first love since he was a small boy, and his experiences in 1848 had only reinforced this. He

had proved his manhood by taking part in a couple of engage-
ments in the Italian theatre, and then taking part in the capture
of Raab (Györ) in the ultimately successful Hungarian campaign
of 1849. What had been proved to him by the events after March
was that he owed his throne to his generals and their troops. In
Redlich's words: 'that material might, physical force, in the shape
of the standing army and military police, constituted the kernel
of the state, at any rate under a monarchy.'[95] During the neo-
Absolutist era Francis Joseph retained personal control over the
military, advised by Quartermaster-General Heinrich von Hess,
and perhaps his closest adviser of all, his ultra-conservative aide-
de-camp, Count Karl Grünne.[96] It was the army which not only
underpinned his absolute rule, but was the instrument of government in many of his formerly rebellious territories, in Italy,
Hungary and Croatia. Yet rule by the military was the most naked
basis of power of all, and deeply ironic for a dynasty which had
prided itself on letting the others wage war.

All of this destruction of history and custom in favour of a
Machiavellian reliance on raw power might not be particularly
pretty, but it did at least have the potential of modernising the
state. There could, after all, hardly be a more dramatic attempt
to break with the past, albeit in an ultra-étatist manner. The clearest and most famous symbolic event of the neo-Absolutist era was
the decision to raze the walls of the medieval inner city of
Vienna in 1857, to make way for what would become known as
the Ringstrasse. There were few more obvious attempts to destroy
the past for the sake of the future. But even here the 'progressive' intentions – to make commerce between the inner city and
suburbs easier and to make Vienna a modern capital dotted with
'modern' buildings fit for a forward-looking empire – were wedded with other, more patently 'absolutist' aims – to open up the
inner city and provide large open spaces where troops could be
mustered in the event of another revolt. Large barracks were built
at either end of the ring of boulevards.[97] Here again a certain
indebtedness to the example of Napoleon III (and his master-
builder Haussmann) is evident.

Neo-Absolutism was an attempt to do without history, to rule
Austria as a *tabula rasa*. As Interior Minister, Bach instituted an
administrative and legal system which for the first time provided
the Austrian Empire with uniform administration. It also appears to have been a relatively efficient administrative system,
with power completely centralised in Vienna. For the first and

last time, Austria was ruled by a completely German-speaking bureaucracy. Each province was divided up into *Kreise* ('cantons'), and districts on a standardised pattern of hierarchically arranged administrative units. In Hungary the historic county system of local government was replaced by a version of this administrative hierarchy of circles and districts, with the middle-rung units retaining the name *Comitate* – county – without, however, being at all similar to the previous, self-governing bodies.[98]

In Hungary the new officials employed in Bach's rationalist system, due to the requirement to administer in German, were often Germans and German-speaking Czechs from outside Hungary. A majority of the chief officials at the local level, the district commissioners, were drawn from the ranks of the Magyar gentry, but the fact that the system had been imposed on Hungary, and that there was such a large influx of what we might term 'carpetbaggers', led to the new officialdom being despised no matter what they did. Known as 'Bach's hussars' because of the uniforms they were ordered to wear (themselves, ironically, a sop to a Hungarian national identity), the officials in fact accomplished an immense amount in terms of administrative and legal reform in the 1850s. They introduced modern legal procedures, operated the legal and administrative mechanisms enabling the peasants' emancipation, implemented efficient tax-collection, and created a state police force – for the first time. A sign of their effectiveness is that most of Bach's administrative system was left in place after 1867.[99]

But it did not do them, Bach, or ultimately Francis Joseph, much good. Bach's hussars were fiercely resented by the local elites in Hungary, who now, having been deprived of their traditional powers, were even more resentful, even more prone to support what in any case was a very powerful national cause.[100] Even the usually neutral masses had been caught up in the gentry-led struggle. When Francis Joseph toured Hungary in 1852, he asked the mayor of a village why the villagers had shouted 'Vivat' instead of 'Eljen' when he had passed. The mayor explained that he had ordered them to shout 'Vivat', because they had all been so used to shouting 'Eljen Kossuth' that he was afraid that some would be unable to remember themselves in time and not do the same if they shouted 'Eljen'. It was not exactly a comforting answer.[101]

The mechanistic uniformity demanded by Bach compounded the problem of loyalty by treating all areas of the empire, whether loyal or disloyal, the same. The crassest example was Croatia, the actions of whose *Ban,* Jellačić, had been crucial in deciding the outcome of 1848 in favour of the Habsburgs. The reward for the Croatians was for their historic institutions to go the way of the Hungarian ones.[102] National equality in neo-absolutist terms meant equality of reward and punishment for friend and enemy alike. This was not a good management of 'political capital', regardless of whether it was good administrative practice.

Wherever Bach's system was imposed, resentment at its imposition compromised much of the benefit that its efficiency produced. Its authority was one stemming completely from the 'material might' of the absolute state, and it had none of the powerful authority which comes from the aura of tradition. Indeed it was specifically designed to contradict traditional authority, supersede traditional authorities. The problem was the same in Lombardy–Venetia, where the bureaucracy administered and the military ruled, and the traditional power elites simply boycotted the reimposed Austrian order.[103]

The large expansion of the police force under Johann von Kempen, especially of the secret police and of the network of informers, was a very bad sign for the well-being of Francis Joseph's regime. It bespoke a general demoralization of the society, a mutual tension of fear and resentment between governing and governed.[104] The reliance on informers connoted a lack of trust of the populace, which amounted to a fear of it, and what it would do if pressed too hard. The classic symptom was not so much the number of informers, as the reluctance to call on the populace to contribute to the common good, to impose taxation sufficient to meet the vast expenditures necessitated by the huge standing army and sitting bureaucracy.

To the extent that it did succeed in its goal of modernisation, neo-Absolutism also faced the problem that it was fostering the causes of its own demise. In the sphere of higher education, the reforms inaugurated under Count Leo Thun were very beneficial, laying the foundation for the high achievements of Austrian scholarship and science in the later nineteenth century. At the same time, the reforms were instituted as a direct effort to catch up with the Prussian performance at secondary and university level in the first half of the nineteenth century. This, together with the lack of suitably educated Austrian pedagogues, led to a large influx of Reich Germans, who, though mostly Catholic, also harboured German liberal sentiments. It was thus Thun, a reforming conservative and enthusiast for the Concordat with Rome, who created the German liberal hegemony which was to typify Austrian higher education for the rest of the century.[105]

In economic matters there was a similar pattern. Here the dominant figure was Karl von Bruck, Minister of Commerce under Schwarzenberg and Minister of Finance 1855–60. Bruck made every effort to rein in government spending to try to reduce the chronic state debt problem. While his efforts were severely hampered by the exigencies of Francis Joseph's foreign policy, he was able to create enough financial stability, and a stable enough currency, for the Austrian economy to resume its moderately upward path from before March 1848. The Bach era used to be seen, through ideologically tinted spectacles, as a time either of economic failure, or of dramatic, 'take-off' growth. According to the latest consensus of economic historians, it seems that until the very end of the 1850s the Austrian economy performed creditably, if not as spectacularly as that of the rest of Germany.[106]

The liberalisation of the laws governing railway construction in 1854 led to a critical expansion in this decade of the Austrian rail network, with the railway industry acting as the economy's leading sector. The institution of the Credit Anstalt in 1855, largely based on Rothschild capital, was also of great benefit to the Austrian credit system. A liberal trade policy, with the creation of the customs union between Hungary and the other Habsburg lands, as well as a Commercial Treaty with the states of the *Zollverein* in 1853 reducing tariffs, also encouraged trade, albeit marginally. The drive to economic modernisation even went so far as the *Gewerbeordnung* (industrial code) of 1859 which virtually abolished the guild system and greatly liberalised Austrian industrial practice. Even if in raw terms of economic growth the 1850s present only a continuation from before 1848, qualitatively there was a marked change, and, as in the development of a modern bureaucracy, the neo-Absolutist era, in sweeping away many of the traditional obstacles in Austria to economic growth, succeeded in laying the groundwork for a much more modern economy.[107]

The main beneficiaries of this economic growth were the groups who peopled this modern, capitalist economy: financiers, industrialists, merchants; and the associated educated and professional classes, the products of the newly reformed universities: physicians, lawyers, professors and more officials. In other words, neo-Absolutist reforms increased and made more prosperous and powerful precisely those groups most sympathetic to the German liberal and national causes. The fact that a crucial part of the Austrian financial system, on which the Austrian state was increasingly reliant as its debt grew, was run by a Jewish financial elite which had seen Jewish emancipation partially withdrawn by this same neo-Absolutist regime, made Francis Joseph's state even more vulnerable to attacks from the liberal opposition.

The basic problem with neo-Absolutism, however, was that it did not fulfil its function sufficiently well of being a power-producing machine. There was economic growth, and there was an improved bureaucratic and tax-collecting efficiency, but not enough to pay for what was most important to Francis Joseph, an army strong enough to execute his foreign policy as a great power. The neo-Absolutist system was a hostage to the fortunes of Francis Joseph's foreign policy and the performance of his army. Unfortunately for Francis Joseph's ideal solution to the problem of power, foreign affairs were to prove its Achilles' heel.

. . .

DEUS EX MACHINA

Neo-Absolutism might produce power to fuel the Habsburg engine of state, but Austria's status as a great power depended on how that engine was steered and whether it could overcome any obstacles in its way. It was thus in the realms of diplomacy and the military that the fate of Francis Joseph's newly recast Habsburg enterprise would meet its crucial test. These were also the areas of policy in which Francis Joseph had taken the most direct control, having been taught as a youth by Metternich that foreign policy was the most important part of a monarch's responsibility. It was to be the failure of diplomacy and the defeat of the army, however, which were to lead to humiliation for Austria and neo-Absolutism's downfall.

There is no doubt about the calamitous outcome of the diplomatic and military events of the 1850s for Austria. What has been questioned is how much of this can be blamed on Austrian diplomatic bungling itself, most notably by Count Karl Buol-Schauenstein, or whether Austria's fall from grace at the hands of the other European powers was an unavoidable victory of greedy expediency over honour, of *Realpolitik* over 'Metternichian' legitimacy. The long-standing historiographical consensus of Austria being at least partly at fault for her own predicament has been challenged by revisionists such as Roy Austensen and Paul Schroeder, who in turn have been challenged by re-revisionists such as Alan Sked, with Roy Bridge challenging Sked's views, but still not vindicating Austrian diplomacy – at least *after* the Crimean crisis.[108]

Whether Austrian policy was to blame, though, leads to another most relevant question for us: whether Francis Joseph, who was formally in control, can himself be seen as directly responsible for the ensuing calamities? He, after all, chose his foreign minister, and he had final say over policy. To claim that he was doomed whatever choice he made would be to deny precisely that freedom of will which most supporters of the Monarchy's chances insist on preserving. Rather than argue over whether Austrian policy was 'Metternichian' or not, it seems more sensible to consider whether it was fitted to the post-revolutionary era of power politics, which Francis Joseph had done so much to bring about through his avowal of Schwarzenberg's policy of brutal suppression and state self-assertion in Hungary, Italy and Germany. Rather than ask whether he and Buol were legitimists or *Realpolitiker*, it is more useful to ask how sensible their policy was, given the reality of Austria's great power position. One does not have to be a *Realpolitiker* to insist on realistic policy.

It was clearly Francis Joseph's personal decision to follow the informal advice of Schwarzenberg in tapping Buol to be his successor as foreign minister. It was also Francis Joseph's personal decision to continue largely to follow Buol's advice right up until 1859. Not that Buol's advice was always followed. Sometimes Francis Joseph would overrule Buol in favour of other factions at court, such as the conservative faction in the military, or the even more pro-Western faction in the domestic administration: not all of Austrian policy was Buol's fault, but all of it was approved by Francis Joseph.[109]

What for many historians is the key event of this period in Austrian diplomacy, the abandoning of the close alliance with Russia, was done with Francis Joseph's clear, if unenthusiastic agreement. Moreover, it was done in full knowledge that this was turning against former friends, to whom a deep debt was owed (for the intervention in Hungary in 1849). It was justified by Francis Joseph with the revealing statement: 'One must above all be an Austrian.'[110]

The reason for this breach between Europe's two leading absolutists was Nicholas's designs on the faltering Ottoman Empire in Europe. Nicholas personally encouraged Francis Joseph to go along with him, offering him control of the Western Balkans if he agreed. But Francis Joseph, on Buol's advice, demurred, because a weakened Turkey was not seen to be in Austria's interests – and ultimately neither Francis Joseph nor his advisers had full trust in Russian intentions. Instead Francis Joseph tried desperately to dissuade Nicholas from his plans for aggression, in vain. The eventual result was the Crimean War, with Russia facing France, Britain and Turkey, and Austria in a state of what might be termed malevolent neutrality, and then alliance with Russia's enemies in December 1854.[111]

Under Buol's urgings Austria joined with the Western powers in imposing such conditions on Russia in the resulting Peace of Paris in 1856 as to 'bring her to heel', including the demilitarisation of the Black Sea and the cession of Southern Bessarabia to the Danubian (Rumanian) principalities. Such moves on Austria's part destroyed what had been the mainstay of Austrian diplomacy: the alliance with Russia. Nicholas I was outraged at the ingratitude of the person he saw as his protégé, Francis Joseph, and this fierce antagonism continued undiminished under his successor Alexander II. Austria could not expect help from the Romanovs for a very long time.[112]

This would not have mattered if the alliance with the Western powers had been firmly secured, but it was not. Perhaps this was impossible, given British liberal pretensions and Napoleonic practicality, but it cannot be said that the Austrians did much to help their own cause with Britain and France. The refusal to help their allies materially by actually declaring war and sending troops against the Russians might have kept Austria from committing itself and expending more troops and money that it could ill afford – in a war against Russia in Galicia it could have lost – but it deeply antagonised the Western powers, allowing them to talk of Austrian unreliability.[113]

The main beneficiary of such talk in contrast, Piedmont–Sardinia, did contribute some troops to the Crimean campaign, a wise investment as it turned out. Similarly, Prussia's ability to avoid joining Austria's aggressive stance towards Russia, gained her favour at St Petersburg and influence over the other German states, unwilling to go to war for essentially Austrian and not German interests.

Austria and Francis Joseph were thus caught between a rock and a hard place, hated by the Russians for their perfidy, held in contempt by the Western powers for their faint-heartedness. The net result of Buol's pro-Western policy and Francis Joseph's wish for freedom of action and 'tranquillity'[114] was to ensure neither.

That Austria should have remained uncommitted to either side was something with which Metternich himself agreed: 'The state of the middle cannot let herself be tugged either in the eastward or westward direction . . . and must never allow itself to be misused as the vanguard of the East against the West, or the West against the East.'[115] This neutral stance was in effect what Buol and Francis Joseph achieved, and it is questionable whether not taking sides would indeed have rescued Austria. It can also be argued though that it was not *what* was achieved so much as the *way* it was achieved that counted. Metternich's complete disavowal of Buol's policies was of the means and manner, not the ends. Certainly it does not speak of skilful diplomacy to have the 'peacemonger' Austria hated by both sides.[116]

Austria's position 'in the middle' could have been made viable if there had been an imaginative response domestically and in Germany to the main fact of the Crimean episode, the breach with Russia. If, for instance, there had been a turn away from absolutism to liberal constitutionalism – or even mock constitutionalism – then, as Redlich claims, there could have been an appeal to German public opinion against that 'tyrannical' destroyer of constitutional government, Nicholas I. Austria's image in French and British public opinion could have been greatly improved, thus influencing, perhaps, the opinion-sensitive Western governments.[117] As it was, Francis Joseph's adherence to absolutism left foreign and domestic policy at variance and Austria unloved by anyone.

Francis Joseph followed what was in effect a policy of neutrality in the war, but it was a neutrality which entailed almost all the costs of war, and few of neutrality's benefits. Above all, its aggressive nature with regard to Russia, from the ultimatum of 3 June 1854 and occupation of the Danubian principalities onward, meant that it was very much an armed neutrality. The Russian-induced crisis in the Balkans and Austria's need to make her threats credible, meant that already in the winter of 1853–54 there was a massive mobilisation of the Austrian army. On paper Austria had the strongest army in Europe, of some 800,000 men, but even partial mobilisation of this force was very expensive, far more expensive than the neo-Absolutist regime could afford. In 1854 the whole year's army budget had been spent in the first three months.[118]

The need to keep this army mobilised well into 1855 had a devastating impact on an already shaky financial situation, ballooning the state debt, devaluing the currency, and showing, instead of the strength of Francis Joseph's regime, its essential weakness. The pressing need to solve the financial crisis by retrenchment led to the demobilisation of most of the army in late 1855, before the Crimean War was even over.[119] No wonder the Austrians were reluctant to send troops into battle against the Russians.

The Crimean War in the short term ended as a great success of Austrian diplomacy. The Russian threat to Austrian interests in the Balkans had been beaten back without Austria having to go to war. In the longer term, by 1856, Austria was in a very perilous position. She had always needed one big ally among the great powers. Metternich had always relied on Russia. Now this was gone, irretrievably. Britain had large ideological differences with Francis Joseph's neo-Absolutist state, and she and France both had strong objections to Austria's continued presence in northern Italy. The support of their cause in the Crimea by Piedmont–Sardinia, and domestic sympathy for Italians, and also Hungarians, suffering in the 'prison of the peoples', meant that neither Britain nor France could be counted on when it came to Italy. Nor was Prussia to be relied on, especially in German affairs. She had already led German resistance to involvement in the Crimean War and the antagonism over the leadership of Germany remained unresolved. By January 1857 it was clear to the British ambassador in Vienna, Hamilton Seymour, that Austria was isolated from everyone, and hence in huge danger.[120]

The post-war diplomacy of Buol and Francis Joseph did nothing to improve these matters. Bridge cites the Neuchâtel affair of 1856–57 as a case in point. In this trivial but indicative episode, Buol refused to cater to Prussian requests for the support of the German Confederation in upholding its hereditary rights in the Swiss canton of Neuchâtel. In other words Austria, in pursuit of her own ends and to put Prussia in her place, was prepared to pass up a golden opportunity to defend dynastic legitimacy and put into practice the German Confederation's Article 47, obliging members to mutual aid in the event of a defensive war. This set a terrible precedent for the events in 1859, when Austria was to call for the aid of the Confederation states, above all of Prussia.[121]

By 1858 it was clear that Austria was in an exposed position diplomatically, and to no one was this clearer than Count Camillo Cavour of Piedmont and Napoleon III, both of whom had revisionist, nationalist ambitions concerning the Vienna settlement of 1815. With Russia now out of the way, and fuming most at Austria in any case, and Britain sympathetic to the concept of Italian national unity, the way seemed to be clearing for a few changes on the map of the Italian peninsula. If Austria could be induced to start a war against Piedmont, then this could also neutralise any threat from Prussia and the German states. The French army, reputedly the best in Europe at the time, could then take on the Austrians, defeat them, give Piedmont large gains in northern Italy and be given in return parts of Savoy. This would achieve for Napoleon the popular aim of French territorial expansion, and the prestigious role of patron of the Italian national cause. This was what was agreed between Napoleon and Cavour at Plombières in the summer of 1858, and this is exactly the trap into which Buol and Francis Joseph fell in the spring of 1859.[122]

Why Austria declared war on Piedmont on 29 April 1859 was itself an example of the problem of Francis Joseph's neo-Absolutism. On the one hand, the state of Austrian finances and of the problems with military organisation meant that the Habsburg army could not be mobilised quickly, nor could such a mobilisation be long sustained. Francis Joseph had actually resisted expansion of the armed forces in early 1859 for reasons of economy, and the ultimatum was issued before the army was fully mobilised.[123] Part of Buol's reason for that ultimatum to Piedmont was the hope that Piedmont would be cowed by the Austrian bullying and so war would be avoided altogether. On the other hand, Piedmont's provocative claims and its military mobilisation were well designed to rouse Francis Joseph's rigid sense of honour and dynastic prestige. As he said in the ministerial conference of 27 April, war against Sardinia–Piedmont was 'a commandment of honour and duty'.[124] Despite the fact that he was at this point in almost daily contact with the old master, Metternich, he could not see that it was also the downfall of his regime.[125]

Even before battle was joined, the Franco-Austrian War was a disaster for neo-Absolutism. There was a run on the banks in May, and Bruck warned that even victory would result in financial crisis.[126] What credit neo-Absolutism had garnered had now vanished, because of another war which the Monarchy could even less afford. We have no idea whether dazzling victories on the field of battle could have reversed this collapse, because there were none. The Habsburg army, under the command of Count Francis Gyulai, Grünne's protégé and not a particularly well-respected general, failed to press home an attack on the Piedmont army before it was joined by the French. There were then two battles, Magenta, after which Gyulai was sacked, and Solferino, where the Austrians were led by Francis Joseph himself. Both resulted in a narrow but decisive Austrian defeat, even though at Solferino – it is often asserted – the Austrians might have won if Francis Joseph had not ordered the retreat prematurely. He did, and the Austrians lost.[127]

Here again, Francis Joseph was directly responsible for the shortcomings which led to the Austrian losses. As head of the military, he had let Grünne use the immense resources of the army budget very conservatively, to produce an army which was well turned out, had loyal and mainly high-noble officers, and could exercise extremely well. But, having for years served more as an agent of domestic political control than a real fighting force, it was terribly organised, poorly led, poorly paid, poorly supplied, and reliant on out-of-date equipment.[128] Francis Joseph had appointed the unfortunately not very competent Gyulai, and had provided the command, or lack of command, in the heat of battle at Solferino himself. If fortune did not smile on the Austrians, one might counter that they should not have been in a situation to rely so much on luck rather than on their own competence.

The military facts of Magenta and Solferino were compounded by a subsequent bout of ill-considered diplomacy. Francis Joseph could arguably still have gained Prussian support against France, if enough concessions had been made to the Prussians within the Confederation. Partly for reasons of Habsburg prestige, Francis Joseph refused to do this, preferring to negotiate with Napoleon III directly at Villafranca. The terms of this settlement were on paper better than could have been expected. Austria retained Venetia and the Quadrilateral, giving up only Lombardy. Even the rights of the legal (Habsburg) rulers in the Central Italian states were retained. Yet events on the ground, in the central states and elsewhere, meant that by 1860 Sardinia–Piedmont had clearly become the nascent Italian national state, Venetia more a liability than a springboard for revenge.[129]

The calamities of the summer of 1859 destroyed Francis Joseph's neo-Absolutist regime. Buol had already been sacked in May, when the consequences of his diplomacy had become evident days after the declaration of war. Bach, Kempen and Grünne followed by the end of the year. Bruck's dismissal was so insensitive that it led to his suicide in April 1860.[130] The only prominent member of the government not sacked was Francis Joseph himself. Popular unrest was a factor here, both in Vienna and even more so in Hungary, but it was the financial crisis, greatly exacerbated by the war's events, which was the main impetus for change. No more foreign loans could be raised unless there was 'effective budget control' and for mid-nineteenth-century bankers this meant some form of taxpayer representation, in other words a form of representative assembly. With the expanded Reichsrat of 31 May 1860 a new era of Francis Joseph's reign began.[131] Neo-Absolutism was finished.

Francis Joseph himself was largely responsible for this first great failure of his reign. His own hubris, more charitably described as immaturity, brought down his attempt at absolutism. Perhaps Schwarzenberg's example had made things look too easy, and fooled Francis Joseph into thinking he could manage on his own. Perhaps, however, it was 'a natural deduction from the absolutist idea' itself, as Redlich claims.[132] Francis Joseph said of receiving advice: 'The man who can praise me to my face I must allow to blame me likewise; which however may not be.'[133] There is a serene majesty about this refusal of flatterers, but it also bespeaks immense over-confidence in his own abilities, as if he was duty-bound not to allow himself to be criticised. This is indeed a 'natural deduction from the absolutist idea', but it was a disastrous one for a headstrong young man such as Francis Joseph. As the Russian ambassador to Vienna, Peter von Meyendorff, noted on 1 June 1854, two days before the fateful ultimatum to Russia, the emperor was 'blinded by his self-will and the foolish assumption that he can judge and decide everything entirely by himself.'[134]

The truth was that Francis Joseph was not clever enough, or far-sighted enough, let alone tough enough, to be the absolute monarch he styled himself to be; nor was the Habsburg Monarchy strong or rich enough, 'great' enough, to perform the role he and his advisers, and Habsburg tradition, demanded of it. In their minds, Austria was a first rate, and indispensable, great power, the anchor of legitimacy and the international settlement. In reality, as Roy Bridge has put it, Austria was 'only an impecunious second-class Great Power', without the wherewithal to act alone successfully on the international stage.[135]

Metternich in his heyday had seen this, and acted accordingly. Neither Buol nor Francis Joseph could see the wood for the trees long enough to realise the fix they were getting into. Metternich had harsh words for Buol: 'The fatal consequences of any and every action are hidden from Count Buol. He sees what is right in front of him; of what is coming he sees nothing.'[136] Yet this is also an unspoken criticism of Buol's master, Francis Joseph. Redlich was more explicit in pointing out the emperor's inability to see the long-term view, citing the Crimean crisis as an occasion when 'the immediate and tangible determined him, as usual'.[137]

It is deeply ironic that Francis Joseph, with such an elevated idea of his historic mission of maintaining the Habsburg legacy, had the instinctive response of a positivist utilitarian. He not only relied on his common-sense perception of the 'immediate and tangible' in deciding policy, reducing complex issues to rigid formulae, but also treated his populace as a function of *Hausmacht* (dynastic power). There was little heed paid to national sensibilities, instead the young Francis Joseph treated his peoples as if they were another branch of the army.[138] He did little if anything to make himself popular, and in his early years was seen as a cold, militaristic fish, nicknamed 'Red Legs' for his obsessive uniform-wearing.[139] The high-handedness, insensitivity, political myopia and over-confidence made for a disastrous combination. Just how disastrous is shown by the fact that a couple of narrow military defeats, which a sound state would have easily withstood, sent the whole neo-Absolutist system crashing, so weak were its foundations of loyalty in the populace.

Count Alexander von Hübner, in a heartfelt essay written during the crisis, blamed Francis Joseph's mistakes on the reluctance of his advisers to tell him the truth. Yet it was up to Francis Joseph to which advisers he listened, and whom he believed. The fact that Francis Joseph had believed the flattery and wishful thinking of his advisers, thinking he could majestically see through the 'untruths' when he could not, stemmed from his own puffed-up image of his abilities, as did his oft-remarked obstinacy, his refusal to accept unpleasant advice.[140]

It is not the case that neo-Absolutism was destroyed by the *deus ex machina* of foreign affairs. If the Habsburg Monarchy was the victim of the turn towards *Realpolitik* after 1848, Francis Joseph as Schwarzenberg's pupil had done his share to bring this about, casting off legitimacy at home as well as abroad. That the Monarchy became the isolated and hence prime target of revisionist *Realpolitiker* and that in its new form it proved militarily not up to the task set it, can also be laid at Francis Joseph's door. The young emperor, given his background and upbringing, could not perhaps have been anything but a convinced absolutist, but he was, and it was his inability to see the true strength, or rather weakness, of his position, his inability to seek and obtain critical counsel, or listen to it, which led to many of his mistakes. In other words, it was Francis Joseph's own attitudes, his own character flaws, which led to the collapse of his system.

Pride comes before a fall. The commander of what had appeared the strongest army in Europe a few years before was not noticed when he attended the Viennese opera in the autumn of 1859, the worst social disgrace a restless, resentful political nation could give its emperor.[141] Hungary was in turmoil, the state's finances were in ruins. The crisis of Habsburg authority, of the legitimacy of Francis Joseph's rule, was not over – it had only just begun – but change was inevitable.

. . .

NOTES AND REFERENCES

1. E.C. Corti, *Vom Kind zum Kaiser: Kindheit und erste Jugend Kaiser Franz Josephs I. und seiner Geschwister*, Pustet, Graz 1950, pp. 7–11; J.-P. Bled, *Franz Joseph*, trans. T. Bridgeman, Blackwell, Oxford 1992, pp. 1–3.
2. Corti, *Vom Kind zum Kaiser*, p. 154.
3. Ibid., p. 119.
4. Ibid., p. 143.
5. Ibid., pp. 194–200.
6. Ibid., pp. 212–20.
7. Ibid., p. 240.
8. Ibid., pp. 82, 204.
9. Ibid., p. 119.
10. Ibid., pp. 46, 81, 202; J. Redlich, *Emperor Francis Joseph of Austria: A Biography*, Macmillan, New York 1929, pp. 20–1.
11. Corti, *Vom Kind zum Kaiser*, p. 195.
12. Ibid., pp. 41, 125–7.
13. Ibid., p. 244; Redlich, *Emperor Francis Joseph*, p. 22.
14. Corti, *Vom Kind zum Kaiser*, p. 109.
15. A. Sked, *The Decline and Fall of the Habsburg Empire 1815–1918*, Longman, London 1989, pp. 30–1; A.J.P. Taylor, *The*

Habsburg Monarchy 1809–1918, Penguin, Harmondsworth 1948 (1964), pp. 53–5.

16. Sked, *Decline and Fall of the Habsburg Empire*, pp. 34–6, 74.
17. W. Heindl, *Gehorsame Rebellen: Bürokratie und Beamte in Österreich, 1780–1848*, Böhlau, Vienna 1989, pp. 178–209 (Studien zu Politik und Verwaltung).
18. Sked, *Decline and Fall of the Habsburg Empire*, pp. 71–4.
19. G. Barany, 'Ungarns Verwaltung 1848–1918'. In A Wandruszka, P. Urbanitsch (eds), *Die Habsburger Monarchie 1848–1918* (6+ vols). Österreichische Akademie der Wissenschaften, Vienna 1975, vol. 2, *Verwaltung und Rechtswesen*, pp. 316–21.
20. Sked, *Decline and Fall of the Habsburg Empire*, pp. 35–6.
21. Ibid., pp. 32–6.
22. O. Jászi, *The Dissolution of the Habsburg Monarchy*, Penguin, Harmondsworth 1929, pp. 248–51; cf. L. Namier, *Vanished Supremacies: Essays on European History 1812–1918*, Hamilton, London 1958, pp. 112–22.
23. Taylor, *The Habsburg Monarchy*, p. 55: Taylor uses the phrase 'a manufacture of tradition' and so anticipates the 'invention of tradition' debate by thirty years.
24. Jászi, *Dissolution of the Habsburg Monarchy*, pp. 83, 130.
25. Ibid., pp. 163–4.
26. Jászi, *Dissolution of the Habsburg Monarchy*, p. 379.
27. E. Gellner, *Nations and Nationalism*, Blackwell, Oxford 1983, pp. 8–18.
28. S. Beller, 'Germans and Jews as Central European and "Mitteleuropäisch" Elites.' In P. Stirk, (ed.), *Mitteleuropa: History and Prospects*, Edinburgh 1994, pp. 61–74 (Studies in European Unity).
29. P. Urbanitsch, 'Die Deutschen in Österreich: Statistisch-deskriptiver Überblick'. In Wandruszka and Urbanitsch, vol. 3, pt. 1, *Die Völker des Reiches*, pp. 37–8, 50–4; G. Gottas, 'Die Deutschen in Ungarn'. In Wandruszka and Urbanitsch, vol. 3, pt. 1, *Die Völker des Reiches*, p. 349.
30. Beller, 'Germans and Jews as Central European and "Mitteleuropäisch" Elites', pp. 62–9.
31. A. Sked, *The Survival of the Habsburg Empire: Radetzky, the Imperial Army and the Class War, 1848*, Longman, London 1979, pp. 172–83.
32. T.C.W. Blanning, *Joseph II*, Longman, London 1994 (Profiles in Power), pp. 112–16, 189, 202.

33. L. Péter, 'Language, the Constitution and the Past in Hungarian Nationalism'. In R. Robertson, E. Timms (eds), *The Habsburg Legacy: National Identity in Historical Perspective (Austrian Studies* vol. 5), Edinburgh 1994, pp. 13–22; Barany, 'Ungarns Verwaltung', pp. 316–25.

34. R.A. Kann, *A History of the Habsburg Empire, 1526–1918,* University of California, Berkeley 1977, pp. 294–5; Sked, *Decline and Fall of the Habsburg Empire,* pp. 63–4.

35. Kann, *History of the Habsburg Empire,* pp. 292–3; Jászi, *Dissolution of the Habsburg Monarchy,* pp. 258–65.

36. Kann, *History of the Habsburg Empire,* pp. 295–6; Jászi, *Dissolution of the Habsburg Monarchy,* p. 254.

37. F.R. Bridge, *The Habsburg Monarchy among the Great Powers, 1815–1918,* Berg, Oxford 1990, pp. 26–36.

38. Ibid., pp. 36–7.

39. Sked, *Survival of the Habsburg Empire,* pp. 172–83, *Decline and Fall of the Habsburg Empire,* pp. 57–63.

40. Corti, *Vom Kind zum Kaiser,* pp. 125–7, 254–5.

41. On 1848 generally, see P.N. Stearns, *1848: The Revolutionary Tide in Europe,* Norton, New York 1974 (Revolutions in the Modern World); J. Sperber, *The European Revolutions, 1848–1951,* Cambridge 1994 (New Approaches to European History).

42. Sperber, *The European Revolutions,* pp. 23–6.

43. D.F. Good, *The Economic Rise of the Habsburg Empire 1750–1914,* University of California, Berkeley 1984, pp. 38–73.

44. Stearns, *1848: The Revolutionary Tide in Europe,* pp. 17–28: Taylor, *The Habsburg Monarchy,* p. 64.

45. Sked, *Survival of the Habsburg Empire,* pp. 106, 114.

46. W.L. Langer, *Political and Social Upheaval 1832–52,* Harper & Row, New York 1969, p. 255 (The Rise of Modern Europe).

47. Sked, *Decline and Fall of the Habsburg Empire,* p. 81.

48. Ibid., pp. 80–3; Kann, *History of the Habsburg Empire,* p. 300.

49. Langer, *Political and Social Upheaval 1832–52,* pp. 354–60.

50. Sked, *Survival of the Habsburg Empire,* pp. 124–5; Langer, *Political and Social Upheaval 1832–52,* pp. 370–4.

51. Taylor, *The Habsburg Monarchy,* p. 81.

52. Bled, *Franz Joseph,* p. 37.

53. Taylor, *The Habsburg Monarchy,* p. 75.

54. Kann, *History of the Habsburg Empire,* p. 304; cf. Sked, *Decline and Fall of the Habsburg Empire,* pp. 94–101.

55. H.-H. Brandt, 'The Revolution of 1848 and the Problem of

Central European Nationalities'. In H. Schulze (ed.), *Nation-Building in Central Europe*, Berg, Leamington Spa 1987, pp. 107–34.

56. Bled, *Franz Joseph*, pp. 41–5.

57. Rath, *The Viennese Revolution*, Greenwood, New York 1969, pp. 333–7; Taylor, *The Habsburg Monarchy*, pp. 82–4.

58. Sked, *Decline and Fall of the Habsburg Empire*, p. 55; C.A. Macartney, *The House of Austria: The Later Phase, 1790–1918*, Edinburgh 1978, pp. 111–14.

59. Windischgrätz's plan: Corti, *Vom Kind zum Kaiser*, p. 308.

60. Corti, *Vom Kind zum Kaiser*, p. 329.

61. Bled, *Franz Joseph*, p. 48.

62. Sked, *Decline and Fall of the Habsburg Empire*, pp. 138–9.

63. Redlich, *Emperor Francis Joseph*, pp. 38, 52–4.

64. Sked, *Decline and Fall of the Habsburg Empire*, pp. 141–3.

65. Ibid., pp. 143–4; Kann, *History of the Habsburg Empire*, pp. 310–12.

66. Sked, *Decline and Fall of the Habsburg Empire*, p. 143.

67. Kann, *History of the Habsburg Empire*, p. 310.

68. Ibid., p. 312.

69. E.C. Corti, *Mensch und Herrscher: Wege und Schicksale Kaiser Franz Josephs I. zwischen Thronbesteigung und Berliner Kongress*, Styria, Graz 1952, pp. 21–5.

70. Sked, *Decline and Fall of the Habsburg Empire*, pp. 101–2.

71. Corti, *Mensch und Herrscher*, pp. 43–5.

72. Redlich, *Emperor Francis Joseph*, p. 64.

73. Sked, *Survival of the Habsburg Empire*, pp. 190–204.

74. Sked, *Decline and Fall of the Habsburg Empire*, pp. 150–7; Bridge, *The Habsburg Monarchy*, pp. 45–8.

75. Redlich, *Emperor Francis Joseph*, pp. 74–88; Sked, *Decline and Fall of the Habsburg Empire*, pp. 144–7.

76. Corti, *Mensch und Herrscher*, p. 72; Sked, *Decline and Fall of the Habsburg Empire*, p. 148.

77. Corti, *Mensch und Herrscher*, p. 77.

78. Ibid., p. 78.

79. Sked, *Decline and Fall of the Habsburg Empire*, p. 149; Redlich, *Emperor Francis Joseph*, pp. 88–94.

80. Redlich, *Emperor Francis Joseph*, p. 91.

81. Bled, *Franz Joseph*, pp. 74–5.

82. D. Blackbourn, 'Progress and Piety: Liberals, Catholics and the State in Bismarck's Germany'. In D. Blackbourn, *Populists*

and Patricians: Essays in Modern German History, Allen & Unwin, London 1987, pp. 144–55.

83. Corti, *Mensch und Herrscher*, p. 57; Redlich, *Emperor Francis Joseph*, p. 96.

84. Jászi, *Dissolution of the Habsburg Monarchy*, pp. 100–2; Bled, *Franz Joseph*, pp. 72–84, 90–4.

85. Corti, *Mensch und Herrscher*, pp. 122–5, 143; Redlich, *Emperor Francis Joseph*, pp. 185–7, 202–5.

86. Redlich, *Emperor Francis Joseph*, p. 100.

87. Francis Joseph did, however, continue the practice of free access of his subjects to him through regular audiences, an institution which he kept up for most of his reign: Redlich, *Emperor Francis Joseph*, p. 245.

88. Ibid., pp. 92–3.

89. Barany, 'Ungarns Verwaltung', pp. 339–44; Redlich, *Emperor Francis Joseph*, pp. 236–8.

90. Corti, *Mensch und Herrscher*, p. 69; Redlich, *Emperor Francis Joseph*, p. 215.

91. Bled, *Franz Joseph*, pp. 79–82.

92. Corti, *Mensch und Herrscher*, p. 106.

93. Redlich, *Emperor Francis Joseph*, pp. 241–2.

94. Ibid., p. 105; Corti, *Mensch und Herrscher*, p. 54.

95. Redlich, *Emperor Francis Joseph*, p. 104.

96. Ibid., pp. 43–7, 91–2; Corti, *Mensch und Herrscher*, pp. 265–6.

97. C.E. Schorske, *Fin-de-siècle Vienna: Politics and Culture*. Weidenfeld & Nicolson, London 1980, pp. 27–31.

98. E.C. Hellbling, 'Die Landesverwaltung in Cisleithanien. In Wandruszka and Urbanitsch, vol. 2, *Verwaltung und Rechtswesen*, pp. 195–208; Barany, 'Ungarns Verwaltung', p. 346.

99. Barany, 'Ungarns Verwaltung', pp. 347–60.

100. R.J.W. Evans, 'Austrian Identity in Hungarian Perspective: The Nineteenth Century'. In Robertson and Timms, pp. 30–1.

101. Corti, *Mensch und Herrscher*, p. 96.

102. Bled, *Franz Joseph*, p. 83.

103. E. Crankshaw, *The Fall of the House of Habsburg*, Viking Penguin, New York 1963, pp. 138–40; Sked, *Survival of the Habsburg Empire*, pp. 191–204.

104. Redlich, *Emperor Francis Joseph*, pp. 239–42.

105. H. Lentze, *Die Universitätsreform des Ministers Graf Leo Thun-Hohenstein*, Akademie der Wissenschaften, Vienna 1962, pp. 42, 88–91, 271–3.

106. Bridge, *The Habsburg Monarchy*, p. 64; Good, *The Economic Rise of the Habsburg Empire*, p. 239; Sked, *Decline and Fall of the Habsburg Empire*, p. 166.

107. Good, *The Economic Rise of the Habsburg Empire*, pp. 78–95; Sked, *Decline and Fall of the Habsburg Empire*, pp. 157–66; Bled, *Franz Joseph*, pp. 91–3.

108. Sked, *Decline and Fall of the Habsburg Empire*, pp. 167–75; Bridge, *The Habsburg Monarchy*, pp. 49–69.

109. Redlich, *Emperor Francis Joseph*, pp. 120–3.

110. Corti, *Mensch und Herrscher*, p. 153.

111. Bridge, *The Habsburg Monarchy*, pp. 51–6.

112. Redlich, *Emperor Francis Joseph*, p. 150; Corti, *Mensch und Herrscher*, pp. 150–1, 172.

113. Bridge, *The Habsburg Monarchy*, pp. 56–60; Sked, *Decline and Fall of the Habsburg Empire*, pp. 170–1.

114. Crankshaw, *Fall of the House of Habsburg*, p. 130.

115. Corti, *Mensch und Herrscher*, p. 147; cf. Sked, *Decline and Fall of the Habsburg Empire*, p. 171.

116. Redlich, *Emperor Francis Joseph*, p. 180.

117. Ibid., pp. 170–6.

118. Ibid., pp. 151, 230.

119. Corti, *Mensch und Herrscher*, p. 161; Bridge, *The Habsburg Monarchy*, p. 55.

120. Corti, *Mensch und Herrscher*, p. 184.

121. Bridge, *The Habsburg Monarchy*, pp. 64–5.

122. Ibid., pp. 65–6.

123. Ibid., p. 66; Corti, *Mensch und Herrscher*, p. 208; Sked, *Decline and Fall of the Habsburg Empire*, pp. 173–4.

124. Corti, *Mensch und Herrscher*, p. 221; Bridge, *The Habsburg Monarchy*, p. 67.

125. Corti, *Mensch und Herrscher*, p. 223.

126. Ibid., pp. 224–7.

127. Ibid., pp. 229–34.

128. Corti, *Mensch und Herrscher*, p. 85; Sked, *Decline and Fall of the Habsburg Empire*, p. 175; Redlich, *Emperor Francis Joseph*, pp. 228–30, 268; G.E. Rothenberg, *The Army of Francis Joseph*, Purdue, West Lafayette 1976, p. 55.

129. Corti, *Mensch und Herrscher*, pp. 237–9; Redlich, *Emperor Francis Joseph*, pp. 272–4; Bridge, *The Habsburg Monarchy*, pp. 68–9.

130. Redlich, *Emperor Francis Joseph*, pp. 281–6; Corti, *Mensch und Herrscher*, pp. 245, 256–7.

131. Redlich, *Emperor Francis Joseph*, pp. 288–9.

132. Ibid., p. 161.
133. Ibid., pp. 102–3; Crankshaw, *Fall of the House of Habsburg*, pp. 78, 87.
134. Redlich, *Emperor Francis Joseph*, p. 253.
135. Bridge, *The Habsburg Monarchy*, p. 52.
136. Sked, *Decline and Fall of the Habsburg Empire*, p. 171.
137. Redlich, *Emperor Francis Joseph*, pp. 178, 252.
138. Ibid., p. 247.
139. Ibid., p. 194; Crankshaw, *Fall of the House of Habsburg*, p. 77.
140. Corti, *Mensch und Herrscher*, pp. 247–8.
141. Ibid., p. 248.

Chapter 4

LIBERALISM, 1859–79

. . .

'A LITTLE PARLIAMENTARISM'

In late October 1860 Francis Joseph wrote to his mother: 'Now we are going to have a little parliamentarism, but all power stays in my hands, and the general effect will suit Austrian circumstances very well indeed.'[1] The emperor was trying to make palatable to his absolutist mother – and himself – the new quasi-constitutional settlement which he had reached with the conservative nobility, the October Diploma. As subsequent events were to show, however, it would take far more than the rather meagre concessions made in that initial attempt to rehabilitate the imperial government with its subjects – and its creditors. By the end of the decade Austria would have a constitutional structure beside which the October Diploma would pale, and Hungary would have a completely separate constitution and government of its own. Whether he liked it or not – and the evidence strongly suggests that he did not like it at all – the once absolutist Francis Joseph had become by the 1870s a constitutional monarch.

After the collapse of the neo-Absolutist system in 1859, Francis Joseph's preferred option was no longer available, but the problem which he faced remained even more pressing: how to gain enough power – military, economic, financial or otherwise – to carry out what he saw as his main duty: to maintain Habsburg power. This meant preserving Austria's great power status in the European power system, as well as salvaging as much power as he could for the imperial dynasty within the empire and keeping that empire united. Having failed to gain these ends by force, Francis Joseph was compelled to seek to achieve them by something which he had previously spurned: consent.

The step which he now grudgingly took was to accede to an experiment in constitutionalism. He was never really convinced

that constitutionalism, this new-fangled, liberal mode of government, could ever govern a dynastic, multi-national state such as
his Habsburg Monarchy, but by 1860 events – and his own actions – had conspired to produce a situation in which he was forced
to improvise some new form. This would have both to placate
society, especially the restless Hungarians, and even more
importantly satisfy the financial interests at home and abroad
which could extend him the credit without which his impecunious
regime could no longer continue.

Giving his Monarchy a constitution proved much easier said
than done. Partly as a result of the mistakes made in the eleven
years since he had ascended the throne, and indeed of the
economic and social developments fostered by the neo-Absolutist
regime, the imperial regime was in a far less advantageous position to satisfy the leading political interests of the empire than
previously. Moreover those interests were now both more powerful and more at odds with each other, hence less easy to satisfy.
Economic development had greatly increased the economic, social
and hence political power of the German middle classes of the
empire, and made their nationally-tinged liberal leadership even
more insistent on proper constitutional government. Meanwhile
the Czech national revival had gathered momentum, producing
increased resentment at the continuing German hegemony within
even the Bohemian lands, let alone the empire. The Polish noble
leadership was no happier with the situation, resenting Galicia
being run like a German province. Yet the problems caused by
unrest in these provinces paled beside the continued unrest in
Hungary. There the Bachian Germanophone administration had
done little to break the back of solid, sullen Magyar opposition
to the system imposed by Vienna.[2]

Added to these various and conflicting national group interests
was a struggle, especially among Germans, between aristocratic
and middle-class elites for political power in the newly forming
post-absolutist situation. Ideological, liberal-versus-conservative,
clerical-versus-anti-clerical splits cut across these in turn, so that
the political system was highly complex. The possible constitutional
solutions to this situation were similarly varied and complex, but
there were two main forms. On the one hand, the option favoured
by most of the German liberal leadership was a straightforward
liberal constitution, consisting of government by central (German-
speaking) parliament and a centralised (German-speaking)
bureaucracy. In contrast, the other groups, often with aristocratic

leaderships, saw this prospect as a threat to their interests and looked to historical rights and constitutions on a more local level for protection. Liberal, Germanocentric centralisation and traditionalist, feudally-tinged federalisation became the two poles between which Francis Joseph's attempts at a constitutional settlement swung from 1860.

Francis Joseph gave his empire at least three different systems of government between 1860 and 1867, and would have given the Austrian half of his Monarchy yet another in 1871 if the German and Hungarian leaderships had not stopped him. The October Diploma, with which we started, was an attempt to avoid reliance on constitutions and liberals and to keep most of his imperial powers, by relying on the Hungarian conservatives, led by Count Antal Szécsen, and the conservative-feudal, federalist Austro-Bohemian high nobility. They planned to deliver the social peace and revenues wanted by Francis Joseph to revive Austrian, Habsburg power by restoring the Hungarian constitution, especially the Diet and the county administration, and by setting up equivalent 'estates' assemblies in the other Austrian provinces, providing an aristocratically led federalised state structure. At the centre, a strong Francis Joseph and a weak, 100-seat central assembly would run the imperial regime, dealing with common concerns such as common economic policy, the army and foreign policy.[3]

When this proved unworkable due to massive opposition in Hungary and among the German middle classes, Francis Joseph tried another tack, calling on the German liberal centralist, Anton von Schmerling, to form a government. The result was on the face of it only 'enabling legislation' for the October Diploma, but in reality Schmerling's February Patent provided a completely new governmental structure, which was much more like a real constitution than its predecessor, and which reversed the latter's federalism into a strong, Germanocentric parliamentary centralism. The Reichsrat, which was still formally the same *Reichsrat* which Kübeck had devised back in 1851, was now converted into what amounted to a proper imperial parliament. As in the October Diploma, its members were still elected indirectly, by the various provincial diets and with a carefully devised and notorious 'electoral geometry' which ensured German dominance. Now, however, the balance of legislative competence had shifted powerfully in favour of the central body, which had large – and for Francis Joseph worrisome – pretensions to a properly constitutional status. Admittedly this status remained one formally granted by Francis Joseph, who retained his powers where it mattered, in military and foreign affairs.[4]

Whereas the October Diploma lasted only a few months, the February Constitution did better, it lasted a few years; but it was put aside by Francis Joseph in 1865 in the hope of reaching an agreement with the Hungarians, whose refusal to play along with the Schmerling system had been one of the main reasons for the latter's demise. Austria was without a constitutional system for much of 1865 and 1866, but the events of that year and the following led to the restitution of the February Constitution, heavily amended and now the December Constitution, as part of the dualist, Austro-Hungarian Compromise (*Ausgleich*) of 1867. This in turn was threatened by another of Francis Joseph's attempts to placate a restless sector of his subjects by constitutional revision when he tried to solve the Bohemian problem in 1871 by having the Hohenwart ministry federalise the Austrian half of his empire. Combined German and Hungarian pressure brought this plan to nought. Much to the chagrin of the Czechs, the 1867 settlement remained the constitutional basis of the Monarchy.

How all this came about is explored in more detail below, but for now just a glance at the permutations involved in Francis Joseph's various constitutional attempts suggests why there were such radical shifts in the Monarchy's governmental structures. Until the 1867 Compromise, the attempted restructurings of the Habsburg Monarchy failed to provide Francis Joseph with what he wanted: domestic peace and sufficient revenue and/or credit to provide for a powerful enough army to support the Habsburg claim to great power status. Francis Joseph's 'utilitarian realism' meant that he was prepared to experiment with whatever forms, and deal with whichever groups in the society, even the German liberals, could get him to his goal of rehabilitating his Monarchy from the disasters of 1859.[5] The diversity of his realm, and the conflicts exacerbated by his own absolutist regime, made this task very difficult, for it amounted to robbing Peter to pay Paul or vice-versa (rather than robbing both at the same time, as in neo-Absolutism). As we shall see, even the 'separation' of 1867 only put this basic dilemma on another level.

In one sense, Francis Joseph was himself responsible for the instability of the political scene after 1860, for although simply by accepting a constitution he was making a concession he had sworn as late as 1860 he would never make, the amount of real power he was prepared to cede was never very great.[6] Whereas some of the national and political conflicts might have been assuaged, or at least radically altered for the better, by Francis Joseph being prepared to give the empire's elected representatives real power (for instance in setting army policy) he would not hear of it. Indeed one of the first things he did after the February Patent was to order his ministers to make sure that the Reichsrat interfered neither with his powers over foreign policy nor over the army.[7] Yet he was always surprised, even shocked, that his refusal to let the Reichsrat meddle in army affairs was answered by cuts by the same body in the army budget.[8] This was, he claimed, not good for Austria's international position, but Francis Joseph would always ignore the idea that sharing power with his parliament on this issue might be the best way to correct this behaviour. Instead he could only see this as confirming his beliefs (prejudices) about the danger of too much constitutionalism, rather than see that it might be due to too little.

The major shift in the constitutional structures of the Habsburg Monarchy, between 1865 and 1867, happened however not so much because of the internal management of the Monarchy's various conflicts and contradictions, but because of developments outside of its borders, in another disastrous exercise in foreign policy. Or rather, it occurred because of the concatenation of the two, of the inability of Francis Joseph to restore the Habsburg position either at home or abroad. If the constitutional experiments of the early 1860s were in order to regain Habsburg power after the debacle of 1859, the lasting settlement of 1867 was the result of yet another – and greater – failure.

. . .

GERMAN SCYLLA; HUNGARIAN CHARYBDIS

After the Italian fiasco of 1859, and especially after the introduction of the February Constitution of the Germanocentric Schmerling, Austria's main focus of attention shifted to her other major sphere of interest, Germany. This meant a renewal of the traditional rivalry with Prussia, relations with whom had already been upset by Prussian 'disloyalty' in not coming to Austria's aid against France, and Francis Joseph's publicly accusing Prussia of this crime by omission.[9] Schmerling, an advocate of the idea of a Habsburg-led Great German 'empire of seventy millions', led the Austrian effort to reassert a commanding presence in a reformed German Confederation, which could not but be a challenge to the Prussian-dominated Small German entity of the *Zollverein*. In this contest about the future shape of Germany, Austria could well have succeeded for in the early 1860s she held several political advantages which subsequent events have tended to obscure. She did not, however, and one of the main reasons was the impossibility of detaching Austria's foreign and German policy concerns from her domestic problems. Another was Francis Joseph's refusal – again – to make the necessary concessions to the ideological and diplomatic realities of the new European situation.

Austrian interests in Germany were always compromised by the continuing need to solve the Hungarian problem, if Francis Joseph and his government insisted on keeping Hungary within a united empire. Similarly, Austria's position among the Great Powers, so crucial in any stand-off with Prussia, would remain one of complete isolation as long as she retained her remaining, substantial Italian presence. Russia was still fuming after the betrayal in the Crimean Crisis, and Britain and France, though interested, refused to deal without Austrian withdrawal from Venetia. Yet Francis Joseph, who in 1859 had seen even the granting of autonomy to his largest remaining Italian province as the beginning of the end of his Monarchy (because all his other provinces would want the same status) refused to give it up, or even sell it, both for the sake of imperial honour and the possible domestic repercussions.[10] Austrian foreign policy was thus hamstrung by its fears about its discordant domestic condition, which in turn was to be vastly exacerbated by foreign policy failure. Caught between the rivalry with Prussia in Germany and the domestic travails of Hungarian passive resistance, and hobbled by the continuing insistence on an Italian presence, Austria and Francis Joseph were to end up survivors but much diminished: thrown out of Germany and Italy, and Austria shorn of Hungary, even if Francis Joseph was not.

Unlikely as it now seems, in the early 1860s Austria had the opportunity of becoming the leader of a reformed, liberal Germany. On the one hand the February Patent and Schmerling's subsequent regime presented Austria as a centralised, German-dominated and liberal state, which chimed well with developments along liberal and constitutional lines in most of the other states within the German Confederation. The one major exception was Prussia, where the new Chancellor, Otto von

Bismarck, had cracked down on the parliamentary forces in the kingdom in the Army Bill Crisis. The way might therefore have been open for Austria, if she wished, to take on the mantle of liberal leader of Germany, as opposed to illiberal Prussia. This was never realised, partly because Prussia was too powerful within Germany, but also because of the countervailing pressures within the Monarchy against Schmerling's Germanocentrist regime, from the Czechs and especially the Hungarians; and also because Francis Joseph himself was never fully convinced of Schmerling's plans. As Redlich says, such a plan would only have worked if Francis Joseph had offered himself as a truly liberal monarch, 'if – a Habsburg could ever have been a liberal.'[11]

The truth was that Francis Joseph never embraced constitutionalism unless forced to. In early 1864 he gave Schmerling a severe dressing-down for publicly praising Austria's constitutionalism, despite the fact that it was Austria's constitutional status which was among its leading attractions for the middle German states.[12] It was the same in the German question itself. Schmerling tried his best to sell Austria as a reforming, accommodating leader of Germany, but the most imaginative action that Francis Joseph could think of was to keep on insisting on his 'presidial right' at the Frankfurt Diet. He thus refused to cede Prussia equality within the Confederation, as suggested by political and economic realities, as well as, among others, by Queen Victoria in September 1863.[13] By so doing Francis Joseph was within his formal rights, but was playing into the hands of Bismarck and his conservative allies, by showing how unreasonable and selfish Austrian leadership of Germany would be. Why should Prussia co-operate with an Austria who refused to offer true partnership in return? It might be that if Francis Joseph had made concessions, it would have led eventually to the Monarchy's diminution in any case. By insisting on his rights, refusing any real concessions, he ensured virtual dismemberment.

The great opportunity for Austrian leadership of Germany was the *Fürstentag* at Frankfurt in August 1863, where to general acclaim Francis Joseph celebrated his birthday on the 18th under a black–red–gold canopy, surrounded by all the princes of the Confederation, except one. Unfortunately the absence of the one prince, William I, King of Prussia, made the rest of the meeting more or less pointless, or so it seemed to Francis Joseph and his conservative foreign minister, Count Johann Bernhard Rechberg. They therefore viewed Schmerling's German liberal gambit as a failure, despite signs of some success with German public opinion, and reverted to a policy of conciliating Prussia, which meant being led by the nose by Bismarck into the Schleswig-Holstein Question.[14]

Meanwhile, at home, 'Schmerling's Theater', the German-dominated Reichsrat, had no solution to the continuing Hungarian crisis. There the dissolution of the Diet in August 1861 and the return to a Bachian-style centralised bureaucracy had resulted in a campaign of passive resistance and non-payment of taxes which amounted to a national revolt. The additional boycotting of the imperial parliament by its Czech and Polish members in protest at the pro-German bias of the German liberal majority further weakened its authority. Under Schmerling, however, the Reichsrat continued to press for fuller constitutional powers, especially in defence matters, which Francis Joseph refused point-blank to grant. The parliament's response was to keep cutting back the army budget, at a time when Prussia, without parliamentary approval, was greatly increasing her military expenditures.[15]

The German liberal strategy having failed and now threatening his principal concern, his army, Francis Joseph reversed course yet again and returned – as early as the winter of 1864–65 – to trying to come to terms with the Magyar nobility, now under the undisputed leadership of Francis Deák. Matters advanced so well on the basis of Deák's 'dualist' Easter article that Francis Joseph, under the influence of Count Moritz Esterházy, sacked Schmerling in the summer of 1865, suspended the February Constitution in September and recalled the Hungarian Diet, which met in December of that year. The result had been an opportunity to placate the Hungarians, but at the expense of Austria's German liberal credentials.[16]

By then Austrian policy over Schleswig-Holstein had played Francis Joseph straight into Bismarck's hands. Ironically the very idea of proceeding against Denmark in this matter in 1864, though unavoidable given German national sentiment within the Confederation, was in utter contradiction to Francis Joseph's own policy over Hungary, where, just like the Danish king, he had overturned an historic arrangement of semi-constitutional independence in the interests of unitary state reform.[17] Moreover, by allying with Prussia in January 1864, and siding with her against the middle states in denying the Duke of Augustenburg's liberal-supported claims to the two duchies, Austria further undermined her standing as a potentially liberal alternative to Bismarck's barrack-state. The failure to keep Bismarck in check led to Rechberg's replacement by Albert Count Mensdorff-Pouilly in October 1864, but with a continuation of Francis Joseph's preferred policy of staying with Prussia. This simply allowed Bismarck to pick the optimal time to exploit Austro-Prussian conflicts over their joint administration of Schleswig-Holstein to start the war to expel Austria from a Prussian-dominated Germany.[18]

Austrian inconstancy over Schleswig-Holstein, the suspending of the liberal constitution in 1865 and her other internal problems made her a less than reliable ally in the eyes of many German statesmen. The Bavarian prime minister, Ludwig von der Pfordten, wrote in October 1865 that 'Austria, financially bankrupt, in a state of political anarchy, is at the moment incapable of action. We cannot now nor for a long time count on Austria.'[19] When it did eventually come to war between Austria and Prussia in the summer of 1866, however, the great majority of German states sided with Austria. Austria in effect won the diplomatic struggle within Germany.[20] What it had not won was internal peace or the larger diplomatic game among the great powers.

Insistence on his rights within the German Confederation proved costly to Francis Joseph; insistence on his rights in Venetia proved disastrous. Until virtually the eve of battle, the Austrians refused to give up their hopes of reconquering their lost territories in Italy, and reversing the establishment of the 'illegitimate' Kingdom of Italy. Despite the urgings of Napoleon III, a crucial potential ally, Francis Joseph had refused indignantly any plans of buying Italian neutrality with concessions. Even when the Italians offered to buy Venetia for a handily large sum, given Austria's financial straits, Francis Joseph rejected the offer out of hand as an attack on his imperial honour. The refusal even to contemplate the French and Italian approaches spelt diplomatic doom for the Monarchy. It led to the Italian alliance with Prussia in April 1866, which meant Austria had to fight on two fronts, and also to the threat of French intervention on the side of Austria's enemies, unless the Austrians ceded Venetia. In the end, by the treaty of 12 June, in return for French neutrality, the Austrians agreed to the cession of Venetia if they were successful against Prussia and could gain compensation, for instance Silesia, at its expense. (If it lost, the likelihood was that it would have to give Venetia up anyway.) This meant that when war came thousands of Austrian troops died successfully defending territory which the Austrians had already agreed to surrender if they beat Prussia. In effect what they were defending was not territory but Francis Joseph's imperial honour, which forbade surrendering territory without a fight.[21] On 2 July, on the eve of the Battle of Königgrätz, when the war was in full swing and not going Austria's way, Francis Joseph offered to cede Venetia regardless of the war's outcome, in return for French intercession. By then it was a little late to do what had been necessary all along, and give up Austria's position in Italy to keep hold of her position in Germany. Trying for both, she was to keep neither.

The Battle of Königgrätz (known also by its Czech name of Sadowa), the decisive battle of the Austro-Prussian War, indeed one of the most decisive battles in modern European history, took place on 3 July in Central Bohemia and was a crushing defeat for the Austrians. There has been a great deal of controversy since then about who was to blame for the catastrophe. Immediately after the battle, the Habsburg authorities heaped all the blame on the Austrian commanding general, Ludwig August von Benedek. Subsequently the historiographical mainstream has tended to Benedek's exoneration, holding the conservative military leadership around Francis Joseph, and Francis Joseph himself, responsible for the debacle: both for forcing Benedek to be commander in the northern theatre instead of Archduke Albrecht (to protect Habsburg honour), and for forcing Benedek by a notorious telegram to do battle against his better judgement (to protect Habsburg honour).[22] Much of this version has been found wanting by recent scholarship, and revisionist interpretations now put the blame squarely back on Benedek's shoulders.[23]

The latest evidence suggests that Benedek was far from the aggrieved scapegoat of legend, but it does not exonerate the emperor either.[24] When the war started, for instance, interference by Francis Joseph through his messenger Friedrich Beck asking for assistance for the Saxon Army – to salve Francis Joseph's sense of honour – disrupted Benedek's plans. The infamous telegram in which Francis Joseph asked Benedek 'Has a battle taken place?' may have been understandable, but it encouraged Benedek to make the fateful stand. How else, if one is an ultraloyal servant such as Benedek, is one to respond to one's *emperor*?[25] Benedek performed very poorly, making several serious mistakes, standing *before* the Elbe at Königgrätz being only the most egregious.[26] As it was, many of the factors involved were entirely out of his hands, and on anything but the most immediate operational level, this worst of all Austrian disasters before 1914 was far more due to mistakes in organisation, armament policy, training and financing of the army by its high command, and that ultimately meant Francis Joseph. It was after all the control of the army which was the prerogative most jealously guarded by Francis Joseph after 1859. Therefore the critical weaknesses and disadvantages which that army displayed during that campaign must surely be seen as largely his responsibility.

The most well known handicap, often seen as decisive, was the technological one of not being equipped, like the Prussians, with rapid-firing breech-loading rifles. This Prussian advantage took an enormous toll on the Austrian ranks, and was the primary reason for the initiative in the war shifting so rapidly to Prussia. The Austrian army had considered this innovatory weapon as early as 1851, but on advice from 'experts' Francis Joseph had turned it down in favour of the tried and tested front-loader.[27] Prussia's general technological advantage has also been blamed on the cutbacks on military expenditures in the immediate pre-war years, but this was itself a result of Francis Joseph's refusal to concede any control over the military to those who had to vote its expenditures, the Reichsrat. Then again, as Geoffrey Wawro well describes, it was not only – or even primarily – technological or financial difficulties which were to blame. The Reichsrat's military budgets of the early 1860s should have been more than adequate to fund a technologically up-to-date and very large army.[28]

The real problems lay in the inefficiencies and misguided tactics of the military establishment. In the speed of mobilisation and the efficient use of manpower and resources the Austrian army trailed far behind the Prussians.[29] Some of this was due to Austria's nationality problems, but far more had to do with the nature of Francis Joseph's regime itself. One problem was the army's profligacy. Only about half the military budget went to militarily useful ends; the other half, with Francis Joseph's connivance, went to a bloated military bureaucracy and to the army's role in *domestic* political control.[30] It was for this reason that there were insufficient funds left over for the modernisation of military hardware.

Another major constraint characteristic of Francis Joseph's state was the poor educational level of the army's recruits. This meant that, even if there had been funds for modernisation, the troops would have been unable to follow the more complex procedures required for using modern equipment such as breech-loading rifles. This led to what Wawro describes as the incompetent – 'cruel and unintelligent' – tactics followed by the army high command, namely the virtually exclusive employment of shock tactics, with columns of infantrymen advancing with bayonets fixed against lines of rifles. Movement and *élan* were supposed to compensate for the fact that the Austrian army's 'poorly educated, poorly trained, largely non-German-speaking' soldiers, 'could not shoot accurately or maneuver in open order' (which would have allowed, for instance, for lying prone in the face of rifle fire). While the storm columns did serve a 'social function' as a means of internal control of the troops, they proved disastrous as a military measure, leading to horrific numbers of casualties.[31] Incompetent tactics were thus employed to mask the inadequacies and incompetence of the Habsburg troops, with fatal consequences.

The army leadership, Benedek and his mostly high-noble generals, clearly share some responsibility for this sorry state of affairs. Yet they and their misguided policies were only symptomatic of the deeper problems of a state which went to war with such uneducated and untrained recruits and relied on *élan* to carry the day; and the man who ran this state, who had insisted in 1859 on retaining full control of the army, and who was responsible for the appointment of such incompetent military leaders, was none other than Francis Joseph.

Even if the Austrians had done far better on the field of battle, it is arguable that Bismarck's effective diplomatic encirclement of Austria, with him ready to call on Hungarian, Serb and Rumanian, even Bohemian support against the Habsburg state, would most probably have done for the Austrians.[32] As it was, Königgrätz effectively achieved the expulsion of Austria from the German Confederation, a fact confirmed by the Peace of Prague of 23 August 1866. By this, Austria acceded to the creation of a North German Confederation dominated by Prussia, and to the formation of a Southern German Union, linked militarily and commercially to its northern neighbour, and with no special links to Austria, but nevertheless consisting of independent, sovereign states. Bismarck wisely let Austria off the hook, making no territorial demands for Prussia. The only territorial loss suffered by Austria in 1866 was of Venetia, which she had already surrendered before the war.

On the face of it, Austria had not done that badly and had not even been completely excluded from German affairs. In subsequent years Francis Joseph was to attempt, as he had in Italy after 1859, to recover the Austrian position. From the toehold left by the independence clause in the Prague treaty regarding the Southern German Union states, he sought to regain a say in German affairs by marshalling these states on Austria's side against feared Prussian dominance. Under Beust's guidance, Austria was to succeed quite well for a while in this policy, buttressed by similar French interest in not seeing North and South Germany unite under Prussia.[33] In reality, however, 1866 spelt the end of the Habsburg Empire as Francis Joseph had inherited it. Expelled from Italy, virtually expelled from Germany, domestically split asunder by the Compromise with the Hungarians in 1867, whose drastic nature owed much to Austrian defeat against Prussia, the Dualist Austro-Hungarian Monarchy was a quite different, far less imposing (if perhaps sounder) entity than the united empire, the guarantor of peace and against revolution, which had been Francis Joseph's heritage. It was only in 1870 that the loss of Habsburg power became fully evident.

In that year, Napoleon III, led by the nose by Bismarck and admittedly against Austrian advice, invaded the Bavarian Palatinate, uniting the Southern German states behind Prussian leadership and starting the Franco-Prussian War. This immediately put paid to all attempts by Austria to build Southern Germany into a pro-Austrian, anti-Prussian bloc. The subsequent course of the war, with what Francis Joseph called the 'frightful catastrophes' for the French, culminated in that other decisive battle, Sedan, and the establishment of the German Empire. This destroyed any remaining shreds of hope for Austrian involvement within Germany. Austria looked on, impotent to stop the Prussian juggernaut, partly because of Napoleon III's initial mistake, but also because of her own military unreadiness, the threat from Russia, and large sympathy in both the German and Magyar public for the German (Prussian) cause.[34] In the new regime, dynastic interests could no longer ignore national and nationalist concerns, especially from the Hungarian Kingdom.

The events of 1866 affected not only Austria's international status. Domestically the major consequence was the Compromise with the Magyar leadership in 1867, which resulted in the 'restoration' of the autonomy of the Kingdom of Hungary and constitutional government for the Austrian half left over. For some years Francis Joseph was under the impression that this still left him free to amend his relationship with the peoples not directly affected by his Compromise with the Magyar leadership, most notably the Czechs. With the Prussian victory against France and the end of any hope of retaining influence in Germany, he decided the time was right to realise a goal he had harboured for some time to overturn the German-liberal inspired, centralist constitution in Vienna in favour of yet one more change, to a more conservative and federalist structure, which would satisfy the still disaffected Czechs' claims to the 'historic' 'state right' of the Bohemian crown.[35]

This was the task he set the Hohenwart ministry in February 1871, which under Albert Schäffle's guidance devised the 'Fundamental Articles'. In October this new constitutional settlement was crushed by opposition from two main sources. On the one hand, the German liberals and Beust protested the attack on German rights, and pointed to the displeasure of the new German Empire (buttressed by none too subtle hints from the German Emperor himself).[36] On the other, the Hungarian premier, Gyula Andrássy, offered his vehement opposition, seeing the plan as an attack on dualism. Faced with such opponents, Francis Joseph, who had even promised to be crowned Bohemian king, gave up his newest plan – to the despair of the Czechs.[37] Between German national interests, whether within or beyond the Monarchy's borders, and Hungarian national interests, the events of the last decade had taught Francis Joseph how limited his real power was. By 1879 the straitjacket of the Dual Alliance would be added to the straitjacket of Dualism, the Habsburg emperor caught between German and Hungarian.

. . .

DUALISM

The Compromise (*Ausgleich*) which was to provide the Monarchy's constitutional framework for the rest of its existence was negotiated in the aftermath of the crushing defeat at the hands of Bismarck's Prussia. Legend has it that the key point in the negotiations arose when in the wake of defeat Francis Joseph asked the Hungarian leader, Ference Deák, what his demands were now, and Deák replied that they were the same now as they had been before the war. A grateful Francis Joseph, relieved at not having to make further concessions, responded in the same spirit, and an agreement was soon reached, albeit with the Hungarians achieving the maximum demands of their original bargaining position.[38]

Francis Joseph's reasons for agreeing to the Compromise of 1866–67 went beyond just gratitude at Deák's moderation. Above all, his new, Saxon, foreign minister, Baron Friedrich Ferdinand Beust, appointed in October, was able to convince him that the only way quickly to restore order in the realm and restore any influence in Southern Germany (eventually perhaps in Germany generally) was to satisfy the Hungarians. The only quick way to restore dynastic power was effectively to split the Monarchy in half, and thus relinquish the ideal of the unitary state which had been a central goal of Habsburg policy since the time of Maria Theresa, and also of an emperor, Francis Joseph, whose chosen motto was *Viribus unitis*, 'With *united* powers.' The wish to placate his beloved if difficult wife, Elizabeth, whose admiration for the Magyar leaders, especially Andrássy, had made her an enthusiastic advocate of the Hungarian cause, might also have played some role, but if it did it merely reinforced what was all along Francis Joseph's main concern: how to retain and strengthen his, the dynasty's status and power. If, in the dire straits of 1866, this meant allowing the division of one's empire to gain Hungarian support, so be it.[39]

One of the key peculiarities in a unique constitutional settlement was the nature of the parties. The dualistic Compromise was an agreement between Francis Joseph and the Magyar leadership of the Hungarian Diet. The peoples of the rest of the Monarchy were never formally consulted. The Compromise had been agreed to by vote of the Hungarian Diet before Francis Joseph was crowned King of Hungary in June 1867, in a ceremony whose medievalism struck at least one Western observer as remarkable.[40] It was only in December 1867, however, almost as an afterthought, that the remaining 'lands and provinces represented in the Reichsrat' passed the constitution (actually a series of fundamental laws) by which the Austrian half of the empire was to be ruled until the end of the Monarchy. This initial asymmetry gave a large hint as to how the dualism of the Compromise was to work in practice.

Under the Compromise, the Habsburg Empire of Austria became the Dual Monarchy of Austria–Hungary.[41] Instead of a unitary state, there were now two states, Hungary and the rest of the Monarchy, under a single monarch (who was Emperor of Austria and King of Hungary). The identity problems caused for the non-Hungarian half of the Monarchy are legendary, receiving their most famous treatment in Robert Musil's *The Man without Qualities*.[42] In contrast to Hungary, which as the Kingdom of St Stephen had a definite identity, both as state and nation, the non-Hungarian half hardly had a generally accepted official name. It could not officially be Austria, despite its ruler being the Emperor of Austria, because Austria was either the 'hereditary lands' alone, or the whole, former empire. Informally of course it was called Austria, but semi-officially it became known as Cisleithania (as it will be called in this book), denoting those lands this side of the Leitha River (which ran along part of the border between the Hungarian and non-Hungarian halves). The lands the other side are sometimes called Transleithania, but this is redundant, for they were simply Hungary. The official title of the non-Hungarian half, however, was 'the lands and provinces represented in the Reichsrat'. It is hardly surprising, therefore, if Cisleithania lacked 'national egoism' as Louis Eisenmann charged.[43]

Above, or between the two states – it depended on whether one accepted the Austrian (Cisleithanian) or Hungarian version of the Compromise – there were three Joint Ministries, what remained of the imperial state, for Foreign Affairs, War and Finance (the last to manage the funding of the first two). These ministries, whose existence was seen as deriving from the Pragmatic Sanction, agreed to by the Hungarian Diet in 1723, were to be under the control of the joint monarch, Francis Joseph, but subject to annual account to the Delegations. This body consisted of delegations from the two parliaments of the respective states (the former Hungarian Diet, and the Austrian Reichsrat of the February Constitution – minus its Hungarian deputies), which met annually in the same city, alternately in Vienna and Budapest, but not together. It was one of the maximal conditions achieved by the Magyar leadership in 1867 that there was never again to be a truly imperial parliament. The Delegations met and deliberated separately. There was provision made for joint votes if agreement could not be reached; but by Hungarian insistence such votes were to be held in silence, without any cross-deliberation polluting the sovereignty of Hungary.[44]

By Hungarian design, therefore, collaboration was kept to an absolute minimum. According to the Hungarian interpretation of the Compromise, there was no joint state of which Hungary and Cisleithania were parts, but rather only working relationships between two independent states. In Cisleithania, by contrast, the Joint Ministries and the apparatus of the Delegations continued to be seen as the expression of a legal entity beyond the level of the two states. This was to lead to many arguments over such things as the official title of the various joint institutions, whether they were 'k.k.'*: 'kaiserlich-königlich' (imperial-royal), suggesting a joint state entity with the imperial Austria precedent to the royal Hungary, or whether they were 'k. und k.': 'kaiserlich und königlich' (imperial and royal), which suggested the existence of two separate entities which merely shared common institutions. It is a measure of Hungarian influence that the latter title eventually won out. It is a measure of the problems caused by these legal niceties that the Dual Monarchy only received a suitable, politically acceptable coat-of-arms during the First World War.[45]

In addition to the 'pragmatic' elements of the Compromise system, there were 'dualist' provisions for agreements every ten years between the two states directly (the two parliaments and Francis Joseph with both hats). These related to the still preserved customs union, especially as regards the currency and tariff rates, and, most contentious of all, to the 'quota' (proportion) to be set as regards financing of the joint concerns, predominantly the imperial armed forces. This became a huge political football in the Monarchy's affairs. Originally the quota was set at 70 per cent to be paid by the much richer Austria, 30 per cent by Hungary. As Hungary became richer, but also less content with having to finance a joint army rather than just its own, Austro-Hungarian politics was beset every decade by haggling over the quota and related issues; by the last pre-war decades haggling over the Compromise had resulted in almost constant crisis.[46]

What made co-operation between the two states even more complex, and hindered as much as helped the relationship, was the fact that negotiations were never ever solely bi-polar, between the two states, but rather approximated an infernal triangle, because the prime ministers and parliaments of both states had also to deal with another party, with his own interests in the management of the 'joint' affairs: Francis Joseph. He ostensibly surrendered many of his powers over domestic affairs, especially in Hungary, in the Compromise of 1867. He did so in order to retain his power over the Monarchy's foreign policy and its armed

---

*Hence the often used appellation 'Kakania'.

forces. In this he succeeded almost completely, and in practice more than on paper, because the Delegations, largely due to Hungarian dislike of the institution, proved a broken reed if they were ever seriously intended as a control of Habsburg foreign and military policy. Instead the joint affairs of the Monarchy were run by Francis Joseph in consultation with his joint ministers and the Joint Ministerial Council, known as (and called henceforth in this book) the Crown Council.[47] Although in effect an informal imperial cabinet, usually including the Cisleithanian and Hungarian premiers as well as the Joint Ministers, sometimes the states' finance ministers and the Chief of the General Staff, and anyone else Francis Joseph cared to call on for advice, the Crown Council had no official role within the Compromise settlement, and remained therefore Francis Joseph's own organ of government.

Foreign policy remained *his* foreign policy, and the joint armed forces, especially his beloved army (he never cared much about the navy), remained under his direct control, and continued to swear loyalty to him as Habsburg emperor and not to the Dualist state, let alone to Austria or Hungary. Admittedly, the Compromise also allowed for a 'Landwehr' and 'Honvéd', military entities financed by the two separate states; but these remained auxiliary to the imperial army, their secondary character revealed by neither having its own, separate artillery. (A Honvéd artillery was to prove one of the major aims – and achievements – of Hungarian nationalists in the pre-war years.) What the Compromise preserved for Francis Joseph was his direction of the army and foreign policy.

This was what truly mattered for Francis Joseph. Austrian (German) historians tended, and still tend, to see Francis Joseph as pro-Magyar in his handling of the Dualist system. His holding to his coronation oath as Hungarian king has often been seen as causing 'the confinement of the Emperor within the Hungarian King'. Certainly, he saw the preservation of the Dualist regime, at least after 1871, as an absolute necessity for the Monarchy's viability, and this often resulted in policies designed not to antagonise the Magyar leadership.[48] Yet Francis Joseph's 'pro-Magyar' approach can just as well be seen as based on a typically practical, 'utilitarian-realist' if shortsighted, decision to let sleeping dogs lie, as long as he was left with an adequately financed army. When he wanted to, Francis Joseph had his own power-base within the Hungarian constitution, which he periodically used to dramatic effect. In national questions, however, as Steed notoriously phrased it, Francis Joseph chose to act like an absentee landlord in Hungary, allowing his 'managers', the Magyar nobility and gentry, complete licence with the other national minorities, as long as they gave him what he wanted: a well-financed army.[49] It was not Magyar interests, but his own interests as dynast which were always paramount.

Francis Joseph knew very well what he was doing when he opted for the path of dualism. In the Ministerial Council meeting of 1 February 1867, when the final decision was made to pursue a dualist settlement, Beust defended his pro-dualist policy in terms of stark *Realpolitik*: 'I am quite aware that the Slav peoples of the Monarchy will view the new policy with mistrust; but the government cannot always be fair to all the nations. Therefore we have to rely on the support of those with the most viability (*Lebenskraft*) . . . and those are the Germans and the Hungarians.' Francis Joseph agreed in a characteristically pragmatic manner. To Count Richard Belcredi's assertion that the government should not rely on individual nationalities but be above all of them, and that the Slavs could not be so easily ignored, Francis Joseph countered: 'It might be that the way suggested by Count Belcredi is the less objectionable, but that of Baron Beust ought more quickly to lead to the desired goal.'[50]

Francis Joseph chose the dualist path fully knowing that he was ignoring the interests of a very large proportion of his subjects, the Slavs. The effect of his choice was made even clearer by Belcredi a couple of days later. Asked by Francis Joseph whether his agreeing to the Compromise was impossible, Belcredi said it was if the 'non-Hungarian' lands were to have no say in the settlement: 'For in these [lands] and not in Hungary does the Monarchy have its strongest support and it is there that the will to preserve its mighty unity is indubitably still present. To what will a policy lead, which totally spurns the Slav majority of the population of these lands?'[51]

It was an excellent question, for Francis Joseph's expedient acceptance of the Dualist Compromise, whether inevitable or not, necessarily resulted in attempts at emulation by all the other nationalities, especially the 'historic' nations. The Poles demanded national autonomy in Galicia, and got it, albeit unofficially, running the province as if the entire population was Polish, disregarding the almost as numerous Ruthenes and the Jews. The Czechs, as we have already mentioned, did not get the same sort of deal as either Hungarians or Poles, although they came close in 1871, as mentioned earlier. Hungarian opposition had played a large part in scotching that deal. Within the lands of the Crown of St Stephen, Rumanian attempts to retain some form of autonomy for Transylvania were also prevented by sharp Magyar practices; the Croats similarly demanded at least some sort of national autonomy if they had to be under Hungarian sovereignty, and in some degree got it in the *Nagodba* of 1868, but with crucial flaws which were to allow future Hungarian abuses.[52] The two major domestic chronic problems of the Monarchy were to be the frustrated national struggle of the Czechs, and the increasing pressure on the Monarchy's southern border of the South Slav problem.

Adolf Fischhof, who as a Jewish medical student had been a leader of the 1848 revolution and was later one of Austria's leading liberal political thinkers, once stated: 'Our constitution, instead of being the wax which welds our territories into a whole, is the wedge to drive them apart.'[53] In the short term Francis Joseph might well have been right: to preserve his power and Habsburg status, the Compromise of 1866–67 might well have been necessary. Its consequences for the long term, however, were to be anything but positive.

. . .

FRANCIS JOSEPH AS CONSTITUTIONAL MONARCH

On 22 August 1866, the day before the peace treaty with the Prussians was signed, Francis Joseph wrote to his aged mother Sophie a letter in which he blamed the double-dealing of Austria's enemies for the disaster. 'As for us, we were very honest, but very stupid.' Stupid to believe in the promises of others, that is, not stupid in the way he had managed Austria's resources. While he still claimed that the 'life and death struggle . . . is not yet over', he was clearly in despair at his situation: 'When the whole world is against you, and you have no friends, there is little chance of success, but you must go on doing what you can, fulfilling your duty and, in the end, going down with honour.'[54]

This desperate language was understandable, for not only was his Monarchy in the throes of catastrophic defeat in 1866, but also he personally was wildly unpopular with the populace. The news of defeat had been greeted by pacifist celebrations in the

streets of Vienna.[55] A report of the Police Commissioner Cam-
erina in September 1866 was unusually blunt for an Austrian official. Public opinion in Vienna, he claimed, thought that Francis
Joseph,

> since coming to the throne has been the protector of the
> military and lacks any love for his populace, which is made
> evident by the fact that neither his Majesty nor the Empress
> show themselves to the people, indeed at any such op-
> portunity they seek to keep themselves distant. His High-
> ness is also accused of devoting more time to the pleasures
> of hunting . . . than to the business of government.[56]

The latter accusation was a little unfair, as Francis Joseph was nothing if not a hard worker, but the general tenor of the report clearly
shows to what a low level Francis Joseph's star had fallen with
the public.

It was in this state of severely compromised authority that Francis Joseph made the decision both to settle with the Magyar leadership, and to allow the German political leadership to impose a
liberal constitution in Cisleithania. The dualist Compromise meant
Francis Joseph becoming a constitutional monarch in both
Hungary and Cisleithania. He did not like this at all. Even though
he had to acknowledge the 'historic' nature of the Hungarian
constitution, he was determined, successfully as it turned out, to
prevent any notion that the December constitution of Cisleithania was based on popular sovereignty. Legally that constitution
was and remained a gift of the monarch, granted by his grace.

Although he had to accept in this constitution the concept of
ministerial responsibility, it was a rather narrow, legal one,
concerned with possible illegal acts by individual ministers. It did
not extend to the political form of ministerial responsibility usually thought of whereby cabinets fall if they are voted down by
parliamentary majority. The power to hire and fire ministers
remained with the emperor until the end of the Monarchy. They
answered to him and not the parliament.[57] Nevertheless, after
1867 Francis Joseph felt constrained to operate within the constitution he himself had granted, for there was no other way to keep
the Magyars and the Germans satisfied, and he no longer had
the power or authority to rule on the basis of his dynastic right
alone.

Francis Joseph not only disliked having a constitution, he
particularly disliked the German liberal politicians who had done

so much to drive him to this point. Their whole worldview was in many ways anathema to him.[58] One signal he gave was his constant refusal to wear civilian dress at civic functions in his liberal capital city of Vienna.[59] Yet his practical streak allowed him to condescend to play the role of constitutional monarch and to tolerate the *Bürgerministerium* (Citizens' Ministry) which proudly took control of the Cisleithanian government in late 1867 under Prime Minister Prince Carlos Auersperg, because it was the German liberals who seemed to offer the best means to achieve Francis Joseph's ends.

The Germans and Hungarians were, after all, in his and his advisers' opinion, the two peoples with the most 'viability'. We have seen why the Hungarians would be so described. As for the Germans, they were by far the wealthiest, most politically articulate, and best educated group in the Monarchy, especially after the loss of the Italian provinces. The bureaucracy was a German bureaucracy still, in Cisleithania. Although Austria's Germans were split between liberal and conservative political groups, the rising middle classes, the apparent vanguard of 'Progress', were staunch backers of the liberals and the latter thus appeared at this juncture as the power of the future in Austrian politics. Liberals had an overwhelming majority in the Reichsrat's lower house in 1867. They had the backing of the financial interests on which the still rickety state finances heavily depended. It seemed sensible that Francis Joseph should look to this predominant group to provide him with the money and power he needed to continue his dynastic duty.

The Germans also had the attraction for him, ironically, of delivering the most political power into his hands, because of their support for a centralised state. It has been asserted by some that Francis Joseph was a supporter of federalism in his Monarchy.[60] At times he certainly could adopt this stance. In response to Archduke Albrecht's criticism of his decision to visit Budapest in search of a Hungarian settlement in early 1866, he had Felix Count Crenneville reply that 'he is not the emperor of Vienna, but of each and every one of his kingdoms and lands, and feels himself equally at home in all of them.'[61] He was to adopt a similar stance in 1871 and at various times thereafter, sometimes with real conviction. Usually, however, this viewpoint was just a blind, another means to a goal. His ideal had always been the ultimate form of centralisation, monarchical absolutism. When that had failed he had tried Schmerling's German centralism. When that failed, and Hungary had to be given special status, the next best thing was still the Cisleith-anian centralism of the German liberals, for at least this promised to allow him to remain emperor in an imperial capital, with a central parliament and ministry with which he could still rule at least half his empire as emperor, and from which he could still receive sufficient funds to keep up a decently sized army and hence the great power status of the Habsburgs.[62]

As long as the German liberals appeared the dominant force in Austrian politics, and as long as they gave him what he most wanted, Francis Joseph was prepared to tolerate many policies which were not at all to his liking. He allowed them, for instance, to continue the system of 'electoral geometry', we would call it gerrymandering, which greatly enhanced their numbers in the Reichsrat, delivering the large majority which overwhelmed the federalist opposition of German and South Slav conservatives and clericals (the Czechs had boycotted the assembly from 1863, and again from April 1867; the Polish Club co-operated with whoever was in power in Vienna to secure Polish control over Galicia).[63]

Much to his chagrin, he also allowed the German liberal major-ity to roll back the concessions made to the Roman Catholic hierarchy in the Concordat of 1855. A large batch of anti-clerical legislation, the May Laws, was passed in 1868 reasserting Austrian state control over education and marriage, and provid-ing for the legal equality of religious denominations. In the sum-mer of 1870 he even conceded the abrogation of the Concordat itself, to the horror of his mother, after the Papal Declaration of Infallibility had made the defence of the treaty with the Papacy virtually impossible. In 1874 he further allowed a new set of May Laws which asserted more state control over the Catholic hierarchy.[64] Although he assured the Papacy that he would not permit a *Kulturkampf* to persecute the Church as in the new Ger-man Reich, and prevented consideration of full civil marriage in 1873,[65] he nevertheless presided over a great liberalisation and secularisation of Austrian social, religious and educational life, not the least part of which was the final, complete emancipation of Austrian Jewry as full and equal citizens, as guaranteed by the constitution.

The political, economic, civic and legal life of Cisleithania also experienced a large dose of liberalisation during the barely more than one decade when the German liberals were the dominant force in government. The legal system was transformed so that Austria for the first time became a real *Rechtsstaat*, state of law, with fully separated executive and judicial systems, down to the local level. This was achieved through the establishment of the *Reichsgericht*, Imperial Supreme Court, called for in the constitution and established in practice in 1869 with competence over constitutional rights, and the *Verwaltungsgerichtshof*, Administrative Court, established in 1875 and providing for redress against the administration.[66] A new Criminal Law Code, with a somewhat limited application of the jury system, was introduced in 1873. The *Gemeindegesetz*, Law on Communes, of 1862 had already provided for wide-reaching communal autonomy, and there was a flourishing of the press in the new, liberal environment.[67] The economy, experiencing a post-war boom, was also liberalised by a spate of trade treaties with Austria's major trading partners (without, however, a corresponding liberalisation of labour laws). The Ringstrasse development, which once had symbolised the brave new world of neo-Absolutism, now became the symbol of the breakneck boom of the '*Gründerzeit*' of 1867–73.

Even the military received the benefits of liberal reform. The Army Laws of 1868, passed in Cisleithania and Hungary, realised the Compromise's provisions for a Joint Army, establishing conscription and funding for a heavily scaled back imperial army. These laws, renewable every ten years, provided some parliamentary control over the army's budget and hence indirectly over its administration, and it was under two War Ministers appointed for their acceptability to German and Magyar liberals, General Baron Franz John (1866–68) and General Baron Franz Kuhn von Kuhnenfeld (1868–74), that the much-needed modernisation of the Austro-Hungarian imperial-royal armed forces was begun. The army remained Francis Joseph's prerogative, and the countervailing efforts of the arch-conservative Inspector General, Archduke Albrecht, were able to fend off much of the liberal reform agenda. The army remained an essentially conservative, dynastic force, but even in this Habsburg bastion liberal-inspired reform, though minimal, did occur.[68]

Francis Joseph was therefore prepared to accept a great deal of change at the hands of the German liberal Reichsrat majority. Until 1870 he might also have hoped that his retaining of a German centralist system in Cisleithania aided his chances of retaining or even regaining influence in Germany. Yet there was always that consideration, voiced by Belcredi, that reliance on Germans in Cisleithania ignored the vast Slav sector of the population at the Monarchy's – and monarch's – peril. The Poles could be bought off by granting an informal autonomy to Galicia, which soon resulted in that province becoming a semi-independent 'little Poland', with Polish-speaking administration and universities. The Cisleithanian South Slavs could be ignored for now; but the Czechs, living at the heart of the state's economically most progressive region and quickly advancing economically and culturally, could not be so easily brushed aside, especially as their political leadership had allied with the conservative Bohemian high nobility, which still had Francis Joseph's ear at court.

The national arrogance of the German liberal leadership had not helped matters, and the Czechs, the second most significant national group after the Germans in Cisleithania, were emulating the Magyars in their resistance to the Compromise and their boycotting of the Reichsrat. Already by 1868 Francis Joseph had therefore been considering how to settle with the Czechs as well. Mere feelers in this direction on his part had caused the resignation of his prime minister, Carlos Auersperg, so sensitive were German liberals to attempts to appease the Czechs. Despite this Francis Joseph continued to explore the Czech-federalist option. After all, if the German liberals, whom he disliked, could not guarantee order in his realm, why not attempt to make a deal with the other side? He was in any case more sympathetic with the conservative policy positions of the federalists, and at the same time could gain back for himself some of the political power previously lost. Hence his installation of the Potocki ministry in April 1870, and when that failed, the even more conservative and federalist Hohenwart ministry of February 1871.[69]

As we have seen, this attempt at yet another constitutional makeover was frustrated when Francis Joseph decided that this initial bid for freedom from German liberal shackles was more trouble than it was worth given both German and Magyar opposition. Yet the events of 1870–71 showed the limits of German liberal hegemony in Cisleithania, and revealed both the continuing relevance of Francis Joseph's prerogatives and his willingness to use them. This partly explains why the new liberal ministry, this time under Prince Adolph Auersperg, was both more moderate in its policies and more careful with Francis Joseph. The Crash of 1873, which saw widescale financial ruin and the unearthing of all manner of governmental corruption, was a further motivation for circumspection, as its results, bursting the bubble of boom-led capitalist optimism, had a chilling effect on liberalism's prestige among the public. If 1859 and 1866 had undermined the authority of the dynasty, 1873 did the same for liberalism, leaving the ideology and its political adherents in a weakened condition, exposed to conservative, and dynastic, counter-attack.[70]

In Hungary the story was much the same. In the 1860s and 1870s Francis Joseph behaved very much as the constitutional monarch, allowing the liberal regime of Prime Minister Gyula Andrássy to pass legislation largely paralleling that of the German liberals in Cisleithania. As well as reform of the religious and educational order, the county form of local government was reintroduced to reassert Hungarian liberalism's belief in local autonomy (although the Bachian forms of central bureaucracy were also retained, and fully fledged separation of administration and judiciary at all levels was never achieved).[71] The national question was addressed in the Nationality Law, the creation of Baron Joseph Eötvös, passed in 1868. This would have provided a very liberal and generous settlement of the national problem in Hungary – if it had ever been implemented in the spirit in which it was written. The mini-Compromise with Croatia, the Nagodba, was also passed in 1868.[72] This settlement was not one particularly favourable to the Croats, traditionally one of the Habsburgs' most loyal peoples, and a major reason for the Monarchy's survival in 1848. Yet Francis Joseph was prepared to let the Magyar leadership have their way in this and in many other matters where he might have had qualms. It might be noted that 1868 was also the year in which the Hungarian Parliament passed the Army Law which guaranteed the survival of Francis Joseph's imperial, united army.[73]

Francis Joseph went along with liberal regimes in both halves of his Monarchy, and Austria and Hungary for most of this period gave the appearance of properly constitutional states. Yet this was not at all constitutional monarchy as understood and practised in Britain, for instance. Both in Cisleithania and Hungary Francis Joseph retained very large constitutional powers, which were far from being merely theoretical. In Hungary, in the secret *Punktation* of March 1867, Francis Joseph had insisted on, and the Magyar leadership accepted, various powers which went beyond those of a monarch in a 'parliamentary' system. Apart from various executive powers, such as powers of appointment in the central bureaucracy, there was the crucial power of the royal 'presanction' of legislation. That is to say, Francis Joseph had to give his permission before legislation was presented to the Hungarian parliament by his ministers. This amounted to a royal prophylactic veto, giving Francis Joseph immense negative power over his Hungarian ministers and Parliament.[74] In addition, whereas ministerial responsibility to the monarch was clear, the converse ministerial responsibility to parliament was never clearly established.[75] The post-1867 constitutional settlement in Hungary thus included within itself what George Barany has called 'the disguised continuation of monarchical absolutism'.[76]

What was true in Hungary was even more the case in Cisleithania. We have already seen how parliamentary ministerial responsibility was never established, leaving Francis Joseph in charge of *his* ministers. He also retained the powers of prorogation and dissolution, and although the Reichsrat did have power over the budget, the key constitutional power, even this was compromised by another constitutional provision, the soon to be notorious Article 14. This ostensibly emergency clause allowed the emperor to decree emergency legislation when the Reichsrat was not sitting. As he retained powers of prorogation and dissolution, there was the potential here of a ministry losing a Reichsrat vote of confidence, getting Francis Joseph to dissolve parliament, and then governing by emergency decree, creating a *fait accompli* before the next Reichsrat, elected under government influence, met.[77]

The 'electoral geometry' employed by the German liberals to create artificially high majorities for themselves also had advantages for Francis Joseph. Although made somewhat more 'democratic' by the introduction of direct elections in 1873, the franchise of the Reichsrat still provided for a division of the electorate into 'curiae', whereby rural and urban constituencies were joined by Chambers of Commerce and 'Large landowners'. This last group, 85 of 353 seats in the *Lower* House of the Reichsrat, meant that the aristocracy not only completely dominated the upper, *Herrenhaus*, but also retained a sizeable presence in the Lower. And the votes of these nobles, whether elected from the 'Conservatives' or from the 'Constitutional' (liberal) parties among the aristocracy, were almost invariably at Francis Joseph's command.[78]

Taken together with the consequences of Article 14 and the lack of full ministerial responsibility, this made Francis Joseph's position very strong politically. If one adds his position as 'the keystone of the political structure' of dualism, whereby it was he who, advised by the only informal executive body of the Crown

Council, continued to run – and jealously guard – military and foreign policy, then it becomes clear that Francis Joseph remained, even in the domestic political affairs of each of his states, a formidable presence.[79] When those prerogatives of his in the spheres of defence and foreign policy might ever be threatened, Francis Joseph was in a good position to show just how powerful that presence was. In 1871, over a domestic matter, he had not been prepared to test his full powers against the liberal establishment. When, however, in 1878, his prerogative in foreign policy was challenged by the German liberals, he chose to exercise his powers, to devastating effect. The occasion was the occupation of Bosnia–Herzegovina.

. . .

BOSNIA

The year 1866 saw Austria shut out of Italy; 1870–71 saw Austria–Hungary shut out finally from Germany. Any possibility of a substantial 'colonial' policy had ended with the failure of the attempt by Francis Joseph's brother, Maximilian, to be Emperor of Mexico (an old Habsburg possession), resulting in Maximilian's tragic death by firing squad in 1867.[80] This left the 'Near East', the Balkans, as the Monarchy's one remaining sphere of interest if it was to remain a 'Great power', as Habsburg prestige demanded.

This meant addressing the problem of the ailing Ottoman Empire on the one hand, in which semi-independent states such as Montenegro, Serbia and Rumania were already asserting themselves against their Turkish suzerain, and the far-from-ailing Russian Empire on the other. Russia historically had seen the Turkish Empire not only as the oppressor of fellow Slavs and (Orthodox) Christians, but also as ripe for the picking in terms of geopolitical expansion. If Austria–Hungary was to hold her end up in her last sphere of influence she had to be able at least to stand up to her north-eastern neighbour, even if she were friendly, and this meant finding help elsewhere.

This state of affairs was quickly understood by Beust, who, in a Memorandum of May 1871, recommended to Francis Joseph that the future basis of Habsburg foreign policy should be a *rapprochement* with the new Prusso-German Empire. When Beust was replaced by Andrássy in November 1871, largely due to Francis Joseph's dissatisfaction at his Saxon Chancellor crossing him over the question of a Czech Compromise, the former Hungarian prime minister continued Beust's pro-German policy.[81] Beust had also suggested cultivating good relations with Russia and the emerging Balkan states. Andrássy, 'an out-and-out Hungarian', who had once been executed in effigy by Francis Joseph's regime as a result of the Russian intervention in 1849, was initially neither so keen on conciliating Russia, nor convinced about the benefits of cultivating the Balkan states on the Monarchy's south-eastern perimeter. Viewing these neighbours from a strongly Magyar perspective, he described them in 1873 as 'wild Indians who could only be treated like unbroken horses, to whom corn should be offered with one hand while they are threatened with a whip in the other.'[82]

The energetic Andrássy, who, with his close relationship with Empress (Queen) Elizabeth and Magyar nobleman's flair, was one of the most successful of Francis Joseph's foreign ministers in getting the emperor-king to see things his way, initially wanted to use the Austro-German *rapprochement* of the summer of 1871 to build up an alliance, including Britain, aimed against Russia. British and German disinterest brought such talk to nought, and soon, whether he liked it or not, Andrássy was steering the Monarchy into *détente* with Russia, culminating in the Three Emperors' League of 1873, and cultivation of the emerging Balkan states.[83] In other words, by 1873 Andrássy had essentially adopted Beust's policies, of agreeing with the Russians not to step on each other's toes in the Balkans, and offering states such as Serbia the corn (or at least talk of building railways) and not the whip. To Francis Joseph, whose previous experience had persuaded him against war 'for a long time',[84] things must have seemed set fair for an overdue respite in foreign affairs.

Then came the Bosnian Revolt of 1875. The Monarchy already had, it is true, designs on Bosnia–Herzegovina.[85] This mountainous province was at that time a remote backwater of the Ottoman Empire, with a mixed population of: Orthodox Serbs, the most numerous sector, but not an absolute majority; Catholic Croats; and Muslims, the most prosperous and best-educated sector of the populace, consisting of some Turks, but mostly Slavs who over the years had converted to Islam, the religion of the rulers. There was also a small Jewish population. Apart from very small landed and urban elites, the vast bulk of the population were peasants and largely illiterate. Economically there was little if anything to recommend it, apart perhaps as a route for a railway to the richer markets of the rest of the Ottoman Empire.[86] Strategically, though, the province provided the hinterland to the Austrian province of Dalmatia, important to the Monarchy's continuing naval presence on the Adriatic and in the Mediterranean. It also provided the link between the Monarchy's territories and the Sanjak of Novibazar, the Turkish territory between Montenegro and Serbia.

There was thus something, if not that much, to be said for Austrian acquisition of the territory. In purely dynastic terms any land, no matter how poor or potentially troublesome, could be seen as some recompense to the family heritage for the loss by Francis Joseph of the plum of Lombardy–Venetia and the jewel of Habsburg predominance in Germany. There was a great deal more to be said for not letting any other power apart from the Turks have it. If Serbia or Montenegro were to possess it, this would cut off the Monarchy from the Ottoman Empire. Even if an independent Bosnian regime was installed by the Russians, this would still be an unacceptable strategic threat to Dalmatia.[87] Then there were other, more 'Habsburg' considerations. As Francis Joseph himself remarked to Alexander von Hübner in April 1876: 'If, for instance, there were an independent Bosnia, Croatia and Dalmatia would quickly swim away from us.'[88] The example of Piedmont's successful irredentism was too fresh in the emperor's mind not to make the prospect of an independent Bosnia, or even worse a Serbian Bosnia, a nightmare for him in terms of domestic nationality problems.

It was with such thoughts in mind that Francis Joseph, while on his one tour to Dalmatia, intimated to the province's governor, General Anton Mollinary, that Bosnia would be occupied by the Monarchy if it ever looked like slipping out of Turkish hands.[89] The tour of Dalmatia itself could well have been a preparation for such an eventuality; ironically it may well have created it, for Francis Joseph's presence so close by, raised Bosnian aspirations, and barely a month after his Dalmatian visit Bosnia erupted in revolt, throwing the whole of the Balkan peninsula, and Habsburg foreign policy, into turmoil.[90]

In the crisis which followed, Austria found herself in a situation all too reminiscent of the Crimean debacle, unsure of whether to co-operate with Russia, or to side with the Turks against her, thus antagonising the South Slavs both beyond her southern border, and within it. At first she was successful in avoiding confrontation with Russia by the Reichstadt agreement of 1876, which accepted Austrian annexation of Bosnia–Herzegovina. Russian victories against the Turks in 1877 and 1878, however, resulted in the Treaty of San Stefano of 1878, which, if it had stuck, would have made the Ottoman Empire and the Balkans a completely Russian sphere of interest, thus shutting the Monarchy out from her one remaining theatre of foreign policy. Fortunately for Francis Joseph and Andrássy, this was not only unacceptable to Austria, but also to the other power which had been a traditional ally of the Ottomans, Britain.[91] British interests in the region, always strong, had received an additional boost by the opening of the Suez Canal in 1869, the occasion for Francis Joseph's one extensive trip beyond continental Europe.[92] She was not about to countenance a Russian-dominated Balkan peninsula as outlined in San Stefano. The upshot of the diplomatic stand-off was the Congress of Berlin of June and July 1878, at which Austria–Hungary and Britain, in the personages of Andrássy and Lord Salisbury, achieved a reduction of the potential Russian puppet state of 'Big Bulgaria' on the one hand, and the right of the Austrians to occupation of Bosnia–Herzegovina and the garrisoning of the Sanjak of Novibazar on the other.[93]

The occupation of Bosnia–Herzegovina, Andrássy's great diplomatic achievement, represented an attempt to mollify the Turks. More importantly, it was a domestic political compromise, the need for which went to the heart of the continuing problems with the dualist Compromise. It further exposed the tensions which were to bring to an end the political and constitutional pact between Francis Joseph and the German liberals which had dominated Austrian affairs since 1867. On the one hand, Francis Joseph was very unhappy that Andrássy had not insisted on annexation, for only then could his dynastic goal of territorial aggrandisement, as opposed to the more practical goal of simply keeping other interests out, be fully achieved. Hübner had remarked in his diary in 1876 that 'sometimes Francis Joseph has certain goals in mind, which he pursues zealously,' and acquiring Bosnia–Herzegovina had by 1878 clearly become one of these.[94] On the other hand, however, was German and Magyar public opinion, and that of the domestic party political leadership, who were dead set against even occupation of the poor, Slav-filled provinces, let alone annexation.[95]

The reasons for this opposition say much about the Monarchy's subsequent problems. The first objection was that the occupation – a *de facto* annexation which would probably lead, it was feared, to real annexation – meant the accretion of yet more Slavs to a Monarchy, where Slavs already outnumbered the German and Magyar 'ruling nations'. Perhaps for the first time, the logic of representative government revealed its hostility to acquiring lands inhabited by other peoples. Secondly, the whole balance of dualism could well be upset by the question of which half of the Monarchy was to receive the new provinces. The Magyars did not want more Slavs, but they also did not want Bosnia–Herzegovina going to Austria, which would make the imbalance in population and resources even greater between the two halves.[96] Bosnia was to both German liberals and Magyars a veritable shirt of Nessus, much more trouble than its limited economic and strategic benefits were worth. If Francis Joseph was unhappy at Andrássy's compromise of occupation, the majority liberals in both Cisleithanian and Hungarian parliaments were livid, because it threatened the whole hegemonic edifice built up from 1866.[97]

The botching of the actual occupation in July 1878 only made things worse, and although the provinces were eventually occupied, the public debate which followed, especially in Cisleithania, presented a withering attack on Andrássy and by implication Francis Joseph. After much wrangling and protesting, the Reichsrat did eventually accede to the emperor's wishes, ratifying the treaty and occupation in March 1879, but not without a majority of the German liberals first lambasting the whole enterprise, and opposing Francis Joseph's foreign policy.[98] With this the German liberals had in Francis Joseph's eyes broken the implicit agreement on which his support had rested, for they had dared to interfere, threaten, one of his last remaining major prerogatives, foreign policy. From their viewpoint this was because this foreign policy impinged dramatically on their domestic political situation; from his viewpoint, their attacks on Andrássy's achievement not only threatened to deprive him of territorial compensation for his previous losses, but also attacked the centre of Habsburg dynastic power and status, the ability to act still as a great power.

The result was that even before the ratification was finalised, Francis Joseph had accepted the resignation of Adolph Auersperg's ministry on February 15. He replaced it with one under the nominal control of the liberal Stremayr, but effectively run by his old friend, Count Edward Taaffe, who now moved to conciliate the federalist, Slav and conservative forces dismissed in 1871.[99] In Hungary, Francis Joseph still had to deal with a liberal ministry, albeit under the efficient Kálmán Tisza, but by 1879 the balance of power in Cisleithania, the diminution of liberalism's prestige in the aftermath of scandals and corruption trials of the Crash of 1873, and the splits within the liberals' ranks due to the Bosnian crisis left open the possibility of a new political constellation. Few realised it at the time, but the German liberals' challenge to Francis Joseph's foreign policy prerogative in the Bosnian crisis had sealed their political doom. When crossed, Francis Joseph was to prove quite capable of destroying what had seemed the insuperable German liberal hegemony in Cisleithania.

Taaffe, as Interior Minister, arranged for the return of the Czechs to active parliamentary politics, and lined up the Polish Club, always willing to deal with whoever was in power, as well as the usual assortment of clericals, conservatives and feudalists. Above all he had the backing of the emperor, to whom the landed nobility still deferred. In the elections of June and July 1879 the Liberals, led by Eduard Herbst, did not do at all badly in their urban bases, losing only eight seats in the urban curia. It was in the rural and 'large landowners' curiae, where their political support was most exposed to the influence of the landed aristocracy, and hence to imperial pressure, that they made catastrophic losses, of twenty and twenty-one seats respectively. The result was a loss of the Liberal majority and the formation on 12 August of the Taaffe ministry, composed of everyone else.[100] Francis Joseph had proved a stronger and more determined constitutional monarch than Liberals such as Herbst had bargained for. After 1879 there was never to be another liberal ministry in charge of Cisleithanian government.

Almost at this very moment, when German liberals lost control of Cisleithanian politics, they nevertheless gained what was to become an even firmer anchor for their national interests in the Dual Alliance with Germany. This, ironically, was also a result of the fallout of the Bosnian Crisis. The political turn in Cisleithania, combined with criticism of his Bosnian policy and his wish to go out while he was still ahead, had moved Andrássy to offer his resignation on 6 August 1879. When Bismarck heard of this, for once he lost his nerve. Already feeling unsure of Russia after the 1878 Berlin settlement, he saw the possibility of a feudal-conservative-Slav-led Austria–Hungary concocting a 'Kaunitz coalition' with Russia and France to exact revenge for 1866 as well as 1871.[101] As a result, on 28 August he offered Andrássy, whom Francis Joseph had kept in office, an Austro-German alliance. Negotiations proceeded and the alliance was signed on 7 October 1879. Andrássy resigned the next day, having achieved his initial goal of 1871, an alliance with Germany against Russia.

Admittedly it was only a defensive alliance and it could hardly have been foreseen that it would prove the linchpin of all subsequent Austrian and German foreign policy. Yet it did promise the sort of stability which Austria had been seeking for decades, and it gave Francis Joseph the conservative alliance between the two 'German' powers which he had sought since 1848, although in a radically altered form.[102] Thus 1879 saw Francis Joseph on the verge of casting off his reliance on the Germans and their liberal pretensions domestically, but tying his Monarchy to Germany internationally. This paradox, combined with the continuing central role of the Magyars both in domestic and foreign policy, was to govern his subsequent policies. A few buckles had been loosened, but others had been added: the German-Hungarian straitjacket remained.

. . .

NOTES AND REFERENCES

1. E. Crankshaw, *The Fall of the House of Habsburg*, Viking Penguin, New York 1963, p. 181.
2. J. Redlich, *Emperor Francis Joseph of Austria: A Biography*, Macmillan, New York 1929, pp. 287–8; E.C. Corti, *Mensch und Herrscher: Wege und Schicksale Kaiser Franz Josephs I. zwischen Thronbesteigung und Berliner Kongress*, Styria, Graz 1952, p. 275.
3. Redlich, *Emperor Francis Joseph*, pp. 289–95.
4. J.-P. Bled, *Franz Joseph*, trans. T. Bridgeman, Blackwell, Oxford 1992, pp. 120–3; Redlich, *Emperor Francis Joseph*, pp. 296–307.
5. Redlich, *Emperor Francis Joseph*, p. 345.
6. Corti, *Mensch und Herrscher*, p. 247; Redlich, *Emperor Francis Joseph*, p. 306.
7. Corti, *Mensch und Herrscher*, p. 268.
8. Ibid., pp. 323, 329.
9. F.R. Bridge, *The Habsburg Monarchy among the Great Powers, 1815–1918*, Berg, Oxford 1990, p. 74.

10. Redlich, *Emperor Francis Joseph*, pp. 275–6; cf. Bridge, *The Habsburg Monarchy*, p. 81.

11. Redlich, *Emperor Francis Joseph*, pp. 320–1; Bridge, *The Habsburg Monarchy*, pp. 74–5.

12. Corti, *Mensch und Herrscher*, p. 309.

13. Redlich, *Emperor Francis Joseph*, pp. 321–2.

14. J. Kořalka, 'Deutschland und die Habsburgermonarchie'. In A. Wandruszka, P. Urbanitsch (eds), *Die Habsburger Monarchie 1848–1918* (6+ vols). Österreichische Akademie der Wissenschaften, Vienna 1993, vol. 6, pt. 2, *Aussenpolitik*, p. 35; Corti, *Mensch und Herrscher*, pp. 290–6; Redlich, *Emperor Francis Joseph*, pp. 315–18.

15. Corti, *Mensch und Herrscher*, pp. 323, 329; Bled, *Franz Joseph*, pp. 122–3; Redlich, *Emperor Francis Joseph*, pp. 304–9.

16. Redlich, *Emperor Francis Joseph*, pp. 310–13; Kořalka, *'Deutschland und die Habsburgermonarchie'*, p. 38.

17. Corti, *Mensch und Herrscher*, pp. 304–5.

18. Bridge, *The Habsburg Monarchy.*, pp. 76–7; Kořalka, *Deutschland und die Habsburgermonarchie*, p. 38.

19. Kořalka, *Deutschland und die Habsburgermonarchie*, p. 38.

20. Bridge, *The Habsburg Monarchy*, p. 79.

21. A. Sked, *The Decline and Fall of the Habsburg Empire 1815–1918*, Longman, London 1989, pp. 179–81.

22. Redlich, *Emperor Francis Joseph*, pp. 323–8; Sked, *The Decline and Fall of the Habsburg Empire*, pp. 180–1.

23. G.E. Rothenberg, *The Army of Francis Joseph*, Purdue, West Lafayette 1976, pp. 67–72; K. Koch, 'Das Jahr 1866 und die Benedek Kontroverse', *Etudes Danubiennes* vol. 8 (2): 145–52.

24. See G.D.W. Wawro 'The Austro-Prussian War: Politics, Strategy and War in the Habsburg Monarchy, 1859–1866' (2 vols). Unpublished PhD dissertation (thesis), Yale University, esp. vol. 2, pp. 804–15; see also his shorter, published version, G.D.W. Wawro, *The Austro-Prussian War: Austria's War with Prussia and Italy in 1866*, Cambridge 1996.

25. Corti, *Mensch und Herrscher*, pp. 349–59; Rothenberg, *The Army of Francis Joseph*, p. 70.

26. Corti, *Mensch und Herrscher*, p. 358.

27. Rothenberg, *The Army of Francis Joseph*, p. 66; Redlich, *Emperor Francis Joseph*, p. 328; Corti, *Mensch und Herrscher*, p. 85.

28. G.D.W. Wawro, 'Inside the Whale: the Tangled Finances of

the Austrian Army, 1848–66', in *War in History*, vol. 3, pp. 42–65; Rothenberg, *The Army of Francis Joseph*, p. 66.

29. Sked, *The Decline and Fall of the Habsburg Empire*, pp. 184–5; cf. Crankshaw *The Fall of the House of Habsburg*, pp. 153, 212–13.

30. Wawro, 'Inside the Whale', pp. 45–53.

31. G.D.W. Wawro, 'An Army of Pigs: the technical, social and political bases of Austrian shock tactics, 1859–66', in the *Journal of Military History*, vol. 59, pp. 407–34; Rothenberg, *The Army of Francis Joseph*, p. 64.

32. Kořalka, *Deutschland und die Habsburgermonarchie*, pp. 42–3.

33. Bridge, *The Habsburg Monarchy*, pp. 87, 94–5.

34. Ibid., pp. 96–7.

35. Bled, *Franz Joseph*, pp. 165–7.

36. Kann, *A History of the Habsburg Empire, 1526–1918*, University of California, Berkeley 1977, p. 359; Bridge, *The Habsburg Monarchy*, p. 102.

37. Corti, *Mensch und Herrscher*, pp. 451–2; Bled, *Franz Joseph*, pp. 178–82; Redlich, *Emperor Francis Joseph*, pp. 372–6.

38. Bled, *Franz Joseph*, p. 148.

39. Ibid., pp. 147–9.

40. Corti, *Mensch und Herrscher*, p. 396.

41. On the details and consequences of the Compromise see: L. Eisenmann, *Le Compromis Austro-Hongrois de 1867: Étude sur le dualisme*, reprint 1904 edn, Academic International, Hattiesburg 1971; Sked, *The Decline and Fall of the Habsburg Empire*, pp. 187–97; Redlich, *Emperor Francis Joseph*, pp. 348–54.

42. R. Musil, *The Man without Qualities* (3 vols), trans. E. Wilkins, E. Kaiser, Pan, London 1979, vol. 1, pp. 32–3.

43. Eisenmann, *Le Compromis Austro-Hongrois*, p. 528.

44. O. Jászi, *The Dissolution of the Habsburg Monarchy*, Chicago, pp. 349–53 (Studies in the Making of Citizens).

45. Ibid., pp. 354–5.

46. Kann, *A History of the Habsburg Empire*, pp. 333–4.

47. Jászi, *The Dissolution of the Habsburg Monarchy*, p. 355; Sked, *The Decline and Fall of the Habsburg Empire*, pp. 192–3.

48. Redlich, *Emperor Francis Joseph*, p. 353.

49. H.W. Steed, *The Habsburg Monarchy*, reprint 2nd edn, 1914, Fertig, New York 1969, p. 30.

50. M.H. Brettner (ed.), *Die Protokolle des österreichischen Ministerrates 1848–1867*, Öst. Bundesverlag, Vienna 1973, pt. 6, vol. 2, pp. 401–6; cf. Corti, *Mensch und Herrscher*, p. 387, where the initial quotation is wrongly ascribed to Francis Joseph.

51.   Ibid., p. 388.
52.   Sked, *The Decline and Fall of the Habsburg Empire*, p. 208.
53.   Redlich, *Emperor Franz Joseph*, p. 397.
54.   A. Palmer, *Twilight of the Habsburgs: The Life and Times of Emperor Francis Joseph*, Weidenfeld & Nicolson, London 1994, pp. 146–7.
55.   Bridge, *The Habsburg Monarchy*, p. 84.
56.   Corti, *Mensch und Herrscher*, p. 382.
57.   Kann, *A History of the Habsburg Empire*, p. 340; Eisenmann, *Le Compromis Austro-Hongrois*, p. 499.
58.   Redlich, *Emperor Franz Joseph*, p. 370.
59.   Corti, *Mensch und Herrscher*, p. 268.
60.   O. Habsburg, *Kaiser Franz Joseph*, Werner, Vienna 1966, pp. 8–9.
61.   Corti, *Mensch und Herrscher*, p. 336.
62.   Redlich, *Emperor Franz Joseph*, pp. 374–5.
63.   Bled, *Franz Joseph*, pp. 163–5.
64.   Corti, *Mensch und Herrscher*, pp. 414–15; Kann, *A History of the Habsburg Empire*, p. 357; Bled, *Franz Joseph*, pp. 158–63.
65.   Corti, *Mensch und Herrscher*, p. 480.
66.   E.C. Hellbling, 'Die Landesverwaltung in Cisleithanien'. In Wandruszka and Urbanitsch (eds), *Die Habsburger Monarchie 1848–1918* (6+ vols). Österreichische Akademie der Wissenschaften, Vienna 1975, vol. 2, *Verwaltung und Rechtswesen*, p. 218.
67.   Kann, *A History of the Habsburg Empire*, p. 358; Hellbling, 'Die Landesverwaltung in Cisleithanien', p. 213.
68.   I. Deák, *Beyond Nationalism: A Social and Political History of the Habsburg Officer Corps 1848–1918*, Oxford 1990, p. 59; Rothenberg, *The Army of Francis Joseph*, pp. 74–89.
69.   Bled, *Franz Joseph*, pp. 163–7, 178–82; Kann, *A History of the Habsburg Empire*, pp. 356–60.
70.   Bled, *Franz Joseph*, pp. 182–5.
71.   Kann, *A History of the Habsburg Empire*, p. 364; G. Barany, 'Ungarns Verwaltung 1848–1918'. In Wandruszka and Urbanitsch (eds), *Die Habsburger Monarchie 1848–1918*, vol. 2, *Verwaltung und Rechtswesen*, pp. 343–4, 391–7, 421–3.
72.   Kann, *A History of the Habsburg Empire*, pp. 362–4; Sked, *The Decline and Fall of the Habsburg Empire*, pp. 208–9.
73.   Redlich, *Emperor Franz Joseph*, pp. 357–9.
74.   Barany, 'Ungarns Verwaltung', pp. 403–5; L. Péter, 'The Dualist Character of the 1867 Hungarian Settlement'. In G. Ránki

(ed.), *Hungarian History – World History*, Indiana, Bloomington, 1984, p. 151.

75. Barany, 'Ungarns Verwaltung', p. 407.
76. Ibid., p. 403.
77. Kann, *A History of the Habsburg Empire*, pp. 339–40.
78. L. Höbelt, *Kornblume und Kaiseradler: Die deutschfreiheitlichen Parteien Altösterreichs 1882–1918*, Geschichte und Politik, Vienna 1993, p. 17.
79. Péter, 'The Dualist Character of the 1867 Hungarian Settlement', p. 147.
80. Bled, *Franz Joseph*, pp. 168–71.
81. Bridge, *The Habsburg Monarchy*, pp. 98–102.
82. Ibid., pp. 105–6.
83. Ibid., pp. 106–11.
84. Ibid., p. 87.
85. On Bosnia see N. Malcolm, *Bosnia: A Short History*, Macmillan, London 1994.
86. Malcolm, *Bosnia: A Short History*, pp. 119–34.
87. Bridge, *The Habsburg Monarchy*, pp. 112–13; Palmer, *Twilight of the Habsburgs*, pp. 195–8.
88. Corti, *Mensch und Herrscher*, p. 490.
89. Bridge, *The Habsburg Monarchy*, p. 113.
90. Palmer, *Twilight of the Habsburgs*, pp. 199–201; Bridge, *The Habsburg Monarchy*, pp. 111–14.
91. Bridge, *The Habsburg Monarchy*, pp. 114–26.
92. Bled, *Franz Joseph*, pp. 173–5.
93. Bridge, *The Habsburg Monarchy*, pp. 126–7.
94. Corti, *Mensch und Herrscher*, p. 495.
95. Bridge, *The Habsburg Monarchy*, pp. 126–31.
96. Corti, *Mensch und Herrscher*, p. 514.
97. A.J.P. Taylor, *The Habsburg Monarchy 1809–1918*, Penguin, Harmondsworth 1948 (1964), p. 167.
98. Bridge, *The Habsburg Monarchy*, pp. 131–2.
99. Bled, *Franz Joseph*, pp. 190–2.
100. W.A. Jenks, *Austria under the Iron Ring 1879–1893*, University Press of Virginia, Charlottesville 1965, pp. 31–6; Höbelt, *Kornblume und Kaiseradler*, pp. 20–1.
101. Bridge, *The Habsburg Monarchy*, p. 133; Kořalka, *Deutschland und die Habsburgermonarchie*, p. 74.
102. Bridge, *The Habsburg Monarchy*, pp. 134–5.

Chapter 5

MUDDLING THROUGH, 1879–97

. . .

IN THE IRON RING

There could have been few better birthday presents in Francis Joseph's lifetime than the ministry which his old boyhood friend, Count Edward Taaffe, formed for him on 12 August 1879, just in time for the emperor's forty-ninth birthday. He had been on the throne already for over thirty hectic years, and he must have fervently hoped that Taaffe could provide the political balm which none of his previous ministers, or he himself, had possessed to calm the national and constitutional problems of at least the Cisleithanian part of his empire. Although at first the imminent demise of his regime was predicted, especially by the German Liberal opposition, Taaffe was able to hold on to an often razor-thin majority in the Reichsrat and provide his emperor with over a decade of more or less stable government. Meanwhile in the Hungarian kingdom the regime of Kálmán Tisza, prime minister since 1875, provided a similar political stability, albeit with diametrically opposite national and political consequences.

After the dramatic events of the reign so far, the Taaffe era could appear almost pedestrian in its lack of eventfulness. There were no more radical shifts in political power, no new constitutions, the economy motored along fairly nicely, the army and bureaucracy settled down now that the reform era of the Liberals was over. Abroad there were no major wars, only a few spats in the Balkans and Austrian diplomatic jockeying, albeit within the confines of the Dual Alliance. It seemed that Taaffe's style of *Fortwursteln* – muddling through – an apt description also of Austrian foreign policy, was doing just what the now middle-aged emperor-king wanted, to maintain peace at home and Habsburg great power status abroad.

At the same time this period saw the developments which were to culminate in the rending of the Cisleithanian constitutional fabric, chronic political instability in Hungary, the exacerbation of the nationality conflict to state-threatening levels, and a radical divergence between the characters of the two constituent states. The Taaffe era was symptomatic of the role of Francis Joseph's Monarchy as a whole, and it poses to the historian the same basic question: is it to be praised for the relative peace which it secured compared to what followed, or was that subsequent crisis itself to be blamed on the decisions and policies pursued, or not pursued, during the period in question? And especially for this book, if the latter is the case, how much of the responsibility for the path not taken can be put at Francis Joseph's door?

In one respect at least, Francis Joseph had actually a greater responsibility for the policies followed by the Taaffe ministry than he had had for those of his Liberal ministries before 1879. The great significance of 1879 was that the emperor and the German Liberals had tested their political strength, and the election results of that year and the successful formation of the Taaffe ministry had shown that the most powerful player in Cisleithanian politics remained the emperor. This should have been obvious before 1879, but had not been, at least to the German Liberal leadership. Taaffe, unlike the Liberal premiers, was indisputably Francis Joseph's man, and made no bones about it, delighting in describing himself as a *Kaiserminister*, the emperor's minister, above parties but beholden to the sovereign.[1] On the other hand, the political landscape of Cisleithania was so complicated and contradictory that the room to manoeuvre for Taaffe and his emperor was severely circumscribed, and the situation was further limited by circumstances in Hungary and abroad.

In this situation one can well argue that Taaffe, Tisza, Count Gustav Kálnoky, the foreign minister, and Francis Joseph, the main players, did as well as could be expected of them and that anything more 'dynamic' would have simply brought on the crisis earlier. The question remains, though, whether some more imaginative approach might not have turned these circumstances to greater advantage for Austria–Hungary. Francis Joseph, in some respects, was indeed to profit politically from the problems brought on by 'muddling through', but at what expense to the viability of his empire?

The key political fact in Cisleithania after the election of 1879 was that the various German Liberal parties and their allies controlled 174 seats in a Reichsrat Lower House of 353 members, but no more, whereas Taaffe's coalition ragbag of Czechs, Poles, German Conservative Clericals, Slovenes, Croats and Rumanians together controlled only 168 seats, but had the backing of the emperor.[2] They might not have a full majority (the difference was made up by independents), but nor did they have a solid majority against them. Taaffe therefore could survive as long as he had the emperor's backing, and was able to placate or cajole enough of his coalition partners to prevent them jumping ship and joining the Liberals. Indeed he could often get his way with his coalition partners by threatening himself to go to the Liberals for support. He managed this complex finesse for over a decade, reducing the 'governing party' Liberals to just another political interest, and greatly enhancing the political power of his imperial master along the way.

While his successful policy of 'well-tempered dissatisfaction' left most of his coalition partners, by definition, dissatisfied, the concessions which he did make at the expense of the German Liberals' constituency subtly yet decisively shifted the balance of power within Cisleithania. Despite the closeness of the 1879 election result, by the end of Taaffe's rule the path of political development had changed profoundly from one of clear German dominance to one in which the other Cisleithanian nationalities, especially the Czechs, were approaching parity. At the same time, the constitutional balance had clearly shifted from a parliamentary style of governance back to the traditional Habsburg emphasis on the state bureaucracy. In 1878 Cisleithania had still appeared a state governed by a German Liberal parliamentary majority; twenty years later, German Liberalism was a spent force on the defensive, parliament a shambles, and Cisleithania was being governed by the emperor and his officials. The Taaffe era was thus crucial in the transition from a political system combining German centralist hegemony and responsible parliamentary government to the opposite combination, of both a more equal, multi-national dispensation of power, but also one in which the people's representatives were once again not responsible for government, but instead looked to the imperial administration for favours – and direction.

In the first year or so after the election, it was neither clear that Taaffe would long survive as prime minister, nor that he would rule without having the Liberals, at least the more moderate faction, within his coalition. Indeed both Taaffe and Francis Joseph preferred to include Liberals, as long as it was on the emperor's terms.[3] The votes of moderate Liberals were needed to pass the ten year extension of the Defence Bill by the required two-thirds margin, as was at length achieved after some arm-twisting by Francis Joseph in December 1879.[4] Moreover, although Liberals were a minority in the Lower House, until 1882 they remained a majority, albeit a very loyal majority, in the Upper Chamber of the Herrenhaus.[5] Until January 1881 there was in fact a number of Liberals or Liberally-inclined officials in Taaffe's ministry, but Liberal intransigence and imperial obstinacy meant that from then on Taaffe governed solely on the basis of the German Clerical-Conservative-Slavic coalition known as the 'Iron Ring'.

The legislative agenda of Taaffe's ministry came to reflect that ministry's composition of all formerly 'out' elements in Austrian politics, which virtually meant everyone who was not German Liberal. It was thus German national and Liberal ideological interests that paid the price for the functioning of Taaffe's coalition. The subsequent horse-trading in national interests had been pioneered, ironically, by the Liberals. In return for the votes of the Polish Club in the Reichsrat they had already ceded control, amounting to informal autonomy, to the Polish noble leadership in Galicia.[6] Polish became the province's official language, and both its universities, at Cracow and Lemberg (Lwow), were Polonophone by 1879, despite Ruthenes being a very large minority in the province (43 per cent to the Poles' 46 per cent), and a majority in its eastern half.[7] The reward for Polish support of Taaffe's regime, apart from more and better cabinet posts, amounted to a maintenance of this already very Polonophile status quo. Seen in this perspective, Czech demands for their own university, and the admission of Czech as a language of administration, could be justified on the grounds of keeping parity with the Poles, to say nothing of the Magyars; and this argument from Polish example was indeed used to justify the foundation of a separate Czech university in Prague, resulting in the splitting of the venerable Charles University into German and Czech parts in 1882.[8]

Similar arguments could also be used to justify the Stremayr Ordinances of 1880, which made Czech an 'external' language of the 'political', that is to say imperial bureaucracy (as opposed to the provincial, autonomous administrative hierarchy controlled by the provincial diets). On the face of it this seemed reasonable, as it allowed Czechs to conduct business with the government in their own language, while the 'internal' administrative language of the imperial authorities in Bohemia and Moravia, that used among officials, remained German, as did the 'most internal' language, used for communication between central office and the localities. Given the relative status and prestige of German and Czech, though, it severely undermined the German position. German had been virtually a necessity for anyone, German or not, to get on in their careers, whereas Czech had been only recently revived as a literary language, and was still despised by most of the German educated classes as a peasant language. Many Czechs spoke German, few Germans spoke Czech. The effect of this seemingly innocuous and equitable provision was therefore to put most of the official jobs in Bohemia with contact with the public in the hands of the much more bilingual Czechs.[9]

Of course the Czechs were not at all satisfied with the partial victory of the Stremayr Ordinances, but then it was Taaffe's method to keep every partner not happy, but rather just interested enough to keep him in power. Thus the Czech politicians were fed further sweeteners at German expense, such as the electoral 'reform' of the landed curia of the Bohemian Diet in 1882, which ensured that what had been a solid German majority (quite at variance with the demographic, but in accord with the social and economic reality) now became an unshakeable Czech one.[10] Croats in Dalmatia were allowed to have Serbo-Croat as the official language of the province's autonomous administration in 1883. Slovenes were allowed an expanded use of Slovene in the Carniolan administration.[11]

German Clericals and Conservatives were paid off by an erosion of the Liberals' cherished secular public education system. Clericals were appeased by a provision making it compulsory for teachers to have 'special competence' in the religion of the majority of their pupils, effectively ensuring that teachers be Catholic, or at least Christian (not Jewish). (Galicia was exempted because of the consequences of Jewish or Ruthenian majorities in many of the schools.) Conservatives were rewarded with loopholes in the compulsory eight-year length of children's education, although the opposition from within the Iron Ring, from parties such as the 'liberal' Old Czechs, kept these concessions minimal.[12]

Following the Bismarckian example to the north, Taaffe also tried in effect to co-opt the lower classes, whether of the *Mittelstand* (lower middle class), peasantry or working class by backing away from the more extreme forms of the *laissez-faire*

'Manchester' liberalism of his German-Liberal predecessors. His coalition thus reformed the very free-market 1859 Industrial Code, introducing much more regulation, and proficiency tests, for the various artisanal trades in 1885.[13] Peasants were the supposed beneficiaries of their children being allowed to leave formal schooling at age 12 rather than 14, and supposedly also gained by the rise in agricultural tariffs.[14] Meanwhile, the perceived threat of proletarian socialism received a similarly Bismarckian treatment. On the one hand Taaffe had an emergency Anti-Terror Law passed in 1884, and an Anti-Socialist Law passed two years later (and kept in force until 1891). On the other hand, skilfully advised by the prominent official (and converted Jew) Emil Steinbach, he had enacted limits on working hours and the use of child and female labour in factories and mines, and instituted systems of sickness and accident insurance for industrial workers.[15]

As with Bismarck, one intention of such social legislation was to undermine the political strength of his Liberal opponents. Most Liberal politicians actually supported what amounted to the foundations of a welfare state, accepting the argument that the previous era of 'deregulation' had been too cut-throat and insecure an environment for an efficiently functioning economy. It was also Liberals who did most to soften what at first had been draconian measures against the socialist movement, and who eventually were at the forefront in calling for the measures' repeal in 1891. However, the fact that agricultural and forestry workers received far less insurance coverage than their urban counterparts says much about who was in power (Conservative owners of landed and forested estates) and who was not (Liberal factory owners). Moreover the electoral reform of 1882, which added the lower-middle-class 'Five Gulden men' to the electoral rolls, was an attempt to undermine German Liberal political support in the urban and rural constituencies, just as Francis Joseph's creation of new peers in 1881, all of them of the Right, took the majority in the Herrenhaus from the Liberals.[16]

When the election was eventually held in 1885, the Five Gulden franchise reform did not harm the Liberals as much as electoral 'compromises' against them in the Bohemian landed curia and the Tyrol, but the net result was a further diminution of German Liberal power and hence a wider margin for the wheeling and dealing methods which Taaffe had by then made his trademark. It was under Taaffe that Austrian politics began to take on the contours of the bazaar, of a trade of support for favours.

It was thus quite in keeping with Taaffean politics that the premier turned a blind eye to the rise of political anti-Semitism in Austria during the 1880s, as long as the Jewish establishment continued their vociferous support of his Liberal opponents.[17] Upholding civic order and the rights of religious minorities thus became a matter to bargain over, not a duty of government. Perhaps most revealing about what lay at the base of Taaffe's system in its heyday was Steinbach's open praise, in the debate on the ill-fated electoral reform bill of 1893, of the absence of a strong majority in the Reichsrat as guaranteeing 'the crown's full sovereignty'.[18] It was precisely the inability of a strong enough, cohesive enough majority to emerge in the Reichsrat, which made the sort of role of Taaffe as 'Kaiserminister' not only necessary, but possible. The power of the monarch within the Cisleithanian political system relied on the fractiousness of the legislature. Taaffe's 'Iron Ring' worked because his coalition partners were sufficiently *dis*united not to band against him. Once again the 'divide and rule' potentialities of a multi-national political structure worked for the agent of the dynasty.

Almost the exact reverse solution was found for managing the other 'half' of Francis Joseph's realm, Hungary. There Kálmán Tisza established as firm a control of Hungarian politics as Taaffe of Cisleithanian, but by merging his initially oppositional followers with the established Deákist ruling party, creating in 1875 a Liberal party hegemony which was to last for three decades. Instead of breaking the lock of the 'ruling nation' on power, Tisza's manoeuvre greatly enhanced it, providing an unassailable dominance of Hungarian politics by one nation, the Magyars, despite the fact that demographically they were only a minority in the multi-national Hungarian state, not that much larger a presence than the Germans within Cisleithania.

Tisza's record until 1890 was what might have been expected of the German Liberals if they had carried on in power in Cisleithania. He combined a policy of crass state Magyar chauvinism in national issues with liberal economic and social policies. The year 1883 saw the beginning of the rule of Count Károly Khuen-Hédervàry as Ban of Croatia and the assertion of a large degree of Magyar control in supposedly 'autonomous' Croatia-Slavonia.[19] The Education Acts of 1879, 1883 and 1891 made the teaching of Magyar compulsory in schools, and this strategy was combined with various other forms of coercive 'Magyarisation', such as the closing-down of Slovak and other minority-language high schools, and the persecution of minority-language publications, to make Hungary into a Magyar-speaking nation-state. Magyarisation was only partially successful, and indeed the greatest success, among Hungarian Jewry and Hungarian Germans, was the result not so much of coercion as of voluntary assimilation to the 'state' language.[20] Economically, Tisza's *laissez-faire* policies encouraged strong economic growth from the late 1870s, and prepared the ground for the emergence of a strong Hungarian industrial sector by the end of the century.[21] Socially, perhaps the most striking contrast to Taaffe's policies was the Calvinist Tisza's continuation of liberal policies in religion and education, and especially towards Hungarian Jewry. Much of the economic progress in Hungary, and the emergence of Budapest as an impressive national capital, was indeed based on the alliance of the Magyar county gentry politicians, the backbone of Tisza's Liberal party, with an urban, capitalist bourgeoisie which was predominantly Jewish. Protection of the interests of the latter produced reciprocal deep loyalty to the former. This explains both why Hungary retained the reputation in Jewish circles for being a liberal state, despite the chauvinism of Magyarisation, and why, unlike their Cisleithanian counterparts, the Hungarian authorities cracked down hard on political anti-Semitism when it raised its head during the Tiszaeszlar Affair of 1882. It was this alliance which managed to pass liberal legislation in late 1894, when Alexander Wekerle was premier, making civil marriage compulsory, allowing mixed marriages, and declaring the equality of religions, in effect disestablishing the Catholic Church in Hungary, and forced Francis Joseph, despite his strenuous objections, to give his sanction.[22]

He did so for the same reason that he let Tisza follow his both chauvinist and liberal policies: as long as the Hungarian leadership delivered him the votes on military spending and left him in charge of foreign policy and the military, then he would even stomach religious policies which went against his convictions. Tisza's power with Francis Joseph, which formed the model of the king's relationship with his Hungarian premier much as Taaffe set the model of *Kaiserminister* in Cisleithania, rested on two things: his ability to get the necessary votes in parliament; and his skilful manipulation of Francis Joseph's fear that, unlike in Cisleithania, there was no acceptable alternative.

How Tisza had delivered these votes did not bear close inspection. His regime perfected the rigging of elections, tightening

up the electoral franchise, subverting the previously decentra-
lised county administrative system into a political machine, and
employing its own 'electoral geometry'. Tisza's agents, the 'Ma-
melukes', delivered the votes in the small, peripheral and ironically non-Magyar constituencies, which overwhelmed the often
oppositional Magyar constituencies in the central plain.[23] At the
same time hardly any candidates of the national minorities were
elected, making the Hungarian parliament an almost exclusively
Magyar body in a country with a non-Magyar majority.

This also meant that the main opposition to Tisza was not to
his 'Right', as it had been for the German Liberals in Cisleithania, but rather to his 'Left', in the form of the even more chauvinist and anti-Dualist 'Moderate Opposition' and 'Independents'.
Tisza had started out in 1877 trying to use Hungarian opposition to the Compromise as a bargaining counter in dualist negotiations over the Austro-Hungarian Bank. He had been faced down
by Francis Joseph then, and had grown to accept the dualist settlement as beneficial to Hungarian interests.[24] Yet the tactic of self-
interested mediation remained basically the same: to gain
concessions and compliance from the king by promising loyalty
over the army question, but also pointing to the alternative of
an even more demanding, rambunctious group, who would not
be so modest in their demands. Given this framing of his choices,
it is not too difficult to see why Francis Joseph chose to play the
role of 'absentee landlord', and let Magyar chauvinists and anti-
clericals such as Tisza have their way, for there apparently *was*
no alternative.

The two 'ruling' nations of the Dual Monarchy therefore
experienced widely different fates by 1890.[25] In Hungary the Magyars continued to rule unassailed. In Cisleithania Taaffe's Iron
Ring system had severely undermined the position of the Germans
as the 'state people'. In some respects, Cisleithania continued
to be a 'German' state. The language of the Habsburg administration, of the Court, of the Army, of most of the media and most
of commerce, continued to be German. Most of the members
of Taaffe's cabinet continued to be Germans, albeit not so much
'national' as Habsburg Germans. Yet what had been the leading
political representation of German national interests, the loose
and shifting constellation of factions known as the German Liberals, had lost legislative power to a federalist-Slav coalition and
this had profound consequences for the position of the Germans

within Cisleithania, and hence equally important implications for the political structure of that state.

From now on the German interests were on the defensive, and had lost their position of clear political hegemony. Although Germans might continue to run the state, these were either bureaucrats with a higher allegiance to the state and their emperor, or people with greater ideological loyalties (conservative and dynastic), than national. Gone therefore were the days when the German Liberals could assume that they were the natural defenders of the constitutional rights of the 'People' against the emperor's prerogatives. Instead of pressing for more parliamentary power, in a parliament where after 1885 they were in a permanent minority without imperial backing, what had been the German Liberal camp began to shift over to the position of the German Nationalist leader Otto Steinwender, whose vision of a proper German party was no longer to claim responsibility for the state itself, but rather be one national interest among many – and let the nationally neutral imperial authorities run the state.[26]

Cisleithania's Germans began the long process which shifted the balance of nationalism and liberalism inherent in German Liberalism decisively towards nationalism.[27] They began to put most of their resources into defending the 'national property', for instance with the foundation in 1880 of the *Deutscher Schulverein* (German School Union) to protect German-language schools. Shorn of their control of the Bohemian Diet in 1882 they pressed for a national partition of that province to save what could be saved for the German areas of the Sudetenland; shorn of their majority in the Reichsrat they pressed for the confirmation of German as the official state language and would soon end up looking to the (German-speaking) Habsburg central bureaucracy for favours and support, just as all the other nationalities had done.

It is interesting, if idle, to speculate on what would have been the shape of Cisleithania and Austria–Hungary if the German Liberals, like the Magyars, had been able to retain their parliamentary majority: whether there would indeed have been a move to further expand parliamentary power, whether a national understanding under parliamentary auspices would have led to the often dreamt of transformation of Austrian politics with a new German-Czech liberal bourgeois hegemony.[28] The clash with Francis Joseph over Bosnia and Taaffe's success, however, ensured this remained a fantasy, which the German leadership abandoned.

Unlike their Magyar counterparts, they gave up the attempt to provide Cisleithania a properly responsible government, on Western parliamentary lines. And, given the large variety of national and ideological groups in the Reichsrat, there was no other obvious political formation to replace them – except the emperor himself.

. . .

THE EMPEROR IN POWER

One of the leading defenders of the German cause during the Taaffe era was, ironically enough, Francis Joseph. On several occasions, in the debates during the 1880s over the language of administration, and during the negotiations for a Bohemian Compromise of 1890, the emperor had demanded the preservation of German as the 'internal' and 'most internal' language of administration in Cisleithania.[29] In 1882 he also made clear his wish that German be taught at all secondary schools, so that all future bureaucrats would have command of this unifying language. (This wish was never realised by Taaffe's cabinet, because the counter-proposal was made that German students also learn the other language of their respective provinces, for instance Czech in Bohemia, something so anathema to Bohemian Germans that they had put a clause into the constitution defending against just this eventuality; so nothing came of the idea.)[30]

His reasons for defending German interests – he also wanted to ensure that many Germans were elected in the 1885 elections – were quite different from those of his German Liberal opponents, however. When he wanted Germans elected in 1885, he wanted Conservative and Clerical Germans elected, instead of Liberals. When he wanted German taught in schools and retained as the administrative language, and bewailed the decline in German proficiency in Bohemia and Galicia, this was because of his wish to preserve the cohesion of his bureaucratic and military system.[31] In contrast, the body which attempted to defend German in schools, the German School Union, enjoyed Francis Joseph's disapprobation as a hive of nationalists. Bismarck was not far wrong in asserting in 1881 that Francis Joseph would have much preferred to have relied on Germans as his ministers, if only they had co-operated, for he clearly disliked the consequences he perceived would flow from Taaffean decentralisation and the break-up of the German linguistic monopoly in the Habsburg bureaucracy.[32] The problem was that he would only have them back on his terms, which the bulk of the liberal and national German political nation refused, leaving them out of power and Francis Joseph at the head of what would be a decreasingly cohesive administration.

Nevertheless, the Taaffe era found the emperor-king with more power than he could scarce have hoped for back in the late 1860s. He was the chief official in an increasingly powerful and expanding bureaucracy. The army was fully under his control and being run along conservative lines to his liking by Archduke Albrecht and General Friedrich Beck, as was foreign policy by his able and long-standing Foreign Minister, Count Gustav Kálnoky. He was surrounded by what remained a glittering, if increasingly old-fashioned court. In many ways it was the apogee of his reign, and by this period the style for the rest of his rule was set.

Francis Joseph took his role as first bureaucrat of the state very seriously. He became famous for his dedication to the work of monarchy. Rising at 4 a.m., and dressing usually and characteristically in the uniform of an army lieutenant, he would be at his desk by five reading official documents, which spanned the full range from importance to triviality. One of the flaws for which all his biographers chide him is his inability or unwillingness to leave the trivia to others. As with his grandfather, Francis I, Francis Joseph became an expert at the art of pushing paper, often with the same procrastinating and obfuscating results. At eight, audiences with his ministers and others would begin, and last with interruptions for the rest of the day.[33] During the ministerial audiences the emperor would stand to attention and treat the minister as his subordinate, *his* minister. He was also always careful to respect the competence of the minister in question, which meant, however, that a minister overstepped his brief at his peril. This made for a certain trust between the emperor and his ministers. Seen another way, though, it also meant that the only man who really knew everything that was going on at the various levels of Austro-Hungarian, Cisleithanian and Hungarian government was Francis Joseph himself.[34]

For all the disadvantages created by his predilection for detail, Francis Joseph's careful perusal of the most obscure promotion, the most insignificant bureaucratic regulation, meant that there were few if any who knew more – in more depth – than he, or who had longer experience of the intricacies of the bureaucratic machine. This was of great value at a time when the battles in the Reichsrat and Taaffe's functioning as *Kaiserminister* resulted in much greater power for the Habsburg officialdom.[35] Not only had Francis Joseph taken the majority in the Reichsrat from the German Liberals, he also was able, through Taaffe, to restore to the executive, headed by himself, the direction of policy which parliamentary ministries had threatened to assume. Now most ministers were the sort of people Francis Joseph instinctively trusted, 'tried high officials' who, as the prime minister himself, regarded themselves as 'instruments of the imperial will,' rather than representatives of the people.[36]

Parliamentary interference in the running of military affairs had also been fended off. Archduke Albrecht, the Army's Inspector General, and Beck, elevated to Chief of the General Staff in 1881, ran the army on decidedly conservative lines, with Beck effectively subordinating the constitutional Ministry for War to himself.[37] Beck came to be seen as the vice-emperor, and the fact that after Albrecht's death in 1895 he ran the army, subordinate in effect only to Francis Joseph himself, speaks volumes for the constitutional control, or lack of it, over the army. This remained very clearly the emperor's prerogative, indeed the one remaining institution and symbol of a united Habsburg Monarchy. The army took up a large amount of Francis Joseph's time, and military manoeuvres were the main occasion for Francis Joseph's visits around his empire. He was hardly ever seen not in uniform, and all visits around his realm had to include a garrison visit and a parade. The army remained central to his understanding of his function as emperor, and he retained a close grip on running it.

Paying for it was another matter. The price which Francis Joseph paid for control of the armed forces was parliamentary resistance in both Cisleithania and Hungary to increased military expenditures. Why spend good money on someone else's army? The Hungarians, as the crisis of 1889–90 was to show, did not regard the dynastically loyal army, with German as the language of command, as theirs. The German Liberals had never overly supported an army of which they had been unable to gain control. And to most other nationalities in Cisleithania the army, with a predominantly German-speaking officer corps, represented nothing more than German hegemony.[38] It was indeed not their army, nor that of the Germans, but Francis Joseph's, and the result was that the military budget stagnated, compared to the other great powers. By 1890, Austria–Hungary was spending less on its military in absolute terms than Italy, a much smaller, less populous state.[39]

130

This was not due to economic stagnation. The economy was doing quite well, the budget went into surplus for the first time in decades in 1889, and in 1892 Austria–Hungary adopted the Gold Standard, reflecting her new-found financial strength. Instead, as ever, there was neither the political will nor cohesion in the empire's complex and conflicted structure of governmental institutions to allocate the necessary resources. Francis Joseph was still in control of Austrian military power, but a Dualist settlement originally meant to enhance his ability to wage war was now sapping it.[40]

At the height of the Bosnian Crisis, Francis Joseph interrupted a delegation of Reichsrat deputies by saying: 'You speak constantly of Andrássy's policy. Do not forget that it is my policy.'[41] Under Andrássy's successors, this was even more the case with Francis Joseph's other clear prerogative, foreign policy. Under Baron Heinrich Haymerle, Kálnoky and Count Agenor Goluchowski, Austrian diplomacy clearly followed the emperor's wishes. Austrian interests were now, after the occupation of Bosnia–Herzegovina, almost solely concentrated on the Balkans. This was not as grand a game as previously in Italy and Germany, but still enormously complicated, and made more so by the emergence of independent, or effectively independent, states in previously Turkish territories. The Austrian Foreign Ministry became involved in an elaborate board game, where the clear opponent was Russia, and the pieces on the table were labelled Serbia, Rumania, Montenegro, Bulgaria, Greece and what was left of European Turkey; but just who one's allies were was often cloudy.

On paper the Dual Alliance should have made Germany Austria's primary ally, and this was certainly how Francis Joseph wanted it. Having established a version of his ideal Central European conservative alliance, he was now clear that, as he confided to his friend Albert of Saxony in 1887, 'I regard the closest understanding and tightest co-ordination with Germany in all political and military questions as the guiding star of our policy.'[42] This explains his great enthusiasm in 1895, when William II, rather condescendingly, promised to come to Austria's aid militarily if her status as a great power were ever threatened. Francis Joseph thought this to be the 'most important declaration as to the scope of the alliance since its foundation'. If William II had truly meant it, and stuck by it, it would have been. The problem was that at the same moment Count Alfred Schlieffen and the German General Staff were backing away from effective military support of Austria against Russia in the event of war, because they saw German interests better served by planning to attack France first.[43]

Germany, after all, had her own interests, and her own (bigger) games to play; Austrian interests usually figured only marginally in such schemes. Until his firing in 1890, Bismarck had often been more interested in keeping on friendly terms with Russia than in supporting Austria. Between 1889 and 1893 Austria benefited greatly from having a pro-Austrian policy in place in Berlin, but from 1894 the paths again diverged, with Germany now emerging more as an economic rival in the Balkans than a diplomatic ally. From 1896 to 1909 there was not even any military co-ordination between the German and Austrian General Staffs, much to the chagrin of the Austrians.[44] Yet Austria was effectively locked into being a dependent ally of Germany, regardless of the Wilhelmine regime's unreliability, because that was how Francis Joseph wanted it.

In 1882, Italy also became an ally, in the Triple Alliance (with Germany) of monarchical solidarity against French republicanism. Yet Italy was always regarded somewhat askance in Vienna, because of its irredentist aspirations to the Austrian territories of Southern Tyrol and Istria.[45] The great power which Austria looked to most during this period as a counterweight to Russia in the Balkan peninsula was Great Britain. The initial moves by Haymerle to reach an understanding with the British had run out of steam due to Gladstone's lack of interest, resulting in a move toward compromise with Russia, which was embodied in the Three Emperors' Alliance of 1881. After Haymerle's death in that year, his conservative successor, Kálnoky, followed a pro-Russian line until the Bulgarian Crisis of the mid-1880s led to the collapse of that understanding. In response Kálnoky came up with an informal agreement with Britain, the Mediterranean Entente of 1887, to work to counter Russian influence in the Near East. This continued after his resignation in 1895, until frustration with British vacillation in her Near Eastern policy resulted in Kálnoky's successor, Goluchowski, ending the agreement in 1897.[46]

By 1897 the Austrian diplomatic version of 'muddling through' had resulted in a *rapprochement* with her main rival, Russia, as a response to the falling off of support from either Germany or Britain. Yet it was clear that this situation was fairly unstable. Only a couple of years earlier, Francis Joseph had predicted that war with Russia was inevitable, and the ups and downs of Balkan affairs meant that the relative peace ensured through the *détente* with Russia would be fleeting. Austria was not very well placed for the predictable end of that *détente*. On paper, Austria had alliances with Serbia and Rumania, and had often enjoyed friendly relations with a Bulgaria more impatient of Russian 'patronage' than accepting of it. Yet Austria's essentially conservative approach to the region, her efforts to preserve the pro-Turkish status quo, combined with the external implications of her domestic nationality policies, especially in Hungary, did not operate well in a theatre rife with the most volatile forms of nationalism.

Both the alliance with Serbia of 1881 and the secret alliance with Rumania of 1883 were alliances with monarchs, not with peoples. Francis Joseph generally had good relations with the Balkan monarchs. The Serbian king, Milan Obrenovič was so pro-Austrian that in 1885 he offered Francis Joseph the opportunity to incorporate his kingdom into the Habsburg Monarchy, not for the last time.[47] (The offer was declined.) Serbian and Rumanian public opinion, on the other hand, was strongly nationalist, and anti-Austrian. The Serbians had the humiliation of Bosnia in their gullet, and the Rumanians were increasingly antagonised by the anti-Rumanian policies of the Magyarising Hungarian authorities. The Serbians, disgusted in any case by the inefficiency and corruption of the Obrenovič dynasty's 'government' thus tended to look to their big Orthodox brother Russia for help, and the Rumanians, like the Italians, were hard to trust, given the irredentist problem. This context meant that the Austrians could hardly avoid being on the defensive in their last sphere of interest, for they had not caught up, perhaps constitutionally could not catch up, with the nationalist politics of the times.

A similar story could be told of the world in which Francis Joseph mainly moved, the Court. Under Francis Joseph the Habsburg Court came to be known for its strict ritual, its pomp, its exclusivity, and increasingly for its anachronistic nature. This was the result of the emperor's intentional effort to restore to his court the 'majesty' lacking under Ferdinand, and thus, it was hoped, the authority which went with majesty. By all accounts majesty was indeed restored, and had the desired effect. The imperial family and the court aristocracy preserved their immense social prestige, and the strict ceremonial associated with such events as the *Hofball,* the Washing of Feet on Maundy Thursday, and most famous of all the Corpus Christi Procession, were eminently successful exercises in symbolic politics.[48]

These symbolic politics emphasised both the majestic superiority of the emperor and his entourage, and also the sublime condescension of the Christian emperor in his concern for his peoples. The narrow exclusivity of the Court (proof of nobility for eight generations was required of ladies for admission) raised the Court majestically high above the rest of society. At the same time, Francis Joseph's twice weekly general audiences, where anyone could potentially talk to his monarch, created the image of an all-embracing sovereignty which did so much to boost the emperor's popular image. The humility and simplicity of the emperor's legendary domestic life, with the iron bed and his daily bureaucratic chores, was so symbolically effective precisely because of all the pomp and circumstance which accompanied the hosting of dignitaries, court occasions, imperial tours and the daily ceremonial of court life. In the carefully designed public image he was both a simple man, a 'Christian, humble before God', and an emperor by divine right.[49] The perfect Catholic monarch.

All this had large drawbacks, though. In an age in which the high aristocracy was no longer the only upper class in the state, but rather found its status challenged by an increasingly wealthy and powerful 'Second Society' of newer nobility, high bureaucracy and a *haute bourgeoisie* of finance, commerce and industry, the Court was not fulfilling its original representative and co-opting functions when it kept these very influential groups out. In Britain and Germany, where the Court was not as exclusive and some access was provided to the new wealth, one might have to suffer the pomposity and 'snobbishness' associated with the 'parvenu' (successful) entourage of a William II or Edward VII, but this relative openness did allow the respective courts to stay up with modern Society, and in offering the incentive of acceptance provided a means of leverage over that Society. This was not the case with the Habsburg Court. There, social exclusivity combined with the ageing emperor's old-fashioned tastes and increasing resistance to technological innovations to produce a sense of anachronism.

An 1899 account of the admission ceremony to the Teutonic Order commented that it was 'one of those picturesque and medieval functions, which in this prosaic nineteenth century are only to be witnessed in all their pristine splendor either at Vienna or at Madrid, and which would appear stagey and even ridiculous anywhere else'.[50] The Teutonic Order was only one of many ensconced at the Habsburg Court. 'It is the presence of the knights and ladies of these various orders, in their picturesque array,' related the report in 1899 further,

> that gives so medieval a flavor, and unique an aspect, to all the state functions and great ceremonies at the Court of Vienna. One turns from the black-robed ambassador of the Sovereign Order of Malta, with his Elizabethan ruff, and with a great white cross woven into the breast of his sombre doublet, to the gigantic Archduke Eugene, whose snow-white doublet and flowing white robes are decorated with huge black crosses; and then after chatting for a while with a knight of devotion of the Order of Malta, in his scarlet uniform and sword-belt representing the Crown of Thorns, one suddenly finds oneself confronted by a barely seventeen-year-old archduchess, whose smiling, sunny and mischievous face is surmounted by an episcopal mitre, the ecclesiastical effect being increased by the crozier which she bears in her hand. Add to this the Mary Stuart caps, dresses and ruffs of the canonesses, the fur-trimmed velvet kaftans and attilas of the Hungarian magnates, whose buckles and sword-belts, as well as scimitars of barbaric magnificence, are adorned with superb jewels, – their costume being exactly what it was in the days of Empress Maria-Theresa – and you have at the Court of Vienna a scene that carries you back to the middle ages, and would seem strangely out of place and anachronistic were it not for the setting offered by the imperial palace.[51]

The sense of time having passed the Court by was enhanced by a curious consequence of 1866. The German monarchs and princes defeated by Bismarck's Prussia had been welcomed to the Viennese court, the court after all of the former Holy Roman Emperor, and because of their mediatised status had taken precedence at the Habsburg Court.[52] Francis Joseph's consort at many state occasions, when ladies were present and Elisabeth was not, was the Duchess of Cumberland, the wife of the eldest son of the dispossessed King of Hanover, and hence the royal female guest highest in protocol.[53] Even with the Dual Alliance, Taaffean stability and economic prosperity, this aspect of the composition of the Habsburg Court continued as a reminder of a more glorious age, now past. It was also a reminder of the fact that, in a multi-national state becoming increasingly so as the other nationalities developed economic and intellectual elites of their own, the Court remained an overwhelmingly German one, further reducing its ability to represent the interests and voices of the empire as a whole.[54] By excluding the newly emerging national and social elites, the Court ceased to provide a centre of cohesion for the Monarchy's peoples.

If the Court became isolated from the rest of society, so too did Francis Joseph. Surrounded by court functionaries, army officials and ministers, the emperor-king had a detailed knowledge of the official version of his empire, but had few opportunities to discuss policy matters directly with the sectors of society excluded from Court society. The twice-weekly general audiences were good show, but did little if anything to inform him about what was really happening in the empire, outside of the governmental structure. Similarly his quite frequent visits to the provinces were more occasions for displaying the majesty of empire to the regions than allowing the emperor to learn about the parts of his realm. Each visit saw a transportation of a travelling version of the Court and many trappings to accompany the emperor, and also to surround him. The unvarying rituals of each of these imperial visits created the impression of the state's uniformity, and hence further sheltered Francis Joseph from reality.[55] The insulation of the Court, and the careful exaltation of the monarch, created an aura of majesty, a sense of the emperor being above party and national politics, but it also left the emperor isolated, an old-style monarch in an increasingly modern state.[56]

In 1881 one informed critic wrote:

> Our emperor has no friends; his character, his nature does not allow it. He stands alone on his promontory; he discusses the official business of everyone with his servants, but a real conversation is carefully avoided. Therefore he knows little of the thinking and feeling of the populace, the views and opinions of the people . . . He believes that we are enjoying one of the happiest epochs in Austrian history. He is told so officially, and in the newspapers he reads only the sections marked in red, and so he is kept from any purely human contact, from any non-partisan, truly thoughtful advice.[57]

Crown Prince Rudolph, the author of this criticism, was more frustrated than most at the developments at Court and in politics under the Taaffean dispensation. The relations between the emperor and his heir provided one more problem area in the 1880s.

Rudolph provided a twofold problem for Francis Joseph. First, his outspoken support of liberal causes, combined with his deep distrust of Prussia–Germany and the Dual Alliance, made him a political thorn in the side of his father's government. The adversarial stance of the heir and his entourage was an oft-repeated occurrence in modern European history, but it was nevertheless troubling. Rudolph and his left-liberal advisers, such as Karl Menger and Moritz Szeps, had an intense aversion to the anti-Liberal politics of the Iron Ring, thinking its attempt to subvert the public education system particularly egregious.[58] Rudolph saw the Bosnian adventure and the prospect of Balkan expansion as 'one foot in the grave' for the empire, and in 1888 warned against the consequences of the German alliance.[59] He was also very pro-Magyar, although not as blindly so as sometimes supposed. In 1886 he wrote with great insight about the problems caused by Magyar persecution of the minority nationalities in Hungary, especially how it encouraged irredentism among Serbs and Rumanians in the kingdom.[60] It is unclear how his sometimes confused and self-contradictory ideas would have translated in practice into the complexities of Austro-Hungarian reality. As in many such cases the liberal aspects might well have given way to more traditional emphases, such as the love of military affairs which he shared with his father. Nevertheless, he provided a focus for the Liberal opposition to his father's policies.

Francis Joseph dealt with the (loyal) political opposition of his son by more or less ignoring him, shutting him out of almost any positions of responsibility in government.[61] This might well have contributed to the second problem posed by Rudolph, his increasingly scandalous and erratic behaviour. As with almost all ruling houses in an age of ever better communications, and challenges to traditional authority, the Habsburgs were quite aware of the necessity of presenting the image of being the upholders of what would now be called 'family values', something which the dynasty's chief 'theoretician', Archduke Albrecht, emphasised in 1877.[62] Francis Joseph quite agreed. By the Habsburgs' Family Statutes its absolute ruler, he ruled the family with great strictness.[63] Often brutal behaviour by archdukes to lesser folk was tolerated, but publicised sexual indiscretions were harshly dealt with, especially when combined with *lèse majesté*, as in the case of the expulsion from the archducal ranks of one of the most attractive family members, Archduke John, for marrying a commoner.[64] Standards had to be kept up.

When it came to himself and his immediate family, however, Francis Joseph's record as paternal family man was decidedly spotty. Until the 1890s he was reputed to have had several extra-marital liaisons, at least one of which, with Anna Nahowski, has been well documented.[65] It was also common knowledge that the empress, Elisabeth, was hardly ever resident in Vienna, but spent most of her time in Corfu or travelling. Francis Joseph would occasionally join her abroad, visiting the French Riviera in the 1890s, some of the rare occasions when he was photographed in civilian attire.[66] The estrangement from the woman he still deeply loved was partially assuaged by the equally famous relationship which he developed with the actress Katharina Schratt from 1886.[67] This seems to have been a platonic relationship, remarkable for nothing so much as its domesticity, but that the apostolic monarch, the arbiter of dynastic and social morality, should seek solace from a broken marriage in the conversation of a Burgtheater actress was a decidedly peculiar, and peculiarly Austrian phenomenon. Rudolph's marital problems after his marriage to Stephanie of Belgium in 1881 were thus not out of the ordinary, and to his own son Francis Joseph seems to have exercised the sort of indulgence he usually reserved for himself. Nevertheless the antics of the heir-apparent were reaching such a point by the late 1880s that they were causing serious concern for the dynasty's image, and, combined with Rudolph's politics, were creating tensions between father and son.

Yet the problems posed by Rudolph alive were nothing compared to the horrendous consequences for Francis Joseph and his dynasty of Rudolph's death by suicide at Mayerling on 29 January 1889.[68] Although it appears fairly clear that Rudolph did shoot himself after shooting his lover, the young Marie Vetsera, in a lovers' pact, the double suicide has retained an aura of mystery which has given 'Mayerling' almost mythical status. The botched attempt of the Taaffe regime to cover up the fact of suicide (a huge scandal for this most Catholic of dynasties) only added suspicions of conspiracy to a plot ready made for the morbid curiosity of the public, to which the many books (and several films) on the subject attest. Whether the tragedy was caused by frustrations over Rudolph's personal life, his health, or the conservative bent of his father's policies, whether he was mentally ill – whether it was a suicide at all – have been gone into in the greatest, and often most imaginative, detail. It would be superfluous to add to such speculations here. That said, the death of the heir to the imperial throne did have most significant consequences. It was first of all a body blow to Francis Joseph. He seems, despite their differences, to have deeply loved his son. He had him entombed in the Capuchin Crypt, the ancestral resting place, despite all the signs of suicide. A letter to Schratt of 5 February speaks of 'the best son, the most loyal subject', and makes clear how hard he took the loss, trusting once again to divine providence to see him through.[69]

As before when disaster had struck, Francis Joseph gamely battled on, doing his duty, keeping the Magyars in line, annotating his papers, but at least one sympathetic observer, Alexander von Hübner, saw a deep and abiding impact on the emperor:

> The emperor is no longer what he once was before the catastrophe of Mayerling. He does not have the same interest in his affairs. Until the death of the Crown Prince he worked for the Monarchy, but also to prepare the way for his son, whom he idolised. Now, with the son's disappearance, there is an immense absence in the father's existence. It is a sense of duty which makes him deal with the business of state, but his heart is no longer in it.[70]

As we shall see, Francis Joseph carried on for almost another three decades, devoting himself to the business of monarchy, but it is worth considering Hübner's point seriously, for it might well be a clue to the increasing stasis which was to mark the ageing Francis Joseph's rule. The dynastic succession, at least in the direct line, was now irreparably broken. The next heir was only a nephew, not well liked. Perhaps the loss of the direct heir was much more significant in what was still, after all, first and foremost a dynastic enterprise.

Moreover, the loss of the erratic, but once immensely promising Rudolph was also a body blow to the public image of the Habsburg dynasty as a potentially modern and progressive element of the Austro-Hungarian future. Already in 1884, the Magyar official Benjamin Kállay had confided to Hübner his fearful prediction that the future of Europe belonged not to monarchy but to republicanism. Hübner had commented: 'Those are the words of a man who is as little a republican as I am, but they are typical of the ideas of the time. Let us face the fact that no one believes in kings anymore, and I do not know whether they believe in themselves. If they believed in themselves, the republics would have no chance.'[71] In 1884 Francis Joseph clearly believed in himself, and could look to his son and heir for the providential confirmation of the divine right of monarchy. But after Mayerling the future of the Habsburg dynasty was clouded, the prospect for a modern, forward-looking Habsburg dynasty diminished. After the 'golden epoch' of the 1880s, change was to take on much more threatening aspects, which an ageing emperor, still with a great deal of power, but bereft of his son and set in his ways, would increasingly be unable to manage.

. . .

TOWARDS THE BADENI CRISIS

By 1890 the power structure of the Habsburg Monarchy, already intricate, had become almost unmanageably complex. Cisleithania was rife with the geometries of national and social conflict; Austria–Hungary was riven by the partly national, partly constitutional conflict between the two halves; the disparity between the developments of the two states in the national question created an imbalance within the imperial structure; and at all times domestic policies came up against the limits and influences of foreign policy, and vice-versa. As the century drew to a close, the Monarchy represented not so much a 'gorgeous mosaic' as a patchwork quilt with more than one seam coming undone.

In Cisleithania the previously fairly straightforward German Liberal hegemony had given way to a situation where no one national group was in clear control. Instead conflict between the nationalities had come out into the open, encouraged by Taaffe's 'levelling of the playing field' in the spheres of the bureaucracy and education, and indeed exploited by the regime to increase executive, that is to say imperial, power. Economic growth was also causing large economic and social changes which had the effect of further exacerbating the troubled political environment in Cisleithania. Within the German camp, being the most economically and socially advanced, the changes were particularly dynamic, and very threatening not only to the Liberals but also to the emperor.

From the more nationalist 'Left' of the Liberals' ranks a separate German Nationalist movement emerged which was severely to undermine the Liberals' support in its core middle-class constituencies. As its Linz Programme of 1882 shows, this movement was initially as much 'left-wing' in its social policies as it was radical in its nationalism, and many left-wing, nationally inclined Jews were among its founding members. Its leader, however, Georg von Schönerer took the movement in a radically, racially anti-Semitic direction, exemplified by his demagoguery in the Nordbahn Affair of 1884–85. Although Schönerer's imprisonment in 1889 for leading an attack on a liberal newspaper's offices compromised his personal political career, his message, in somewhat more moderate but still racially anti-Semitic form, was successfully exploited by other former Liberals, such as Karl Hermann Wolf and Otto Steinwender. It was Steinwender's 'People's Party' which was to capture and transform most of what had been the 'Liberal' camp into a much more nationalistically oriented one.[72] Attempts to found a truly left-liberal, democratic party, in contrast, never got beyond the confines of Vienna.

To the Liberals' 'Right' emerged an equally devastating new political movement, Karl Lueger's Christian Socials. Lueger conjured his movement out of a ragbag of clerical, radical and anti-Semitic elements of Viennese municipal politics. By 1890 his party had begun to threaten Liberal control of the imperial capital's administration, which it indeed captured in 1895. He also employed a scapegoating, anti-Semitic demagoguery which resonated with many sectors of Viennese society, especially – but not only – among the economically squeezed urban lower middle classes, newly enfranchised in 1882. Although its ostensible target was 'Jewish' capital and 'Jewish' liberalism, this brand of populist, anti-Semitic clericalism appeared as much a threat to the traditional organs of Catholicism in Austria, among them Francis Joseph. The emperor, alarmed at the movement's radicalism, was to refuse three times to sanction Lueger's election to mayor of Vienna, before finally giving way in 1897.[73]

With one mass party on the anti-clerical, nationalist and anti-Semitic 'Left' and one on the clerical, populist and anti-Semitic 'Right', the third was unambiguously on the political Left. The socialist movement re-emerged after decades of suppression, reunited and refounded in 1889 under the leadership of Victor Adler, interestingly one of the Jewish signatories of the Linz Programme. In 1890 this 'revolutionary' party of the urban proletariat was as feared by the Liberals and the imperial authorities as either of the other two new mass parties. Ironically, because of its universalist principles, its secularism and Adler's insistence on order and discipline, this movement was to prove both a refuge for many liberal causes, and a supporting force for the Monarchy.[74] Nevertheless, the emergence of a powerful working-class mass party along with the Christian Socials and the German Nationalists transformed the constitutionalist, gentlemen's-club world of the German Liberals and Clerical-Conservatives. It changed into a world of mass politics which was far more interest-based, radicalised, and volatile than its predecessor, potentially far less amenable to imperial suasion.

Similar developments occurred in Cisleithania's second most developed national society, the Czechs. There the long-established bearers of the national cause, the 'Old Czechs' were being pressured by the Young Czechs. The members of this latter party were in some ways equivalent to the German Nationalists in their anticlericalism and 'radical' (left-liberal) politics, although anti-Semitism was not such an explicit plank of their programme. (Nevertheless, anti-Semitic tendencies against supposedly 'pro-German' Jews were far from absent.) The internationalist socialism of Adler's Austrian socialist party gained some ground among the Czech working classes, but the dynamic force in Czech politics from the late 1880s was the Young Czechs, and their left-liberal, radical politics resulted in a form of nationalism which was far less conciliatory, far more strident than that of their Old Czech rivals.[75]

In Galicia and the Southern Slav parts of the Monarchy economic and hence social change was relatively mild, but these regions were peripheral. It was the Bohemian crownlands which really mattered, and there, both among Germans and Czechs, social and political change meant a radicalisation of the national question, one might even say a nationalising of politics in general.

The other great 'national' conflict in the Monarchy was, formally at least, really a constitutional one, within Hungary. Kálmán Tisza had been able, as we have seen, to control and indeed to exploit the pressure from the Hungarian opposition for more Hungarian independence. He had thus often been able to get the Hungarian king to exert his influence over the Austrian emperor to grant Hungarian wishes. As king and emperor were the same person, this had led to the accusation that Francis Joseph was making concessions to the Magyars at Austrian expense, but until 1889 the costs were bearable, and in return had produced Magyar political stability and relative reasonableness. This pressure to improve the position of the 'real', historic Hungarian constitution within the 1867 settlement, had, however, begun to get beyond even Tisza's political managerial skills. He had managed to get the economic Compromise of 1887 passed, but when the renewal of the Army Bill came up in early 1889 the question which had always been central to disputes about the Dualist settlement and had caused most resentment at supposed Austrian domination of Hungary, the common army and its language of command, ignited a furore of Magyar nationalist resentment.

Exacerbated by crass actions such as the army authorities' laying of a wreath in 1886 on the grave in Budapest of the loyalist 'martyr' of 1849, General Heinrich Hentzi, Magyar sensibilities took umbrage at the continuing enforcement of the use of German as the army's language of command, and, for instance, at the requirement that all reserve officers sit an examination in German. This was the crisis which distracted Francis Joseph from his grief over Rudolph in early 1889, but it was only a year later, after considerable popular resistance, even violence, that it was resolved, and the Army Bill passed in early 1890. In order to get the bill passed, Francis Joseph had had to make several concessions – to his other royal self – including the symbolically important change of the army's title from 'imperial-royal' (k.k.) to 'imperial and royal' (k.u.k.). The effort had also exhausted Tisza, who, shortly after the bill's passage, resigned, closing a long chapter in Hungarian politics, and opening a far less certain one.[76] By 1890, therefore, the dualistic arrangement, although newly secured, had once again proved a source of conflict and tension.

The Magyar opposition in the Hungarian parliament resented the dualistic settlement because they saw it as making Hungary too dependent on the common 'arrangements' of the remnant Habsburg Monarchy, in other words on the Austrian emperor. Yet in many respects the arrangement worked to put Hungarians in charge of Austria. This was due mainly to the developments of the nationality question in the respective states. Francis Joseph's own tendency to cave in more quickly to the Magyar leadership than the Cisleithanian one, because the former had once beaten him and the latter had not, was no doubt one of the reasons why 'Hungary governed Austria through the Crown'.[77] Francis Joseph's deference to Magyar wishes was itself partly due, however, to the way in which the Magyars had successfully imposed on the Kingdom of St Stephen the frame of a uniform nation-state, while Cisleithania, the other half, was clearly on the way to being a 'nationalities-state' with little or no *national* coherence.

The Hungarian parliament was often the scene of discord and strife, but it was discord and strife *within* the ranks of an almost uniformly militant nationalism. Magyarisation might not have been very successful in demographic terms, but government policies ensured that Hungary functioned as an almost purely Magyar state. Even Croatia-Slavonia, supposedly an autonomous state, was ruled with cleverness if not much subtlety by the Magyar Ban, Khuen-Héderváry, as if it were under Budapest's direct control. A Hungarian, the Joint Finance Minister, Kállay, was also the *de facto* ruler of Bosnia–Herzegovina, and similarly used his position to influence Bosnian development in a pro-Magyar direction (for instance in the routeing of railways).[78] The Magyar political elite might quarrel among themselves on the niceties and degrees of their chauvinism but they presented a united phalanx to the rest of the world, and especially to their Cisleithanian counterparts.

These in contrast, already by the 1890s, were riven by the conflict of national interests, which meant that any consensus in the Reichsrat was difficult to reach at the best of times. This meant that in the decennial negotiations over the Compromise provisions the Cisleithanian side hardly ever presented a united front. This made them ripe for the picking when it came to further Magyar demands on economic, constitutional or military matters. It also made the Magyar leadership far more attractive to an emperor-king who had always been attracted to those who had enough 'viability' or 'political strength' to deliver on a deal.

In 1897 Count Andrássy, the son of the former revolutionary and foreign minister, claimed that the Magyars were destined to play a leading role in the Dual Monarchy, because 'we [Hungarians] form a unified state of great antiquity; Austria is a mosaic of nationalities and provinces without an inner unity.'[79] In demographic reality there was actually not much difference between the ethnic composition of the two states, but in political reality he was quite right. Yet this meant that the tail was in effect wagging the dog, for Hungary was much the less populous of the two halves, and far less wealthy or developed. Hungary paid only a third of the empire's expenses yet had half the say, often more than half, in how it was run. If the Magyars resented dependence on 'Austria', the Cisleithanian populace had an even stronger case for resentment of Magyar political hegemony in the Habsburg Monarchy's joint affairs, and, moreover, their continuing influence, if only as a veto power, on internal Cisleithanian affairs. Any attempt to change the status of the Czechs or the South Slavs sooner or later ran up against the Compromise, and, as 1871 had effectively demonstrated, nothing major could be changed within Cisleithania without the Magyars giving the nod first. In contrast the Magyars were given virtual *carte blanche* in their internal affairs.

All of these various layers of tensions meshed in often disconcerting ways with the Monarchy's foreign policy. In the Balkans some of the best laid plans of Francis Joseph and his Foreign Ministers were periodically compromised by Hungarian mistreatment of the Croats and Serbs under their control, whether in Hungary, Croatia or, indirectly, Bosnia–Herzegovina. Hungarian fears of their South Slav minorities, obversely, had considerable impact on how Austria–Hungary dealt with its Balkan neighbours, especially in economic terms. No wonder Kálnoky could frustratedly say of the Magyar leadership 'the gang need watching'.[80]

There was also a strong relationship between domestic and foreign policy when it came to the Dual Alliance. The existence of this alliance both emboldened Austrian Germans in their resistance to compromise with the other nationalities, and disgruntled the Czechs despite the concessions made by Taaffe's regime at German expense. Moreover, Francis Joseph's determination to maintain this alliance as the central pillar of Habsburg foreign policy meant that the erosion of the German position in Austria could only go so far. The German government, Bismarck and then William II in particular, were not chary of showing their disdain for Taaffe's 'anti-German' policies and let it be known that they were not prepared to accept a 'Slavicised' Cisleithania.[81] Although the Taaffean system had given the imperial authorities more room for manoeuvre, they were still stuck within the confines of what Germany and Hungary would accept. In 1885, commenting in his diary on the chaos of the Reichsrat, Hübner wrote: 'This whole parliamentary comedy is wretched. The emperor does what he likes, i.e. what Bismarck in Varzin and Tisza in Budapest like.'[82] This was neither entirely true nor fair, but there was a grain of truth in it. There were set limits on what Austria–Hungary, Francis Joseph, could do, abroad or even at home. Furthermore, the very complexity of the 'mosaic monarchy' began in the 1890s to devalue Austria–Hungary in the eyes of the German policymakers.[83]

There were even more abstruse connections. Germany and the Magyar leadership were usually in agreement on most foreign policy issues. This was a common thread running through late nineteenth-century Central European international relations. Yet even here foreign and domestic policy could clash severely. Thus in 1891 the German government complained bitterly to Francis Joseph at Magyar internal policy in Transylvania against the Rumanian population – because Rumania was an important German ally.[84] The same sort of considerations affected the treatment of the Italian minority in Cisleithania, in case it adversely affected the Triple Alliance with Italy. Meanwhile the still alienated Czechs looked to fellow Slav Russia and also to France for support. Inter-national rivalries and conflicts *within* the Monarchy had increasingly strong links with international relations outside its borders.

It was within this vortex of interconnected tensions that the Taaffean system, which had seemed so ideal to the emperor, unravelled in the 1890s. At the centre of events was the conflict between the Germans and Czechs in Bohemia, with a sideshow in southern Styria. This is understandable, for not only were the Bohemian crownlands the most important because most prosperous lands of Cisleithania outside of Vienna, but this was the one remaining major region where German interests were still being threatened – and defended. German had once been the official administrative language of the whole Monarchy. By the 1890s, however, it had retreated from Hungary, from Galicia, from Dalmatia, even in practice from Slovene Carniola, as the various national groups had been bought off by Francis Joseph and the Viennese authorities, and as the German-speaking populations of the urban linguistic 'islands' had either been assimilated into, or demographically overwhelmed by, the surrounding and immigrating nationalities. There were still conflicts over the use of German in the Tyrol (Italians) and Styria (Slovenes), but it was in the Bohemian crownlands, and especially Bohemia, that the clash over the status of the Germans in a multi-national state was most hotly contested and most significant.

The beginning of the end of Taaffe's ministry came with its inability to make the Bohemian Compromise of 1890 stick. This agreement, between the German Liberals on the one hand, and the Old Czechs and Czechophile Bohemian nobility on the other, would have been an immense achievement of Taaffe and his emperor if it had held. It would have preserved many of the aspects of German hegemony, such as the use of German as the internal administrative language, which Francis Joseph wanted, while its division of the crownland into German and Czech administrative areas both protected German interests and represented German recognition that they could never again regain their previous position of dominance in the province, or the state.[85] The deal was seen as advantageous to the Germans, but it was especially satisfactory for the emperor.

Unfortunately the Compromise failed for the very reason that it had seemed feasible in the first place: the threat, soon realised, of the takeover of Czech politics by the left-radical Young Czechs from their Old Czech rivals. It had been fear of the Young Czechs which had spurred both Francis Joseph and the Old Czechs to seek an agreement with the Germans.[86] Before the Compromise could be put in place, however, it had been made irrelevant and unrealisable by Young Czech electoral success, and vehement opposition to its provisions. Instead of national peace, Bohemia was the scene in the early 1890s of street violence and widespread political resistance. In response to Young Czech success, Taaffe attempted to bring moderate German Liberals into his coalition, by promising to implement the main provisions of the Compromise, especially the redrawing of judicial districts along national lines, by decree. This elicited the response of Young Czech obstruction of the Bohemian Diet, and a summer of virtual chaos and eventually martial law in Prague.[87]

By 1893 the control of Cisleithanian politics was slipping from Taaffe's grasp. For once he decided against muddling through and stunned the Reichsrat in October 1893 with a plan, drawn up by Steinbach, for electoral reform which envisaged universal (but not equal) male suffrage. It was a colossal failure, for it antagonised all existing parties, especially the German Liberals and the German Clericals, pressured as they already were by the more radical German Nationalists and Lueger's Christian Socials. Rather than commit political suicide, the Liberals and Clericals, formerly the polar opposites of the German political scene, banded together and, with added support from the also threatened Polish Club, brought down Taaffe instead. Kálnoky, also determined to see Taaffe off, weighed in by portraying the reform as a threat to the Triple Alliance.[88] For what was to prove the last time, and much to his chagrin, Francis Joseph was forced by parliamentary party leaders to dismiss his old friend Taaffe, and accept a new ministry, composed of the unlikely combination of German Liberals and Hohenwart Conservatives, as well as the ever-present Poles.

The resulting Coalition was always a rather strange agglomeration, with a Conservative, Prince Alfred Windischgrätz, as premier, and a German Liberal, Ernst von Plener, as Finance Minister and leading light. It lasted barely two years, doing little to further the political fortunes of either main partner. Indeed, having the responsibility but not the power of government compromised the Liberals' position among their German constituents, making them lose ground to the more radical nationalist camp and contributing to catastrophic defeat in the Viennese municipal elections of April 1895.[89] Those elections instead brought Karl Lueger's radical-populist Christian Socials to the brink of power in the Habsburg capital in the wake of a very nasty, anti-Semitic campaign. The Viennese situation meant that Cisleithanian politics were already in crisis when the Coalition ministry eventually fell in June 1895 over the attempt to institute a parallel Slovene class at the *Gymnasium* in Cilli (Celje) in Styria.[90]

Francis Joseph cannot be said to have been very unhappy over this, as the failure of the ministry – forced on him in the first place – had only confirmed his prejudices about the ungovernability of Cisleithania by parliamentary-party means.[91] On the other hand, he was very concerned about the radicalisation of Cisleithanian politics. He regarded the Pan-German nationalists and the Young Czechs with barely hidden scorn, and deemed Karl Lueger and the Christian Socials as almost as unacceptably radical as the nationalist groups. When Lueger's party again won a solid majority in the Viennese City Council elections in September, the time had clearly come for decisive action, preferably some new, imaginative approach to deal with a rapidly changing, and deteriorating, political scene. The emperor instead fell back on previous methods. He chose someone who he thought had enough backbone to force the ever more fractious political parties of Cisleithania to see sense, or as Redlich puts it, would lead a 'strong non-parliamentary government in which the assembly he despised would find its master'.[92] It was a fateful decision.

When Francis Joseph appointed him prime minister in September 1895, Count Casimir Badeni had the reputation of being an effective and firm governor of Galicia, qualities which made him attractive to the Austrian military high command, on whose recommendation he had been chosen.[93] Yet Badeni was not simply the oafish 'strong man' of historiographical legend; rather, recent research shows him to have been a quite thoughtful, if unrealistic, politician, more swept away by events outside his control than the bull in a china shop. Within the spectrum of Galician politics Badeni had been actually quite liberal, and his initial strategy appears to have been to govern with a 'liberal' coalition of German Liberals and Young Czechs.[94] While this meant engaging the Young Czechs, and easing up on measures such as the imposition of martial law in Prague, it also meant being friendly to the Germans. At first relations with the German Liberal parties were therefore good, especially when Badeni recommended Francis Joseph not to sanction Lueger's election as mayor of Vienna. The strategy begged the question, though, of how to effect the long-sought but seemingly impossible German-Czech national reconciliation.

Moreover, the quickly changing fortunes of Cisleithanian politics overtook Badeni's 'liberal' strategy. Already in April 1896, much to the chagrin of the Liberals in Vienna, Badeni had felt it necessary to strike a deal with Lueger over the Viennese mayoralty. Relations with the German Liberals were still good enough for them to vote for the electoral reform of May 1896. This nevertheless saw another diminution in the German Liberals' position. It was not as radical as the 1893 proposal had been. It merely added 72 seats from a fifth, universal male suffrage curia, to the already 353 seats from the established Reichsrat. This partial concession to the pressures of social change had, though, the effect of reducing the number of German seats (of all ideological persuasions) to a minority, 202 of 425, for the first time. (In 1873 Germans had held two-thirds.)[95] With further inroads to be expected from the 'clerical' Christian Socials and the prospect of Socialists in the new Reichsrat, it was clear that the 'German Left', increasingly nationalist, was being backed into a desperate defensive posture.

Badeni, however, blithely continued to negotiate with both Czechs and Germans for a compromise, which he envisaged as a trade-off of expanded Czech language rights in the Bohemian administration on the one hand, and an effective division of Bohemia into two national halves, along the lines of the 1890 Compromise, on the other. One problem with this idea was that the former could be achieved by ordinance, the latter only by action in the Bohemian Diet, far from a sure bet. Another problem was that the German leaders never signed off on it, although they also seem neither to have made clear, nor mostly predicted, the degree of opposition such an agreement would generate – especially if only the first part of the trade-off was on the table. The fact that no major German group would guarantee support for his ministry was enough, however, for Badeni to see the failure of his strategy and for him to tender his resignation before the language ordinances were even published.

Francis Joseph did not accept his resignation, however, which left Badeni to patch together a new strategy from the ruins of the old. His job was made only harder by the outcome of the March 1897 elections on the basis of the new franchise. Although the socialists were the most spectacular gainers, the large gains by the Christian Socials, the Young Czechs and Steinwender's nationalist German People's Party were what made the election so significant, reducing further the liberal element in the German camp and resulting in a majority for the 'Right' in the new Reichsrat. Badeni thus found himself faced with the opposite of what he had wanted, the prospect of governing with a Right coalition of German Clericals, Christian Socials, Czechs and Poles, which, almost behind his back, formally constituted itself as the new parliamentary majority coalition. At first he resisted the logic of this arrangement, vowing at the end of April not to become a 'prisoner' of the 'reactionary majority', but soon enough the consequences of publication of the language ordinances on 5 April and the vehement opposition that resulted from the Germans eventually left him little choice but to be exactly that. He did, after all, need a majority in the Reichsrat in order to govern effectively, especially with the renewal of the Compromise with Hungary coming up, and part of that majority was the Czechs, and that meant the language ordinances.[96]

The language ordinances' main item was the provision for all business of the Habsburg administration in Bohemia and Moravia to be able to be conducted in both German and Czech. To facilitate this they also required all Habsburg officials in the crown lands to have knowledge of both languages by 1901.[97] On the face of it this does not seem that onerous, but to Bohemian Germans to accept this was in effect to surrender to complete Czech dominance of the crown lands. For the asymmetry between the two languages (see above) meant that the net effect of the ordinances would be an administration with hardly any German officials. In a state where bureaucrats were so important, the 'national property' of German Bohemia, the industrial and political centre of the German middle classes, appeared to be in mortal peril.

The initial response of the German deputies was to submit a flurry of emergency resolutions to nullify the ordinances, all of which failed. (Christian Social abstention in these votes was rewarded by Lueger's mayoral confirmation.)[98] After that they brought the Reichsrat's business to a halt by continuous filibustering. Obstruction of the Reichsrat by continuous debate and procedural manoeuvre had been introduced by the Czechs in the last years of the Windischgrätz coalition.[99] But the Germans now took it to hyperbolic proportions. At first the obstruction was 'technical' in nature and largely confined to the Progressives (German Bohemian Liberals) and the Pan-Germans of Schönerer and Wolf. As the outrage of the German populace was communicated to their deputies more and more joined in, so that by the summer recess all of the German Left, including Steinwender's People's Party were aboard. Badeni sent the deputies home early for the summer for a cooling-off period, but the crisis only worsened as no settlement was reached, positions hardened and tempers flared.

When the Reichsrat came back in the autumn the need to pass the Compromise legislation meant that matters became crucial, then critical. The attempt by the majority on 25 November to impose new procedures to beat the obstruction, the 'Lex Falkenhayn', created scenes which resembled more an insane asylum than the august deliberating chamber of a parliament. By this time, with the constitution itself in danger from the strong-arm tactics of Badeni and the majority Right, even the Socialists were part of the German obstruction. When deputies were expelled from the Reichsrat by use of the police the resistance overflowed into the streets and squares of German towns all over the country. Bosnian troops fired on a crowd in Graz. Lueger – once a Badeni ally – refused to vouchsafe for the safety of the capital's streets. Cisleithania appeared on the verge of revolution.

Even German Clericals had now joined the ranks of the obstructionists in the battle for national 'survival'. Across the border the German press was up in arms at the persecution of their national brethren, and the government made quite clear that the attack on the German position within Cisleithania was unacceptable.[100] The limit of German tolerance, on both sides of the Monarchy's borders, had been reached. The combination of domestic violence and the admonitions of the all-important German ally had their effect. On 29 November Francis Joseph accepted Badeni's resignation, but it would take more than that to quiet the unleashed storm.[101]

Redlich wrote of the Badeni Crisis: 'From this moment the Habsburg realm was doomed.'[102] This is an exaggeration of hindsight, but an understandable one. What was fairly clear was that the political system of Cisleithania had reached an impasse, and that parliamentary government was, if not dead, then very sick indeed. Francis Joseph, by opting for Badeni and sticking with him for so long, had done more than most to bring this unsatisfactory situation about, where the Compromise had yet to be agreed, Cisleithania was in chaos and his German ally intervening in the domestic affairs of his state. Yet, ironically, he was one of the main beneficiaries of the Cisleithanian breakdown. With parliament prostrate from the national conflict, only he remained as a focus of order, of authority. It was scant consolation for the international embarrassment and political paralysis of the Badeni crisis, but from this point on even more of what remained of the power of the state accrued to Francis Joseph, because when it came to authority in Cisleithania, especially moral authority, he was the only thing left.

. . .

NOTES AND REFERENCES

1. J. Redlich, *Emperor Francis Joseph of Austria: A Biography*, Macmillan, New York 1929, p. 421.
2. W.A. Jenks, *Austria under the Iron Ring 1879–1893*, University Press of Virginia, Charlottesville 1965, p. 35.
3. Ibid., p. 37.
4. Ibid., p. 49.
5. Ibid., p. 56.
6. J. Redlich, *Österreichische Regierung und Verwaltung im Weltkriege*, Hölder, Vienna 1925, pp. 50–2.
7. E.C. Hellbling, 'Die Landesverwaltung in Cisleithanien'. In A. Wandruszka, P. Urbanitsch (eds), *Die Habsburger Monarchie 1848–1918* (6+ vols). Österreichische Akademie der Wissenschaften, Vienna 1975, vol. 2, *Verwaltung und Rechtswesen*, pp. 249–50.
8. Jenks, *Austria under the Iron Ring*, p. 72.

9. Ibid., pp. 59–62.

10. Ibid., pp. 115–16; L. Höbelt, *Kornblume und Kaiseradler: Die deutschfreiheitlichen Parteien Altösterreichs 1882–1918*, Geschichte und Politik, Vienna 1993, pp. 141–4.

11. Hellbling, 'Die Landesverwaltung in Cisleithanien', pp. 252–4.

12. Jenks, *Austria under the Iron Ring*, pp. 128–39.

13. Ibid., pp. 184–5.

14. D.F. Good, *The Economic Rise of the Habsburg Empire, 1750–1914*, University of California, Berkeley 1984, p. 226.

15. Jenks, *Austria under the Iron Ring*, pp. 162–76, 191–218.

16. Ibid., pp. 67–8, 105–12.

17. J.S. Bloch, *Erinnerungen aus meinem Leben*, Rikola, Vienna 1922, p. 159.

18. Jenks, *Austria under the Iron Ring*, p. 295.

19. J.K. Hoensch, *A History of Modern Hungary, 1867–1986*, trans. K. Traynor, Longman, London 1988, p. 34.

20. Ibid., pp. 30–1.

21. Good, *The Economic Rise of the Habsburg Empire*, pp. 226ff.

22. W.O. McCagg, *A History of Habsburg Jews, 1670–1918*, Indiana University Press, Bloomington 1989, pp. 123–38; Redlich, *Emperor Francis Joseph*, p. 459.

23. C.A. Macartney, *The House of Austria: The Later Phase 1790–1918*, Edinburgh 1978, p. 209; A.J.P. Taylor, *The Habsburg Monarchy 1809–1918*, Penguin, Harmondsworth 1948 (1964), p. 207.

24. Macartney, *The House of Austria*, p. 209.

25. Cf. O. Jászi, *The Dissolution of the Habsburg Monarchy*, Chicago 1929, pp. 346–7 (Studies in the Making of Citizens).

26. Höbelt, *Kornblume und Kaiseradler*, pp. 30, 35, 181.

27. Redlich, *Emperor Francis Joseph*, p. 418.

28. Höbelt, *Kornblume und Kaiseradler*, p. 19.

29. Jenks, *Austria under the Iron Ring*, pp. 95, 265.

30. Ibid., p. 83; R.A. Kann, *A History of the Habsburg Empire, 1526–1918*, University of California, Berkeley 1977, pp. 339–40.

31. Jenks, *Austria under the Iron Ring*, pp. 117–18.

32. Ibid., p. 79.

33. J.-P. Bled, *Franz Joseph*, trans. T. Bridgeman, Blackwell, Oxford 1992, pp. 200–2; A. Palmer, *Twilight of the Habsburgs: The Life and Times of Emperor Francis Joseph*, Weidenfeld & Nicolson, London 1994, p. 276.

34. Redlich, *Emperor Francis Joseph*, p. 407.

35. Ibid., pp. 420, 423, 440.
36. Ibid., p. 421.
37. I. Deák, *Beyond Nationalism: A Social and Political History of the Habsburg Officer Corps 1848–1918*, Oxford 1990, pp. 59–60; F.R. Bridge, *The Habsburg Monarchy among the Great Powers, 1815–1918*, Berg, Oxford 1990, p. 149.
38. Cf. Deák, *Beyond Nationalism*, pp. 183–5; although Deák disputes the official figure of 80 per cent of officers being German, he acknowledges that this proportion was German-*speaking*, and that over half of all officers were *nationally* German.
39. Ibid., p. 75.
40. Bridge, *The Habsburg Monarchy*, pp. 193–5; Deák, *Beyond Nationalism*, p. 64.
41. Bled, *Franz Joseph*, p. 205.
42. E.C. Corti and H. Sokol, *Der alte Kaiser: Franz Joseph I. vom Berliner Kongress bis zu seinem Tode*, Styria, Graz 1955, p. 92.
43. Bridge, *The Habsburg Monarchy*, p. 211.
44. Ibid., p. 211.
45. Ibid., p. 178.
46. Ibid., pp. 221–3.
47. Corti and Sokol, *Der alte Kaiser*, p. 55.
48. Bled, *Franz Joseph*, pp. 211–12; Anonymous, *The Private Life of Two Emperors: William II of Germany and Francis-Joseph of Austria* (2 vols), Nash, London 1904, vol. 1, pp. 218–20.
49. Cf. Albrecht's account of the morality of the Habsburg family, in Franz Joseph, *Meine liebe, gute Freundin! Die Briefe Kaiser Franz Josephs an Katharina Schratt*, ed. B. Hamann, Überreuter, Vienna 1992, p. 158.
50. Anonymous, *The Private Life of Two Emperors*, p. 122.
51. Ibid., p. 129.
52. P. Vasili, *Die Wiener Gesellschaft*, Leipzig 1885, pp. 72–90.
53. Anonymous, *The Private Life of Two Emperors*, pp. 184, 193.
54. R.A. Kann, *Dynasty, Politics and Culture: Selected Essays*, ed. S. Winters, Social Science Monographs, Boulder 1991, pp. 58–9.
55. Bled, *Franz Joseph*, p. 221; Redlich, *Emperor Francis Joseph*, p. 409; Anonymous, *The Private Life of Two Emperors*, p. 264.
56. E. Crankshaw, *The Fall of the House of Habsburg*, Viking Penguin, New York 1963, p. 294.
57. Rudolf, *Majestät, ich warne Sie: Geheime und private Schriften*, ed. B. Hamann, Amalthea, Vienna 1979, p. 10.
58. Redlich, *Emperor Francis Joseph*, pp. 410–11.

59. Rudolf, *Majestät, ich warne Sie*, p. 218.
60. Ibid., p. 170; cf. Redlich, *Emperor Francis Joseph*, pp. 435–8.
61. Rudolf, *Majestät, ich warne Sie*, p. 9.
62. Franz Joseph, *Meine liebe, gute Freundin*, p. 158.
63. Anonymous, *The Private Life of Two Emperors*, p. 59.
64. Redlich, *Emperor Francis Joseph*, p. 477; Anonymous, *The Private Life of Two Emperors*, p. 60.
65. Franz Joseph, *Meine liebe, gute Freundin*, pp. 16–18; Anonymous, *The Private Life of Two Emperors*, p. 25.
66. Corti and Sokol, *Der alte Kaiser*, p. 161.
67. Palmer, *Twilight of the Habsburgs*, p. 236; cf. Franz Joseph, *Meine liebe, gute Freundin*, for a full account and the emperor's part of the correspondence.
68. Palmer, *Twilight of the Habsburgs*, p. 260; also see Frederic Morton, *A Nervous Splendor: Vienna 1888–9*, London 1979, *passim*.
69. Franz Joseph, *Meine liebe, gute Freundin*, p. 126.
70. Corti and Sokol, *Der alte Kaiser*, p. 142.
71. Ibid., p. 52.
72. Redlich, *Emperor Francis Joseph*, p. 418; Höbelt, *Kornblume und Kaiseradler*, pp. 30ff.
73. Corti and Sokol, *Der alte Kaiser*, p. 214; cf. J.W. Boyer, *Political Radicalism in Late Imperial Vienna: Origins of the Christian Social Movement 1848–1897*, University of Chicago 1981; R.S. Geehr, *Karl Lueger, Mayor of Fin de Siècle Vienna*, Wayne State, Detroit 1990.
74. Cf. W.M. Johnston, *The Austrian Mind: An Intellectual and Social History, 1848–1938*, University of California, Berkeley 1972, pp. 99ff.
75. Jenks, *Austria under the Iron Ring*, p. 244; J.F.N. Bradley, *Czech Nationalism in the Nineteenth Century*, East European Monographs, Boulder 1984, pp. 30–3.
76. Hoensch, *History of Modern Hungary*, pp. 51–2.
77. H.W. Steed, *The Habsburg Monarchy*, reprint 2nd edn 1914, Fertig, New York 1969, p. 28.
78. Jászi, *The Dissolution of the Habsburg Monarchy*, pp. 370–1; Palmer, *Twilight of the Habsburgs*, p. 213; cf. Taylor, *The Habsburg Monarchy*, pp. 166–7; Kann, *A History of the Habsburg Empire*, pp. 466–7.
79. Corti and Sokol, *Der alte Kaiser*, p. 214; Crankshaw, *The Fall of the House of Habsburg*, p. 299.
80. Bridge, *The Habsburg Monarchy*, p. 205.

81. J. Kořalka, 'Deutschland und die Habsburgermonarchie'. In Wandruszka and Urbanitsch (eds), *Die Habsburger Monarchie 1848–1918*, Vienna 1993, vol. 6, pt. 2, *Aussenpolitik*, p. 86; Bridge, *The Habsburg Monarchy*, pp. 184–5.
82. Corti and Sokol, *Der alte Kaiser*, p. 55.
83. Kořalka, 'Deutschland und die Habsburgermonarchie', p. 99.
84. Ibid., p. 97.
85. Jenks, *Austria under the Iron Ring*, pp. 253–6.
86. Ibid., p. 248.
87. Höbelt, *Kornblume und Kaiseradler*, pp. 61–4.
88. Jenks, *Austria under the Iron Ring*, pp. 299–303.
89. Boyer, *Political Radicalism in Late Imperial Vienna*, pp. 321–49.
90. Höbelt, *Kornblume und Kaiseradler*, pp. 106–15.
91. Redlich, *Emperor Francis Joseph*, p. 443.
92. Crankshaw, *The Fall of the House of Habsburg*, p. 301; J. Redlich, 1929, p. 443.
93. Redlich, *Emperor Francis Joseph*, p. 444.
94. Höbelt, *Kornblume und Kaiseradler*, pp. 116–17.
95. A. Sked, *The Decline and Fall of the Habsburg Empire 1815–1918*, Longman, London 1989, p. 222; A.J. May, *The Habsburg Monarchy, 1867–1914*, Harvard, Cambridge 1951, p. 325.
96. Höbelt, *Kornblume und Kaiseradler*, pp. 151–5.
97. Kann, *A History of the Habsburg Empire*, p. 441; May, *The Habsburg Monarchy*, p. 325.
98. Höbelt, *Kornblume und Kaiseradler*, p. 163.
99. Redlich, *Emperor Francis Joseph*, p. 447; Höbelt, *Kornblume und Kaiseradler*, p. 109.
100. Kořalka, 'Deutschland und die Habsburgermonarchie', pp. 107–10.
101. Höbelt, *Kornblume und Kaiseradler*, pp. 161–6.
102. Redlich, *Emperor Francis Joseph*, p. 448.

Chapter 6

GETTING OLD, 1897–1914

. . .

THE THUNDER OF HEAVEN

The year 1898 should have been one of celebration for the now sixty-seven-year-old Francis Joseph, marking as it did the Golden Jubilee of his reign. On 2 December it would be the fiftieth anniversary of his becoming Austrian emperor. Despite continuing political trouble in the aftermath of the Badeni Crisis, celebrations did indeed start in the summer of 1898, and were building to a crescendo, when on 10 September Francis Joseph was told that his wife, the Empress Elisabeth, had been assassinated by an Italian anarchist in Geneva. His immediate reaction was: 'So I am to be spared nothing in this world!'[1] Unfortunately for Francis Joseph this was to prove less a statement than a prediction.

Over the next decade the political strife in both halves of the Dual Monarchy would become so intense as to make European public opinion wonder about its survival, and the great powers' foreign ministries draw up plans for the eventuality of its demise. The empire and its monarch would survive this crisis, only to be swept up anew in the Balkan quagmire, from which there proved to be no escape. In November 1912 Francis Joseph exclaimed: 'I don't want war. I have always been unlucky in wars. We would win, but lose provinces.'[2] Less than two years later, after the assassination of yet another close relative, his nephew and designated successor Francis Ferdinand, the same Francis Joseph, the self-styled 'peace emperor', was to declare war on Serbia, thus starting a conflagration which was to destroy much of European civilisation, and the Habsburg Monarchy with it. Francis Joseph was thus given the dubious privilege of signing the death warrant of the dynastic empire he had battled his whole life to preserve.

Historians still argue passionately over how the collapse of coherent government in Cisleithania and Hungary was or was not related to the start of the First World War; whether Austria–Hungary was already being riven asunder by the various national and constitutional conflicts before the war; whether indeed it was the hopelessness of these conflicts which pushed the Monarchy to start the war; whether once started the war inevitably spelt the end of the Habsburg Monarchy; or whether none of this is true and the idea of any decline is an error of hindsight: the war and the Monarchy's break-up either an accident, tragic mistake, or the result of external forces with no understanding of the region's needs. The only claim of certainty that emerges from such debates is that the question is very complicated.

In this complex debate about the relationship between the Monarchy's internal problems and its (ultimately disastrous) foreign policy, two aspects seem to call for special attention: the continuing role played by the emperor and the imperial apparatus; and the continually building, ever broadening problems caused by nationalism within a multi-national, dynastic state. These two aspects together came to define the Monarchy, and no matter how much is made of the evidence for supposed viability of the Monarchy despite its national conflicts, what remains very unclear is how modern nationalism could ever have been fully reconciled to the sort of dynastic, imperial framework which the Habsburg Monarchy represented, and which Francis Joseph was determined to preserve.

The problem in the imperial–national relationship was perhaps put best by Berthold Molden, a journalist with close ties to Francis Ferdinand's Belvedere Circle of advisers, in a memorandum of 6 July 1914. Referring to the question of whether better treatment of the Serbs within the Monarchy would be advisable, he looked to a previous Habsburg experience of nationalism: 'the Venetians, in their time, used to say that they did not wish for Austria to govern them well – it should not govern them at all. [. . .] We are confronted with a current of the time, which is intensified by Balkan traditions to which we cannot yield without committing suicide.'[3]

Nationalism inherently calls for self-determination. This does not necessarily mean complete independence, but it does mean the absence of a superior power ruling over the nation. Empire means, if nothing else, ruling over nations. If an empire does not rule over nations, it is not an empire. It is at least conceivable that the nationalities might have been reconciled in Central Europe, but only under the sort of federalist or commonwealth structure which would have meant a change beyond all recognition of the Habsburgs' monarchical role, certainly beyond anything Francis Joseph would have recognised, and certainly an end to the *imperial* nature of the dynasty's position. Conversely, the need to keep the Habsburgs an imperial 'great power' made Francis Joseph always reluctant to give up any control of his military or foreign policy prerogatives, or risk antagonising the political forces which could give him what he most needed: sufficient moneys to finance his army, and hence to maintain Austria's great-power status. This meant both that he could never willingly give up the powers that he had for fear of reneging on his duty to the dynasty; nor could he bring himself to use the power that he did have to challenge and overturn the entrenched elites, especially in Hungary, in the interests of a more equitable and truly multinational distribution of power.

The story of his last years is perhaps not one of the Monarchy's decline, but it is one of stand-off, of the demonstrated incompatibility of the imperial idea, as understood by Francis Joseph, with the nationalism which had come to dominate politics both in Cisleithania and Hungary. In this struggle the Monarchy, that is to say the imperial-royal apparatus, might well have been holding its own, but it was being stymied, not helped, by the nationalist movements within the state. It was, after all, the national conflicts which paralysed both parliaments for most of the period to 1914, with the result that the all-important Habsburg armed forces were starved of much-needed funds until far too late in the day; and it was fear of loss of prestige to Serbia, seen increasingly as a new 'Piedmont', a new irredentist power, in other words, a new nationalist threat to the Monarchy's – the empire's – integrity, which brought about the declaration of war in 1914.[4]

There is much that is laudable about the economic performance, the level of civilisation, the relative rule of law and the relative security which the Habsburg state had brought to Central Europe by 1914, especially in today's retrospect, but the fact that it remained a dynastic empire, led by a monarch and ruling elite intent first of all on maintaining imperial power and prestige, and only secondarily tending to the national conflicts among its subjects, meant that it could not channel the immense forces which nationalism had stirred up by then.[5] In

1859 the former Magyar revolutionary, Bertalan Szemere, admitted that he and the other followers of Kossuth had underestimated the power of 'the idea of nationality' among the minority nationalities in Hungary. 'We took for an artificial noise what was the thunder of heaven.'[6] The same could have been said, ironically, for the young Francis Joseph. Half a century later the noise was ever more deafening, and yet the attempts of both the emperor and his erstwhile Magyar rivals to deal with it remained ineffective; indeed they were to lead to catastrophe.

. . .

ABSOLUTISM – AGAIN?

The chaos and near anarchy unleashed by the Badeni Affair effectively brought an end to even the appearance of parliamentary government in Cisleithania. In any constitutional regime ostensibly run by the people's representatives this would have caused a seizing-up of government. In Cisleithania though, where the constitution had always been somewhat less than parliamentary, granted as it had been by imperial grace and never recognising the idea of popular sovereignty, government went on as it had always done, by way of the Habsburg officialdom headed by the emperor.

It took a little time after the initial shock of the events of late 1897 for the new post-parliamentary system of government to establish itself. Before the relatively stable ministry of Ernest von Koerber in 1900 there were four prime ministers (Paul von Gautsch, Prince Franz Thun, Count Manfred Clary-Aldringen and Heinrich von Wittek) in the space of just over two years. During this period the Reichsrat did get some things done, such as the direct tax reform of 1898,[7] but almost the entire time was taken up by obstruction: German obstruction before the Badeni ordinances were suspended by the Gautsch ministry (they were eventually repealed in 1899 under the Clary-Aldringen ministry); Czech obstruction afterwards. A major casualty was the economic Compromise legislation – one of the prime causes for the Affair in the first place – which could not be got through the Reichsrat. Apart from this huge constitutional problem (patched over by annual provisional agreements), however, the failure of parliament became increasingly inconsequential as ways were found around it, notably by the frequent use of Article 14 of the constitution, the emergency clause noted above.

Under this new system, which eventually amounted to a form of quasi-absolutism, the Reichsrat would meet, obstruction would start, the emperor would prorogue the Reichsrat, in its absence 'emergency decrees' would be passed to keep the government going and deals made between the ministry on the one hand and the parliamentary parties on the other, so that when the Reichsrat reassembled the emergency decrees could be approved. Then, after a brief lull, the obstruction would start and the whole cycle begin again.[8] Government by party politicians became a faded memory as the *Beamtenministerium* (ministry of officials) became the norm. Government was back in the hands of the people Francis Joseph trusted most: it was, according to Joseph Redlich, 'the absolutism of departmental bureaucracy'.[9]

This new system achieved its apotheosis under Ernest von Koerber, a bureaucrat and Francis Joseph's prime minister from 1900 to 1904. Koerber, ably assisted by his aide, Rudolf Sieghart, engaged in a hypertrophic form of Taaffean politics. His therapy for the national conflict in Bohemia was to 'commercialise' politics.[10] After trying to break the parliamentary deadlock by direct German-Czech negotiation in 1900, Koerber then tried new elections, resulting in 1901 in an even more nationally radicalised Reichsrat. He then found his stride by changing the subject, namely to economics rather than national rights. Hence his new gambit was to present an economic recovery programme with plump works projects, mainly railways and canals, for all sides in the parliamentary stand-off. On the basis of this he did manage a truce, so that for the first time for a very long period, the Reichsrat passed two annual budgets in a row.[11]

Yet parliament remained a sham. What was now buying political calm was the wheeling and dealing going on in the backrooms, between Koerber and the various parties over where the works projects were going to be built, who was going to get the favour of the various ministries' powers. It was the government of the bazaar, 'interest' politics at its most naked.[12] Moreover, as the law of diminishing returns went into effect, and those parties who were disappointed in the distribution of economic favours went back to obstruction to get their way nevertheless, Koerber came more and more to trade not in economic but in administrative and educational goods, as Taaffe had done, and with the same effect. Whereas economic matters, with regional results, cut across national interests, these new areas, where the question was which nationality could dominate the personnel of which ministry, or which language should be the language of instruction for a new (Italian) law faculty or (Czech) technical institute, clearly only strengthened this central fissure of Cisleithanian politics.[13] The end result was that Koerber had engineered an economic boom, had managed to get a Compromise agreement with the Hungarians in 1902 and to pass it by decree in 1903,[14] had greatly liberalised the laws on freedom of speech and the press, and had kept the government running relatively efficiently for almost five years, but when he resigned at the end of 1904 after the return of total Czech obstruction, he had not been able to solve the central problem of the Czech-German stand-off in Bohemia.

Moreover his 'success' had been bought at considerable expense to the political health of what remained of representative politics in Cisleithania. Koerber's style, 'more political legerdemain than substance', in which the ministry 'carried on a daily exchange and mart with each party in turn', meant that the public life of parliamentary politics became a showy farce while the real deals and real government went on behind closed, bureaucratic doors. In Redlich's opinion: 'The profound demoralisation of Austrian parliamentary representation dates from this time.'[15] The fact that politicians could behave in a grossly irresponsible manner, because, after all, politics was not serious while the country continued to be run by the 'un-political' officialdom, had a terribly corrupting influence on political life. There was no need to moderate the radicalism of one's nationalist rhetoric, ever popular with the riled electorate, if in the private rooms of the bureaucracy bargains could be struck and one's rhetoric had little or no effect on the functioning of the state. Similarly, German nationalists and Christian Socials, and many politicians of other nationalities, including Czechs and Poles, could cynically utilise the most heinous sort of anti-Semitic rhetoric, advocate the most radical sorts of policies against Jews, in the full knowledge that the Habsburg state would rein in the worst excesses which might result. It was thus that Koerber's system, 'paved the way for unbridled demagogy in Austria, both nationalistic and socialistic'.[16]

Koerber's interest politics had beneficial effects as well. By treating the socialists as just another interest Koerber was able to bring Victor Adler's party into the fold of Austrian political parties; Lueger's Christian Socials, once radicals, were now almost an establishment fixture of this new, interest-driven regime. By dealing in terms of interests with the more radical German Nationalists Koerber was to a degree able to domesticate them as well (although this also meant at least toleration of their anti-Semitic posturing). In effect Koerber was simply taking to its logical conclusion what Otto Steinwender had adumbrated in the 1880s.

Yet the net effect was to make Austrian politics ever more a vertical, hierarchical system – where the parties bargained with the government, that is to say the Habsburg officialdom, rather than with each other (as in a horizontal, democratic system). The government was thus more arbiter than mediator, and the aim of the game was more to put one over on the opponent than to come to a compromise with him. Koerber's system, ostensibly aimed at settling national conflicts, became a classic imperial model of 'divide and rule'. It came both to boost the power of the central bureaucracy, and ensure the *continuance* of the national rivalries, for it meant that no local or regional compromises needed to be made by the parties themselves when the officialdom was there to do it for them. As a result few compromises were made between the parties themselves. Those that were made, under government auspices, such as the Moravian Compromise of 1905, were in effect partitions: agreements not to compromise.[17]

Francis Joseph must have felt quite pleased with this outcome. He must, for once, have felt vindicated. He had believed from the first, and continued to believe, that Austria could not be constitutionally governed.[18] He tended to neglect the fact that his experience showed that it also could not be governed through absolutism, and that his own actions had been a large factor in ensuring that constitutionalism had not worked. Nor did he think too much about other forms of constitution than the centralist-cum-dualist one he had arrived at, for such new ideas threatened the status of the dynasty at home and abroad and in any case yet another constitution at his advanced age was more than he would contemplate, and his advisers knew better than to tax him with such suggestions. Koerber's 'bureaucratic absolutism' on the other hand was just the sort of cobbled-together arrangement that appealed to his pragmatic way of thinking and retained enough of the constitutional framework to get by without undue trouble while keeping the imperial authority in charge.

Indeed the second reason for his affirmation of the new regime was that it boosted the political power of the imperial authorities, and hence himself. Publicly he remained ever hopeful that the Germans and Czechs could be brought to a compromise in Bohemia, but privately he was pessimistic about such a settlement. Moreover, if hearsay of a comment by his daughter, Marie

Valerie, is correct, he did not even want such a settlement, for 'if Germans and Czechs come to an understanding, it will be like Hungary, and the Emperor will lose his power there too.'[19] Whether this was so or not, it is certainly true that the national divisions and the way Koerber's system dealt with them increased the role and power of the imperial arbitrator. Even if he did not want it, the national strife in Bohemia worked greatly to Francis Joseph's immediate political advantage. As an added side-effect, he personally became ever more popular as the one remaining potent symbol of the integrity of the Monarchy, the last court of appeal in a divided polity. While the political system all around him languished in perpetual crisis, the emperor himself now enjoyed more moral and domestic political power than he had for much of his reign.

There was also a great deal for the emperor to be unhappy about in this new system, however. The effective breakdown of constitutional government had immense costs when it came to what mattered most to Francis Joseph: the army and foreign policy. Although the Koerber system, with its liberal use of Article 14, could get legislation passed by decree which enabled government to continue to function, there was in the quality of legislation an 'invisible line' beyond which it could not go without real, parliamentary sanction.[20] Decrees which continued the status quo were acceptable to the Cisleithanian political parties and their constituencies, but the so-called 'ex-lex-situation' became intolerable when it came to major increases of taxation or increases of the conscription quotas. Had the government increased these by decree, then what had been a procedure of questionable legality would have become tantamount to a *coup d'état*, and this was a step which neither the aged emperor was prepared to take, nor the political nation to tolerate. So neither major tax increases nor major increases in army funding and manpower were passed. There were thus important limits to the new 'bureaucratic absolutism', and those limits were felt precisely in the financing and manning of the army, which continued to fall further and further behind those of the other great powers.

This, combined with the spectacle of almost permanent political paralysis, led even Austria's closest ally, Germany, to question whether Austria–Hungary could remain a player in European affairs. In 1905 the German chancellor, Count Bernhard von Bülow considered turning the Habsburg Monarchy into a neutral, 'monarchic, big Switzerland', with an international agreement to leave her to sort out her nationalities problem alone.[21] He soon changed his mind, but that he could think in such terms at all reveals something of Austria's decline in esteem among the great powers.

Bülow's attitude to Austria–Hungary was as much influenced, if not more so, by what had been happening in the other, Hungarian half of the Dual Monarchy. There too questions of national power and imperial power were central, but across the Leitha problems with the army were not a consequence of conflict, but the ostensible prime cause. In Hungary it was not conflicts between nations which the monarch could arbitrate which were the problem, but rather it was the conflict of the (Magyar) nation with its monarch, as Hungarian king but also as Austrian emperor. In this battle Francis Joseph could not be an arbitrator or even an umpire. He was a main player, and target.

Hungary in the 1890s was a state run by a Magyar national leadership brimming with pride. Under Dualism the autonomous Hungarian kingdom had seen by the 1890s a great deal of economic growth, especially in the national capital, and the 1896 Millennial celebrations saw Budapest awash with the symbolism of triumphant nationalism.[22] This pride, tending as it did to hubris, needed outlets, and one popular means of expression was, unfortunately for the Monarchy, the demand for more and more assertion of the 'nation-state's' equal status with Austria, or even independence from imperial Vienna. Such attitudes ignored the fact that Hungary was almost as multi-national a state as Cisleithania, but the shape of Magyar political hegemony and the temptations of politics made the voicing of such demands well nigh inevitable.

The results could sometimes be very petty, and extraordinarily insensitive. In 1898 the funeral of Elisabeth caused a political spat because the inscription on her coffin had originally only described her as 'Empress of Austria'. After vehement Hungarian protests the words 'Queen of Hungary' were added. (Prince Lobkowitz, the Bohemian high nobleman then asked why there was no mention of her being 'Queen of Bohemia'.)[23] On other occasions, though, the pressure to assert an Hungarian identity different, even superior, to that of Austria could result in very major reform which made Hungary, on paper at least, a more liberal, progressive state than her other half. The key instance here was the institution of civil marriage in the mid-1890s, over the strenuous objections of the Catholic Church, the conservative Hungarian magnates, and the emperor-king himself. The problem for the Monarchy was that it was precisely because it was seen as a challenge to the Habsburg establishment that this anti-clerical measure had been adopted and was so popular among Magyar politicians.[24]

The 1890s in Hungary were as unsettled in terms of ministries as they had been in Cisleithania, but the political conflicts which caused this were not between nations, but rather squabbles within the ruling national elite. The squabbles were not about whether or not to demand more power for the Magyar nation-state but rather how much to demand. It was post-Tiszan politics, with a rising Independence Party becoming the main opposition to a Liberal regime which continually pointed to opposition pressure as it demanded more and more concessions from the prostrate Cisleithanian government and the emperor-king.

The failure to get an Economic Compromise Bill passed in 1898 was a classic instance of Magyar politics at work. In the wake of the Badeni Affair, the Hungarian premier, Baron Dezsö Bánffy, had managed to obtain advantageous terms from a weakened Cisleithanian government. As part of the agreement, though, he and the Cisleithanian finance minister, the Czech, Josef Kaizl, had agreed on the Ischl Clause, which would have solved many of the problems of the Compromise by in effect making the customs union automatically renewable unless either parliament voted it down. In effect this guaranteed the union's continuance, as the emperor-king would have the power to veto any such abrogation. Such a cementation of the Compromise was anathema to Magyar nationalists. The Compromise legislation was therefore stalled by obstruction in parliament, and the Bánffy government fell as a result of it. The subsequent ministry of Kálmán Széll refused the Ischl Clause and negotiations over the Compromise dragged on until 1902. Then, according to Alexander Spitzmüller, it was only the emperor-king's threat of abdication which forced Széll and Koerber to finalise an agreement on New Year's Eve, 1902, which was very advantageous to the Hungarians.[25] Kaizl, meanwhile, after the failure of his attempt to buttress the empire's unity, reacted by adopting a very nationalist, pro-Czech line, stuffing the Finance Ministry with Czech personnel.[26]

By 1902 the struggle over the Economic Compromise had been

joined by an even more heated and nationalistically tinged argument in parliament over the Military Bill of that year, which envisaged an increase in conscription contingents to keep up with population growth. It was one of Koerber's achievements that the Reichsrat had agreed to these modest increases, but only if the Hungarian parliament also agreed to them. In the subsequent Hungarian debate the opposition parties tried once again to chip away at the 'imperialistic' nature of the Joint k.u.k. Army to try and turn the Hungarian regiments of it into a genuinely national, that is to say, Magyar-speaking army. This would involve replacing German by Magyar as the language of command of the Hungarian part of the army. Yet overturning the status of German as the language of command alarmed and angered Francis Joseph, for it threatened the unity of his army. On this point, therefore, despite his many concessions to the Magyar leadership, he would make a stand.[27]

The crisis over the Military Bill led to obstruction in parliament, the fall of Széll's government and eventually a government under Khuen-Héderváry. The formidable former Ban of Croatia nevertheless proved similarly incapable of controlling his fellow Magyars. Then, to clear the air, Francis Joseph declared in his Chlopy Order of 17 September 1903, in language almost calculated to wound Magyar sensitivities, his absolute refusal to countenance the undermining of his prerogative over the army, its unity, or its 'existing organisation' (which implied German as the language of command).[28] The result was a crisis to rival the Badeni Affair in Cisleithania, with obstruction and street riots threatening to overwhelm order.

As before with Badeni, Francis Joseph retreated. István Tisza, son of his former Hungarian prime minister, was appointed by him premier in November 1903 after a fragile compromise was reached between the king and the Magyar political parties. In the summer of 1904 Francis Joseph was even prepared to countenance the Honvéd gaining its own artillery, despite warnings by Koerber on the divisive consequences for the Joint Army.[29] There was a lull. By the autumn of 1904, though, the same battles over the new Military Bill had heated up, and Tisza's dubious passage of anti-obstruction legislation caused yet more obstruction and disorder. Tisza's response was to hold an election in January 1905, perhaps the only 'clean' election in Dualist Hungary's history. The result was a devastating defeat for Tisza's

Liberals, a crushing victory for the Opposition parties, the enemies of Francis Joseph's pride and joy, the Joint Army.[30]

Francis Joseph invited the leaders of the Opposition parties, including Gyula Andrássy, the son of his former Foreign Minister, and Ference Kossuth, the son of his former revolutionary nemesis, to form a government, but their conditions for doing so were unacceptable.[31] In June the king appointed another unmistakably loyal general, Baron Géza Fejérváry as premier at the head of a ministry of officials. The opposition responded by calling for what amounted to passive resistance by the county officials, and a tax strike by 'patriots'. Then Fejérváry's Minister of the Interior, Joseph Kristóffy, already known for his interest in expanding the franchise, countered the Magyar elite's opposition with a proposal to expand the franchise from 7 per cent to 16 per cent of the population.[32]

From today's perspective this might not seem that radical, but it was a devastating threat to the Magyar political elite, for it would have given the vote not only to large portions of the lower classes, but, worse still from the Magyar establishment's perspective, to many non-Magyars. After decades in which he had turned a blind eye to the Magyarisation of Hungary and the neglect and suppression of the other nationalities, at first hesitantly and then after a second stand-off in September decisively, Francis Joseph played the minorities card. The interests of the other nationalities and also of the Magyar lower classes were thus hardly pursued for their own sake, but served as pawns in the battle against the Magyar leadership over what was actually a constitutional question about the nature of the 'imperial-royal' connection, and over his dynastic power.

Almost the entire Magyar political leadership, Tisza included, was outraged and horrified by the prospect of radical electoral reform. Yet this was no longer the Hungary of 1848 or even the 1860s. In an increasingly developed and centralised state such as Hungary had become, the old methods of Magyar resistance proved no longer so powerful against a determined executive. The old county autonomy had been eroded by both the needs of modern local administration, leading to a reliance on investments and expenditures by central authorities, and also the needs of a nationalist policy which wanted power concentrated in the safely Magyar parliament rather than the often only questionably Magyar localities.[33] The imposition of new local executive officials (*Föispáns*) on the counties, and the government's order to stop subsidies to offending counties and suspend the salaries of recalcitrant municipal officials thus brought about the effective collapse of national resistance.[34] Fejérváry had hardly any support from the political class but he had the use of the military and the police, and the *absence* of resistance from large swathes of the non-Magyar population and of the Magyar lower classes. He also, crucially, had Francis Joseph's backing. When he dissolved parliament on 19 February 1906 with the use of troops it seemed a veritable *coup d'état* – the decreeing of radical electoral reform – was next, and unstoppable.[35]

One of the favourite counter-factual speculations of Habsburg historiography is to think what would have happened if Francis Joseph had gone through with his threat and instituted electoral reform in 1906 in Hungary. Perhaps it would have broken Magyar nationalist pretensions and replaced the monolithic chauvinism of the Magyar elite with a more interest-based, more multi-national, and more pliable politics, more suited to remodelling and reinvigorating the Monarchy as a whole; or perhaps, given the subsequent experience of a universal suffrage parliament in Cisleithania, it would not.[36] Yet, again, this is idle speculation, for, when the opposition decided to seek terms of conditional surrender, Francis Joseph stepped back from the brink, and a compromise had soon been struck which satisfied Francis Joseph's minimal demands, and left the Magyar political elite still in power.

In the secret deal the Magyar leaders were, it is true, committed to pass electoral reform, as well as backing off on their constitutional assault on the Dualist settlement, but it was obvious from the start that this meant a far less radical change, and as it turned out it meant hardly any change at all. It just might be that this was Francis Joseph's last best hope of profoundly shifting the structure of power in his Monarchy onto a stable basis. Instead he chose to stick with a sobered but still deeply chauvinistic Magyar leadership, probably because he fancied working with the possible alternative, of Magyar socialists and left-liberals, Slovaks and Rumanians, even less. He did manage to preserve the Monarchy's position and his prerogatives in the army, but at the cost of the future, and at the cost of his own standing as the hope of the large masses without a voice in Hungarian politics. It was for this cynical exploitation – and abandonment – of the ideal of electoral reform for purely dynastic gain that Jászi later accused Francis Joseph of being a central contributor to the 'final moral disintegration' of his Monarchy.[37]

In Hungary the former opposition Coalition won a thumping victory in the May elections, and another Wekerle ministry settled down to more moderate policies towards the Compromise, more chauvinism in education and towards the minority nationalities, and obfuscatory procrastination on the required electoral reform bill. Yet events in Hungary had not gone without leaving their mark on the other half of the Monarchy. As the Cisleithanian premier Gautsch (again) had remarked to the heir-apparent, Francis Ferdinand, in November 1905: 'Every day I hear the argument that the Emperor of Austria cannot prevent what the King of Hungary has promised to provide.'[38] The drive to introduce universal male suffrage did not appear in Cisleithania overnight. The movement for reform had been building for years, with the socialist Social Democrats being prominent protagonists. It was only in October 1905, though, when Francis Joseph heeded the logic of his own policy in Hungary, that electoral reform became not only feasible, but likely.[39] With the emperor's explicit backing, combined with ever-increasing popular demonstrations, and with liberal organs such as the *Neue Freie Presse* obviously boxed in by their own ideological logic, the Reichsrat eventually capitulated to the forces of democracy.

It took over a year to get reform passed, a period for once in which national antagonisms took second place to the momentous change involved. (Although the apportionment of constituencies was the subject of endless national haggling, with the Germans getting more than their demographic numbers, but less than their slice of taxation payments, deserved.) The long campaign offered the surreal spectacle of the ruling member of the world's most traditional dynasty in *de facto* alliance with revolutionary socialism. After both the ministries of Gautsch and Prince Conrad von Hohenlohe had fallen, the ministry of Max Beck, Francis Ferdinand's man, managed to pass an electoral reform which introduced universal male suffrage to Austrian Reichsrat elections. (Provincial diet elections remained on the old, curial franchises.) The reform went into law on 20 January 1907.[40]

Why Francis Joseph supported electoral reform in Cisleithania with such dedication has been a matter of much historiographical speculation, especially given his less than determined support for the same in Hungary. One strong suggestion is that, harking back to his memories of Taaffe's proposals, he thought universal suffrage the only way to solve the national conflict. Perhaps he thought, as Radetzky had thought a half century earlier, only an electorate of the common people, peasants and workers, not besotted like the middle classes with national vanities, could elect a parliament which put loyalty to the empire first; at least they might put supra-national, interest-based issues above national rivalry. More pragmatically, perhaps he thought the electoral threat of mass parties would sober the established political parties sufficiently to make them more amenable to imperial legislative necessities. His apparent unhappiness at the very high number of socialist deputies (87 out of a total of 516 Reichsrat deputies) elected in the May elections of 1907 suggests that the latter caculation was closer to his way of thinking than the former.[41] Even more Machiavellian is the suspicion that he used the Cisleithanian example to pressure the Magyar elite further as to the seriousness of his intent, and to keep them in line even after the deal in 1906. He might also have thought that nothing could be worse than the present Reichsrat. Whatever the reason, it was his personal intervention, in Redlich's opinion, which did more than anything to get universal male suffrage passed. Were this true, it indicates just how powerful the emperor still was in Cisleithanian politics.[42]

It did not do the trick, though. The crisis of 1905 was weathered, it is true, without a revolution, unlike Russia. The Magyar leadership had been brought to heel, more or less, and Cisleithania had gained a democratically elected parliament. Initially this parliament did see a slackening of nationalist extremism, as two of the biggest losers were the Young Czechs and the radical German Nationalists, two of the biggest gainers the Catholic and now 'imperially-loyal' Christian Socials and the internationalist Social Democrats.[43] Yet, with thirty parties represented in the Reichsrat, the chances of cohesive functioning were never high. There was a short period of actually working government, in which Beck ruled through a mainly parliamentary ministry, and was able, for instance, to obtain a relatively favourable economic Compromise agreement from the Hungarians in 1907, at the cost of only some constitutional niceties.[44] The old habits of the Reichsrat soon returned, however, as the new nationally-based mass parties proved just as prone to bare-faced nationalist demagoguery as the older ones. Bohemia continued to be a national battleground, with Karel Kramář, the Young Czech leader, stirring the pot by hosting the Neo-Slav Congress in Prague in July 1908. Meanwhile the fight between Poles and Ruthenians in Galicia broke out anew. The

Bosnian Crisis (see below) riled politics still more and led to Beck's resignation in November 1908.[45]

His successor Baron Richard von Bienerth, another official, did his best to keep the lid on national disputes, now breaking out all over Cisleithania, but Czech obstruction once more led to the use of Article 14, for the first time in six years. The elections of 1911 saw the resurgence of German 'Liberals' and 'Nationalists', now allied in the German National Alliance (which saw Jewish liberal deputies excluded in favour of racially anti-Semitic German nationalists in what remained of the supposedly 'liberal' German Left), the diminution of the ministerial Christian Socials and Polish Club. Although the socialists made gains, even their forces had split on national lines, with a separate Czech faction declaring its independence in 1910.[46] The democratically elected parliament had become even more riven by nationalism than the old.

Bienerth's ministry was followed by yet another Gautsch ministry, and then in November 1911, with Bohemia once more in turmoil, Count Karl Stürgkh became premier. With the international situation by this time becoming ever more threatening, Stürgkh was able to get the Military Bill of 1912 passed. Although this was to prove too little too late (see below), this was a major achievement given the fractiousness of the parliament. National conflicts got even worse, paralysing not only parliament but many of the provincial assemblies as well, above all the Bohemian Diet. As a result the none too subtle Stürgkh government, with Francis Joseph's backing, dissolved the Bohemian Diet in 1913, and by a virtual *coup d'état*, which was seen at the time as the return to pure absolutism, introduced an imperial commission to govern the province. When in March 1914 Czech obstruction to protest against this unconstitutional act brought the Reichsrat to a standstill, Stürgkh dismissed the assembly. When Austria–Hungary declared war in July 1914, Cisleithania was being governed more or less as it had been ruled in the first decade of Francis Joseph's reign, as a bureaucratic dictatorship.[47]

The political system was hardly working any better in Hungary, although with a definitely Hungarian twist. After a lull, in which the economic Compromise was passed, the old antagonisms between the king and the opposition, now government coalition, re-emerged. Wekerle's resignation in April 1909 was followed after another crisis by another Khuen-Héderváry ministry in January 1910.[48] The 1910 elections saw all the stops pulled out for the government side, now represented by a Liberal party reconstituted by István Tisza as the 'Party of Work'. The result was, as in his father's day, a victory delivered by the industry and ingenuity of the government's officials. Khuen remained premier, but Tisza was now the power in the land. Co-operation with the monarch and chauvinist domestic policies remained the leading watchwords of the new Khuen administration. Even so, it fell over the Military Bill of 1912, which called for a large increase of the Habsburg army. The new Lukács ministry saw Tisza step from the shadows as President of the Lower House, determined to put an end to the turmoil, and independence, of the Hungarian parliament.

He countered the obstruction of the opposition parties by having new, restrictive parliamentary procedures passed. It was with an iron grip on the parliament, and a large majority for his party, that Tisza succeeded in getting the Military Bill of 1912 passed.[49] At one point, when Kossuthist deputies started a disturbance in the chamber, Tisza had the police eject them. On 23 May 1912, 'Bloody Thursday', he sent in the army to disperse demonstrators and protesting deputies outside the parliament building.[50] Tisza was now virtual dictator of Hungary, managing the country through a 'parliamentary absolutism' which was though – like the Cisleithanian 'bureaucratic absolutist' variant – in the service of, and dependent on, Francis Joseph. On the last day of 1912 Tisza presented to parliament an electoral reform bill, pre-sanctioned by Francis Joseph, which did hardly anything to expand the franchise. The pact between monarch and premier had been made, which continued to 1914 and beyond. As long as Tisza could deliver the votes and moneys of the parliament, Francis Joseph, the 'absentee landlord', would continue to accept the Magyar hegemony which Tisza had made it his life's work to preserve.

By 1914 Cisleithanian government had reverted to a form of absolutism as every palliative had proved unable to mask the symptoms of conflict and deadlock caused by the national problem. By 1914 Hungary was being ruled as a parliamentary absolutism, by a narrow nationalist clique with the assent of the monarch and with the increasingly wide dissent of its disenfranchised and oppressed minority nationalities and lower classes. The basic disparity within the Dual Monarchy had reached hyperbolic proportions, and though it still left Francis Joseph in charge, it was a situation with huge drawbacks for the efficient functioning of the state, and hence of the army and foreign policy which remained his chief interests. By 1914 the adventures of universal suffrage had merely given a fresh overlay to a system which was malfunctioning, and badly in need of rethinking, radical change, but this was just what a now eighty-four-year-old emperor was no longer capable of providing.

. . . .

THE EMPEROR, HIS EMPIRE AND HIS PEOPLES IN 1914

Bismarck is said to have told William I of Prussia at one point in the constitutional crisis of the early 1860s that 'the situation is serious but not desperate'. Karl Kraus, the leading satirist and gadfly of turn-of-the-century Vienna, is said to have described the situation in Austria as 'desperate . . . but not serious'. The above account of politics in Austria–Hungary leading up to 1914 has painted a fairly bleak, desperate, even hopeless picture, of two political systems falling apart at the seams, and falling out with each other, held together by the most tenuous sort of authority, main force and a lack of feasible alternatives.

And yet we might well ask actually how serious this political chaos and national bickering was. After all, the Monarchy was far from being alone in having suffered large-scale disruption of its political machinery. France had survived the Dreyfus Affair, Germany had just experienced the Zabern Crisis and was, by many estimates, in a state of social turmoil. Russia had already had one revolution in 1905 and was similarly unruly by 1914. Even Britain, for all of its vaunted parliamentarism, had just emerged from an extended constitutional crisis concerning the powers of its House of Lords and had perpetual problems with Ireland. By 1914 Britain and France had overcome much of their instability, it is true, but then could not Austria–Hungary have similarly come through its crisis; indeed was it not doing precisely this when, by unlucky fate, the First World War blew up in its face?

This, at least, is the question raised by much of the recent literature on the Habsburg Monarchy and its survivability. Works such as Alan Sked's *Decline and Fall of the Habsburg Empire* point out just how positive many aspects of the Monarchy were by 1914, despite the political noise. Much like post-Second World War Italy, the economy was doing very well despite or almost because of the political shenanigans in Vienna and Budapest. (Low military expenditures left more money for politically determined, but not necessarily unproductive, investments.) It had fallen behind the more developed Western European economies early in the nineteenth century but by 1914 was growing faster than the British economy and was catching up with many others. Moreover, the customs union of the two halves of the Dual Monarchy was spreading the benefits of prosperity to the more backward eastern and southern peripheries, providing a greater degree of economic integration than then present in the United States.[51] While the industrially developed lands of Bohemia and the Vienna area could rival the Western industrialised areas, the general level of prosperity and development was well ahead of any of the lands to the Monarchy's south and east. Economically, the Habsburg Monarchy was a success story.

It was also the scene of a fabulous cultural flowering, recently recognised with enthusiasm in Western Europe and America. This was the world of *fin-de-siècle Vienna, Budapest 1900,* and *Kafka's Prague.* Any society which could produce Sigmund Freud, Gustav Mahler, Otto Wagner, Adolf Loos, George Lukács, Karl Mannheim, Franz Kafka and Ludwig Wittgenstein cannot have been entirely without merit. It is true that much of this cultural brilliance was directed against the society from which it sprang, was indeed a devastating critique of it. It is also true that a very large number of the leading cultural and intellectual figures were of a Jewish emancipatory background, which provided its own encouragement to intellectual achievement; furthermore much of their creativity was spurred by the 'pressure-cooker' of the anti-Semitic atmosphere prevalent in Vienna, as well as, to some extent, in Prague and Budapest. All this proves, however, is that there were positive aspects to the Monarchy's political and social problems when it came to cultural production.[52]

Ironically, the nationality conflict itself was a major contributor to the relatively high level of intellectual and cultural activity in the empire, for two of the main fora of national competition had been education and culture. It had been universities and schools which had been among the major vehicles and prizes of the political game. Although the main aim might have been national advantage, the net side-effect was a heightened cultural level all round. The Czech nationalist drive had especially spectacular educational benefits in the form of a well-educated populace and blossoming intelligentsia.[53]

The state itself played a significant role in this culture-enhancing national competition, either in the case of Cisleithania by trying to buy off and placate the nationalities with generous educational and cultural budgets shared out with an eye to national equity, or in the Hungarian case by lavishing large sums on further-ing the national (Magyar) culture. Magyarisation had, indeed, the ironic result that much more was invested in (Magyar-teaching) educational institutions in the only marginally Magyar peripheries than in the solidly Magyar centre, to the disadvantage of the Magyar peasantry.[54]

Above all, the state authorities maintained a state of law. The politics of both Cisleithania and Hungary was marked by frequent political disturbances, by the occasional imposition of states of emergency in the various provinces, and by abuses of the law by the Hungarian authorities when it came to the national minori-ties. Yet overall the authorities kept the peace and even if the Hungarian legal system never fully acknowledged the legal rights of the individual with regard to the state apparatus or achieved the full separation of the judicial and administrative systems, the Cisleithanian court system did, more or less.[55] Officially there was in Cisleithania full separation of administration and judiciary, and there was judicial review, even if its procedures were never statutorily regulated (until 1926) and the officialdom tended to disregard many of the decisions of the *Reichsgericht* or *Verwaltungs-gerichtshof.*[56] The effect was the appearance of legality. Although doubtless strongly tinged by nostalgia, Stefan Zweig's descrip-tion of this era as the 'age of security' was understandable, given subsequent events.[57]

The state authorities in Cisleithania also did much to protect national minorities and ensure the equal rights of the citizenry when it came to education, culture and language use. The records of the two supreme courts show a fairly honest effort to follow the guarantees of national equality embodied in the 1867 constitu-tion, even if the results hardly ever satisfied anyone.[58] The efforts of the various *Beamtenministerien* to effect national compromise also bore fruit in some cases. In Moravia in 1905 and in the Buk-ovina in 1910 the national feuding, between Germans and Czechs in the former, and Ruthenes, Rumanians, Germans, Jews, Poles and Hungarians in the latter, was settled by agreements to divide up the political system into national curiae. Another national 'Compromise' had been worked out by 1914 in Galicia between Poles and Ruthenes, although it was never implemented. Neither Moravia nor Bukovina were central theatres of the nationality struggle, and all of these 'settlements' were *ad hoc* solutions to local nationality conflicts following no set pattern. That settlements could be found at all was, however, some encouragement and at least shows the authorities' interest in calming the national turmoil.[59]

It is in the light of such developments that Crankshaw could assert that by 1914 'outside Hungary things were going very well', a view which is shared, perhaps surprisingly, by Jászi.[60] Even in the Hungarian half it can be argued that there was an improving climate. The huge crisis in Croatia, in which the constitution had been suspended in 1912, resulted by early 1914 in a settlement between the Hungarians and the Serbo-Croatian opposition.[61] It is possible, therefore, to argue as Sked does that the nationality problem was 'abating' by the eve of war in 1914.[62]

It is also possible to argue that, regardless of the immense discontent of the various national groups within the empire, there was hardly any serious contemplation before 1914, indeed until shortly before the end of the war, of these national groups seeking for solutions outside the parameters of the Habsburg Monarchy. Sked's survey of the various national conflicts does not deny that there were huge problems; it simply points out that none of them really threatened to break the Monarchy apart by themselves. The Magyars might oppress all other Hungarian minorities, but there was no overwhelming threat from the minorities to Magyar hegemony. In Cisleithania there was relative equity, the Italians were well treated as were the Poles. The Czechs were discontented but working within the politics of the Monarchy. Even Kramář, whose Neo-Slavism looked to Russia for support, is quoted as saying, after Francis Ferdinand's assassination, that the Czechs 'lean in no direction outside the empire'.[63] Therefore, Sked argues, nationalism was not a threat to the integrity of the Monarchy.[64]

The problem with such an entertainingly prestidigitatious presentation, as with all those arguments asserting a rosy scenario for the Habsburg Monarchy in 1914, is that it is far too reminiscent of the curate's answer to the bishop about his rotten egg: 'good in parts'. Behind the apparent strengths of the Monarchy there were huge, debilitating, real problems. There is also a large difference between public pronouncements and private beliefs. What Kramář really thought in 1914 about the Czech problem is hardly going to be revealed by a public statement. In contrast there is evidence that his far more moderate counterpart, Thomas Masaryk, thought that the Monarchy was doomed as early as 1910, or so he reportedly confided to his friend Henry Wickham Steed.[65] As Solomon Wank points out, given the international situation and the readiness of the imperial authorities to use military force internally, seeking solutions outside the Monarchy was unrealistic before 1914 for the national leaderships. Yet the long-term goals of many nationalists often pointed to extra-imperial solutions. The Czechs persisted in seeking international recognition for themselves as a nation, not under Austrian auspices. Hence the appearance of a Czech team at the Olympics of 1908 under the banner 'Bohème' and with their own red–white flag.[66]

Other nations within the empire also clearly had long-term plans beyond the Monarchy. The Polish leadership never made any secret of the fact that their long-term aim was to be part of an independent Polish nation-state. The Magyars were clearly dissatisfied with their status in 1914; pro-Russian sentiment among the Ruthenes was considerable by that year; irredentism among Austrian Italians was causing trouble if only in foreign policy (as it was with Transylvanian Rumanians); in the South Slav lands, as we shall see, Croats and Serbs had been so mishandled as to band together and make demands for a trialist revision of the empire and for some of them even to look to triumphant Serbia as a focus of national pride. None of these movements singly were a direct cause of the war and the empire's eventual break-up, but cumulatively they hardly allow the rosy scenario adumbrated above. Even if some of these problems might have been abating, this was only relatively – from dire to critical – and there is no guarantee that they would not have flared up again. Moreover, by 1914 the national and constitutional conflicts of the last decades had done their work.

In 1907 Count Franz Conrad von Hötzendorf, the Chief of the General Staff, had argued that the Austrians need not attend the Second Hague Conference on Disarmament as the Habsburg power found itself in a state of permanent disarmament.[67] He had a point. Until 1912 the wranglings and conflicts of Austro-Hungarian politics absorbed most of the attention and resources of the imperial authorities and this left the military budget hamstrung by the Compromise hagglings while the other great powers steadily built up and modernised their armed forces. In 1912 the threatening external situation of the Monarchy became so apparent that both the Hungarian and Cisleithanian parliaments acted to increase the size of the standing army by 22 per cent (from 405,120 to 494,120). Even then the War Minister,

General Moritz Auffenberg, was still not able to get all the budget increases approved which were necessary to cover the army's expansion in the context of repeated mobilisations during 1912–13. The supplements were to be doled out only in instalments, with the second instalment deferred until 1914. The old problem of financing somebody else's army meant that by 1914 Austria–Hungary was still woefully behind the other great powers in terms of military personnel and *matériel.*[68]

In other words the national (and constitutional) conflicts within the Monarchy were absolutely central not so much to tearing the Monarchy apart but to undermining its very *raison d'être* as far as Francis Joseph was concerned: having a powerful enough army to be a real player in the 'great game' of the European great powers. One could argue therefore that the nationality conflicts were indeed the main force which brought about the Monarchy's decline – *relative to the rest of Europe's great powers* – and that their main victim was, as the embodiment of the dynastic empire, Francis Joseph. This is in effect what one of the most popular presentations of the emperor in his final years would like to suggest, the old man, beset by wicked fate, betrayed by feuding nationalities, nobly soldiering on as the last remaining link of an empire which would fall apart as soon as he left the saddle of command. Such views, that he was the only thing left holding his empire together, seem to have been widespread at the time (voiced at times even by the emperor himself[69]), and go a long way to explaining his popularity among his subjects. Francis Joseph might be a bit doddery, hostile to change, but he was better than the rather terrifying prospect of Francis Ferdinand, or the inevitable crisis which would ensue were the empire to split apart in whichever way it might, and fall prey to Pan-Germanism or Pan-Slavism, or whichever threat suited one's national paranoia.

The problem with this rather endearing image of the old emperor as the last remaining hope of supra-national reason in a sea of nationalist enmity was that he himself, as ruler of the empire for over sixty years, had had as large a role as any in bringing this rather sorry state of affairs about. He was not so much a victim, let alone part of the solution, as one of the main causes of the problem. Indeed the very fact that the empire seemed to depend on Francis Joseph's personal survival for its continuation was a measure of the emperor's failure as a dynast, let alone a head of state. A successful dynast or head of state would leave behind a workable governmental system, which could function regardless of the personality of the successor. Yet this is precisely what Francis Joseph neglected to bequeath.

For years he kept Francis Ferdinand out of any positions of responsibility and then when the heir did start to assert himself from 1906 Francis Joseph only grudgingly relinquished some powers and refused to cede anything of real substance. Moreover he never thought to transfer any more power to the representative assemblies and governments of his empire and kingdom. Crankshaw speculates that by 1914 Francis Joseph was 'much closer to a president than to an autocrat, and he knew it', and if only he had been a little younger and fitter would soon have transformed himself into a truly constitutional monarch.[70] This is very wide of the mark. Francis Joseph still thought of himself as emperor by divine grace, and still thought of his empire as, well – his. It was the persistence of this essentially authoritarian way of thinking which marked his whole career, and it was the persistence of this hierarchical, top-down – imperial – structure of authority which was at the root of the Monarchy's problems in 1914.

By 1914 the dominant political form in both halves of the empire was of state bureaucracy, power from the top down. Hungary had its own national bureaucracy responsible to parliament, and it had the vestiges of county local autonomy. Yet the former had largely been adapted from the Bachian imperial model, and Tisza's 'parliamentary absolutism' left the bureaucracy large powers; as for the counties, the imperatives of Magyar nationalist centralism, combined with the centralising forces of infrastructural modernisation, had led to a sharp diminution of local independence, as dramatically illustrated by the 1905–6 crisis.[71] In Cisleithania the old, imperial bureaucracy had never gone away. The Compromise of 1867 had merely limited the scope of the bureaucracy (excluding it from Hungary) rather than changed its structure.[72] The liberal era had seen substantial reform but this had only marginally affected the bureaucracy's culture, which remained that of an *Obrigkeitsstaat*, authoritarian state.

Many observers were strongly critical of the still overbearing nature of the Habsburg state in pre-war Cisleithania. Most trenchant perhaps was Henry Wickham Steed, who contrasted the Austrian officialdom with the British Civil Service. In Britain, contended Steed, the civil servants were there to serve the people; by contrast in Cisleithania the prevailing attitude among the bureaucracy (and among the populace) appeared to be that the people were there for the state, rather than the state for the people:

'the people . . . is there to be governed'.[73] He was further horrified by the arcane Byzantinism of Habsburg officialdom's
procedures. He conveys something of his horror by simply list-
ing the various procedures through which each document had
to go at each stage of the Austrian bureaucratic process: it was
'präsentiert, exhibiert, indiziert, prioriert, konzipiert, revidiert,
approbiert, mundiert, kollationiert, expediert, and registriert'.
The Vatican, in his opinion, was far swifter.[74]

Living in a bureaucratic age, we might not see this as a
characteristic unique to the Habsburg state, but Cisleithania does
seem to have been particularly 'bureaucratic' even among
continental states, and moreover inefficiently so. This was, as
Waltraud Heindl has pointed out, the state in which Kafka grew
up, and it appears that, while much more honest and efficient
than officialdoms in states to the south and east, the Habsburg
imperial bureaucracy was slipping back into the ossified state of
petty corruption and large inefficiency from which the reforms
of the liberal era had momentarily rescued it.[75] This was yet
another of the bad effects of the collapse of properly representative government, for the sort of resistance to reform innate in
large, bureaucratic organisations was quite insuperable when the
organisation was in effect not answerable to a parliament in too
much disarray to exert control and when the bureaucrat-in-
chief, Francis Joseph, was far too old even to want radical change,
let alone capable of pushing it through.

Steed indeed describes an officialdom which was largely out
of even the emperor's control. Resistance to change and solidarity among officials were summed up by Steed in the phrase
'Justament nöt!', the closing of ranks, the collective resistance
of the officialdom to doing anything which harmed one of their
number.[76] In Steed's opinion the bureaucracy had, by 1914,
become the Habsburg Monarchy's main problem, absorbing a
third of the public revenues and threatening to become 'a class
of privileged drones and educated paupers'.[77] No doubt much
of this is English liberal alarmism at the development of the
modern, technocratic and bureaucratic state. Yet the expansion
of the Habsburg state bureaucracy had been exponential in the
last decades. Employing 80,000 officials in 1870, the central Habsburg state authorities were employing 400,000 by 1910.[78] In
Hungary, the number of state officials in 1870 was just over 23,000.
By 1902 it was nearing 100,000; by 1918 it was to be just under

230,000, a tenfold increase over half a century.[79] Steed's accusations about 'bureaucratism' are made at least partially understandable by such figures.[80]

The hierarchical, bureaucratic nature of Francis Joseph's state has been blamed for several adverse effects on the political culture of the populace. Steed, like so many of his Edwardian contemporaries, saw the Habsburg Monarchy as lacking the sense of individual freedom prevalent in British and American culture, leaving the population politically immature and always looking to government for protection and problem-solving.[81] On the other hand, the top-down structure of power meant that there was precious little identification, trust or loyalty between the government and those governed. Even local and provincial government did not elicit much trust as the restrictive curial franchises meant that the bulk of the population had little if any say in how they were ruled.[82] In such circumstances loyalty to another abstraction, such as the nation, could flourish as a counterweight to an alien, all-imposing state apparatus.

As Jászi commented, the relative lack of civic experience, of self-government on the local level, and the retention, even aggregating of power by the imperial authorities, further meant that any chance there might have been for practical experience of international co-operation on a local level was also missed. If the failure of parliamentary government in Vienna and its replacement by 'bureaucratic absolutism' prevented national co-operation at the state level, the bureaucratic nature of most of local government ensured a lack of national co-operation on the local level as well. While the bureaucracy saw themselves as keeping the empire together, in a sense they also made sure that the peoples of that empire would never get together to solve their problems on their own.[83]

If Francis Joseph's Habsburg state, by its bureaucratic, hierarchical paternalism thus indirectly discouraged any collaboration among the nationalities, it in turn was adversely affected by the nationality conflict in a number of ways. One of these was external. At the communal level the exigencies of modernisation, the expansion of government competences (which came to embrace such fields as the nationalised railway system) and administrative specialisation led to a centralisation of power in much of the Monarchy, with effective power shifting from the autonomous communal councils to the central state's representative, the ubiquitous *Bezirkshauptmann,* and from him to the central agencies, the ultimate source of the necessary resources, power and expertise.[84] Set against this tendency to 'administrative centralism', however, was a countertrend, particularly evident in the larger cities and at the provincial, crown land level, of the emergence of proto-national bureaucracies.

Taking advantage of the 'dual-track' nature of Austrian administration and the constitutional space created for local autonomy by the Liberals in the 1860s, the autonomous administrations of the major cities (particularly Vienna and Prague) and above all of the various provincial commissions (*Landesausschüsse*), which paralleled the centralised state bureaucracy, greatly expanded their areas of competence and their personnel in the last decades of the Monarchy. The alternative bureaucratic empires thus created provided rival power centres to the Habsburg authorities.[85] These could be used as bases from which to launch an assault on the imperial political scene in general, as in the case of Karl Lueger's Christian Social takeover of Vienna and Lower Austria and the resultant Christian Social '*Reichspartei*'.[86] Elsewhere, though, they could be used as the vehicle of nationalist politics. In Bohemia, for instance, the provincial administration was almost entirely staffed by Czechs by 1914. Whereas the imperial 'k.k.' officials were to remain highly loyal to the empire right up until the end, those in the provincial autonomous administrations very quickly looked to local loyalties at the first sign that the Monarchy was splitting apart.[87]

The other effect was internal. The sort of national horse-trading which had come to maturity under Taaffe's Iron Ring had from the start been about one of the most important forms of power in the Habsburg Monarchy: bureaucratic jobs. If the uniformity of the Habsburg officialdom had initially been marred by national diversification at the local levels of government, the centralised nature of real power in Cisleithania meant that eventually what was at stake in the nationality conflicts which paralysed the Reichsrat for decade after decade was which nationality got what jobs not only in the provincial but also the central government. Under Taaffe, but more strongly under Koerber, even jobs in the Viennese ministries were bargained away for political favours, so that what had been a uniformly German-speaking central administration increasingly became a divided, polyglot reflection of the general Cisleithanian political landscape. Like so many Trojan horses, national bureaucracies began to develop within the imperial, supposedly supra-national bureaucracy, often to the dismay of the old, supra-national *and* German-speaking official caste.[88] A two-tier structure developed in the imperial bureaucracy with Germans largely at the top, the lower levels increasingly dominated by the various nationalities, especially the Czechs. The old, German officialdom still had a hold on the higher reaches of the bureaucracy, but even at the centre in Vienna it was slipping. By 1914 almost a quarter of state officials in Vienna were non-German.[89]

There was an ironic moral in this as far as Steed was concerned. Referring to the policies of the Iron Ring, he was to write that Francis Joseph's

> object was to neutralise German influence in Austria by developing the power of the Czechs and other Slavs who were gradually given universities, high schools and other educational facilities that would entitle them to a greater share in the civil services. Once again, Francis Joseph failed to perceive that these concessions might cut both ways, that they would bring the spirit, if not the principle, of nationality into the very heart of his Administration, and that what had been a comparatively homogeneous Habsburg bureaucracy would become a training ground for Czech, Polish and other Slav officials whose devotion to their own races might one day prove to be greater than their devotion to the Habsburg State.

Francis Joseph's solution to the constitutional challenge of the German Liberals in 1879, in other words, was seen by Steed as the beginning of the end of the uniform Habsburg officialdom, and by implication of the Habsburg state.[90]

This sort of creeping invasion and disaggregation of the central Habsburg bureaucracy by the nationalities might well have been avoided, or not have had the divisive effects that it did, if the Habsburg Monarchy had been successfully reformed on federalist lines, or at least those that took account of the nationality problem. There were many published suggestions as to how this could be brought about, one of the most famous being that of the Austromarxist Karl Renner, and his system of personal autonomy, where national identity became a matter of personal choice and nationalism a matter of culture rather than politics.[91] The federal restructuring of the empire, despite its own set of demarcationary problems, was the most likely way towards some sort of reconciliation between the nationalities' aspirations and the fact and desirability of the Habsburg Monarchy's continued existence. Such federalist decentralisations of empires have a very mixed record and it is unclear, given the depth of national rivalries, whether even federalism would have produced a workable solution. Yet such an outcome was imaginable. As Jászi, echoing Fischhof, was to point out, a progressive federal Monarchy, with a prospering economy, a relatively efficient and law-abiding bureaucracy, in which each nation could feel its rights protected, would have been an almost irresistible magnet of attraction to the various emergent states of the Balkans, just as the European Union is to the Central and Eastern European states of the present day.[92] This would not only have made the Monarchy viable, but it would also have made it a real 'European necessity', as it always pretended to be, and a real power on the European stage.

All such speculation is, however, idle, for it ignores the realities both of the dualist Compromise and even more significantly of the sort of state – an empire – Francis Joseph thought he was ruling. Federalism, or even the much more limited solution to the South Slav problem of 'trialism', was not feasible given the veto of the Hungarian leadership under dualism. Federalism, even in Cisleithania alone, would have challenged Hungary's status as an equal partner in the Monarchy. Trialism, whereby the South Slav lands in both parts of the Monarchy with Bosnia–Herzegovina added would have formed a third equal partner alongside Cisleithania and Hungary, was quite out of the question for Hungarians as it would have attacked the integrity of the Lands of the Crown of St Stephen (which included Croatia-Slavonia). Given the Austrian Germans' disdain for federalism in the first place, the German-Magyar phalanx against it – or even trialism – was probably insuperable. If one then adds the pressure from Berlin against any weakening of the German or Hungarian, or strengthening of the Slav, position within the Monarchy, then any such attempts to decentralise, 'de-imperialise' power in the Habsburg state were near enough doomed in any case.

Despite this, if there had been a ruler with sufficient will and wiles, federalism was no more extreme a measure than universal male suffrage, and something might yet have been achieved by appealing to the other nationalities and other forces in Habsburg society, if the monarch had wished. Yet Francis Joseph did not so wish. In reply to one proposal of imperial reform the aged emperor is said to have replied: 'En théorie, en théorie, peut-être; mais, en pratique, il faut avoir été Empereur soixante ans.'[93] He was partly right. By the last decade of his reign no one else had more knowledge or more sense for the affairs of his Monarchy than the emperor himself. This allowed him to see some things very clearly. In 1904 he confided to Margutti: 'The Monarchy is not an artificial creation but an organic body. It is a place of refuge, an asylum for all those fragmented nations scattered over central Europe who, if left to their own resources would lead a pitiful existence, becoming the plaything of more powerful neighbours.'[94] Francis Joseph had thus learnt something in sixty years.

The problem was that he also brought with him the preconceptions of sixty years ago. Along with sixty years of experience went the baggage of a view of monarchy and empire not even fit for the mid-nineteenth century let alone the early twentieth. The moral of his depiction of the Monarchy as home to the small nations of Central Europe was that *they* should therefore be grateful for being in *his* empire, be happy to be ruled by his dynasty and thus do his bidding. The emperor-king was perhaps more aware than he had been of the role of his Monarchy as a multinational state, yet his priority remained what it had always been, to use the resources of his empire to maintain the imperial prestige and power of the dynasty. For him the Habsburg Monarchy could never be merely a 'big Switzerland'; it remained a matter of *Hausmacht* first and foremost.

Ultimately it is difficult to dispute those of his biographers who stress the way in which Francis Joseph regarded the nationality problem more as an opportunity for power than as a problem to solve. He was guided by what Steed called the 'exalted opportunism' of the Habsburg tradition, which always put dynastic advantage first, often to the detriment of national understanding, if the latter worked against imperial power. Within the imperial-dynastic frame, therefore, as we have seen, the nationalities question became a Machiavellian game of 'protection' and back-stabbing. As Steed put it cynically: 'An Austrian people need never despair as long as it can find means, in case of need, to frighten the Government. The impotent, or those for whom the State has "no use", are alone in a hopeless position.'[95] Yet this Baroque Hobbesianism was unlikely to foster workable long-term solutions.

The national question was, if not 'natural', at least inevitable given the Monarchy's composition and the forces making for nationalism in the nineteenth century. Yet, as Jászi argues, it need

not have been insoluble, if those forces could have been chan-
nelled productively (for instance on a federalist model):

> The real evil which shattered the intellectual and moral forces
> of the monarchy was the fact that this very natural process
> was undirected, the growing national forces were uncana-
> lised by any statesmanlike conception, either in internal or
> external policy. With the exception of Kremsier and the
> Hohenwart experiment the national problem was never
> treated as the most fundamental problem of Austria but only
> as a matter of tactics. The chief political task never was how,
> out of the decaying feudal castle a comfortable, modern
> house could be created for all the peoples of Austria but
> rather how this unhygienic slum could be further rented
> with the help of superficial and cheap alterations.[96]

If Jászi is right, then a major culprit in the Monarchy's inability
to change from a vehicle of power interests to a refuge for the
nations of Central Europe has to be the man who ruled it for
over half a century as an empire, as a base for dynastic ends. If
the Habsburg Monarchy was a botched state, much of the reason
for that has to be put at Francis Joseph's door, because of his
persistence in pursuing dynastic-imperial ends in a multi-
national state.

Whether Francis Joseph was a 'slum landlord' or Steed's slightly
kinder 'absentee landlord' by 1914 it was rather late to start changing things, and it was quite unclear whether the only likely alternative was any more attractive. Francis Ferdinand, Francis Joseph's
nephew and heir, was much more feared than loved by the
populace. In retrospect some historians have come to see him,
despite his militarism and reactionary conservatism, as a force
for both peace and reform within the Monarchy. It is unknown
what would have happened if he had ascended the throne,
whether his espousal of radical reform along the lines of a form
of federal absolutism would ever have taken place given vehement Hungarian opposition. Even if it had, it is far from clear
that it would have improved the chances for the Monarchy's
eventual survival; conversely, success on Francis Ferdinand's part
might well have led to a further curtailing of political freedom
in the Monarchy.[97]

From 1906 he was given some say in government and those in
his Belvedere circle increasingly predominated in the higher circles

of government, among them Aehrenthal, Conrad von Hötzendorf and Max Vladimir Beck. Yet relations between Belvedere and Schönbrunn were never warm, partly due to Francis Joseph's high dudgeon at Francis Ferdinand's marriage to Sophie Chotek, a mere high noblewoman, and thus not fit by imperial rules to be the empress. (The morganatic marriage was only allowed by Francis Joseph after Francis Ferdinand renounced all rights to the throne of his children by it.) Moreover Francis Ferdinand's brand of radical conservatism was not one with which the aged, now traditionalist, emperor much sympathised. Therefore the emperor continued to keep his heir out of positions of real power; when Belvedere nominees became members of the government they became the emperor's men, obeying his, and not the heir's command. Beck, originally a Belvedere man, came eventually to adopt policies so at variance with Francis Ferdinand's views that the latter's intriguing contributed to Beck's downfall as premier.[98] The heir-apparent was thus not without some power, especially on an informal level, but Francis Joseph was still, despite his years, at the helm of government.

Yet he was by 1914 almost purely a force of inertia. His isolation from the real world, already encouraged by the nature of the Court and the structure of government, had only increased with the frailty of age. In 1913 the Austrian-German writer, Joseph Baernreither, noted:

A wall of prejudices cuts the emperor off from all independent-thinking political personalities. Not only every atmospheric but also any fresh political draft is kept from him by the ring of courtiers, military and medical personnel which surrounds the monarch. The powerfully surging life of our times barely reaches the ear of our emperor as distant rustling. He is kept from any real participation in this life. He no longer understands the times, and the times pass on regardless.[99]

At a time when reform seemed more urgent than ever the man who still ruled was too isolated, too old, too tired, to listen. Margutti reports that he simply would not allow the words 'Trialism' or 'Federalism' spoken in his presence.[100] With his empire in flux the emperor was becoming ossified and out of touch, unable to provide the energetic leadership needed to solve the Monarchy's internal problems, unwilling to give others the chance.

He himself knew that he was an 'anachronism'. When he met

Theodore Roosevelt in 1910 he described himself as 'the last monarch of the old school'.[101] The problem was that he had never been that good at learning the lessons even of the old school, and he did not understand the lessons of the new. Take his statement, quoted above, from 1912: 'I don't want war. I have always been unlucky in wars. We would win, but lose provinces.' This shows admirable love of peace, but it is also the talk of an old-fashioned imperial dynast, worried about losing provinces rather than resources or population. Moreover, he had still not understood, apparently, that loss of provinces was not the worst outcome. A far greater problem for his Monarchy, which was ostensibly run on lines of representative government and national equality, was the acquisition of yet more provinces, which would mean more of the 'wrong sort' of people, especially South Slavs, something completely unacceptable to Germans and Magyars alike. If he still considered his Monarchy an empire, then Bosnia–Herzegovina had been his one imperial acquisition. It had caused immense trouble when it was occupied in 1878 and had continued since to be a thorn in the side of the Dualist Compromise. It is fitting that it was the South Slav question, and events in and around Bosnia, which was to start the war which destroyed the empire.

· · ·

THE OTHER FOOT

In 1888, Crown Prince Rudolph had anonymously warned his father about the dangers of Balkan expansion: 'You have put one foot forward into the Balkans; that is putting one foot into the grave, which your supposed friend [Bismarck] has dug for you.'[102] Austrian foreign policy after 1897 was to prove Rudolph's intuition all too right.

The dilemma facing the Habsburg Monarchy and its ruler had been put succinctly as far back as the crisis over the occupation of Bosnia–Herzegovina itself, by another anonymous work, published in 1880: after the relegation from real great-power status due to thirty years of mismanagement, the imperial authorities could either withdraw Austria–Hungary from 'great-power manoeuvres' and concentrate on financial and economic recovery, or uphold Habsburg prestige and great-power status and forfeit any such recovery.[103] In effect, Francis Joseph, the ruler, never made this choice, at once adopting a pacifism induced by budget and internal political constraints and yet striving to maintain the Habsburgs' prestige as a great power. This refusal to choose between domestic recovery and external status had the direst consequences when faced with a situation which showed similar resistance to being defined as either a domestic or foreign policy matter: the South Slav question. It was, as Rudolph had predicted, in the Balkans that Francis Joseph put the other Austro-Hungarian foot in the grave.

As has been gamely argued by many, if the Habsburg Monarchy had simply had domestic discord to deal with, it might well have survived. One might even claim that, had its foreign policy not been affected by domestic concerns, its role as 'European necessity' would have preserved it.[104] Yet to think that foreign and domestic policy in the Monarchy could actually have been separated in this way shows a deep misunderstanding of the Habsburg state and especially of the mindset of its ruler. As Samuel Williamson has put it, the Monarchy was a special case, for 'foreign policy provided the essential *raison d'être* of the Dual Monarchy'.[105] To his credit, Alan Sked, who might at times appear to think the Monarchy 'viable' in 1914, is nevertheless quite clear in his view that the link between foreign and domestic policy, embodied in Francis Joseph, ultimately caused the empire's demise. It did so, in his opinion, because Francis Joseph could not allow the prestige of the Monarchy, its honour, to be impugned by Serbs. It was thus the *perception* of the South Slav question, foreign and domestic, seen through the prism of Habsburg imperial tradition, which caused Austria to go to war in July 1914.[106]

In some ways the cause of the First World War, as it relates to the Habsburg Monarchy, tragically revisited the Habsburg problems with Lombardy–Venetia and Piedmont in the 1850s. Not only was the existence of the Monarchy linked to foreign policy by its status as 'European necessity' and Central European 'refuge', but foreign and domestic policy were inextricably interwined due to the position of the South Slavs under dualism, and the position of the Monarchy in the Balkans; and what linked them so fatally was the irredentist relation between Serbia and the Monarchy's South Slavs: Serbs but also Croats and even Slovenes. It was not internal dissension which was Austria–Hungary's terminal problem, but rather irredentism – of Italians, Ruthenes, Rumanians, but above all South Slavs.[107] It was the status of Serbia as the Piedmont of the Balkans which exacerbated Austrian policy enough to start a world war.

That said, it took special circumstances for Austrian fears about the South Slav and Serbian threat to lead to a declaration of war. The period from 1897 to 1908 shows that there was no necessary connection between the Monarchy's internal dissension and a hostile foreign policy. Indeed, precisely because these years saw the Monarchy prostrated by the national and constitutional conflicts in both its halves, there was little or no incentive for the Monarchy to take an aggressive posture – as long as the other great power most directly concerned in the Balkans, Russia, was prepared to be co-operative. Fortunately for the Monarchy, the Russians were concentrating during this time on expansion in the Far East and were indeed willing to join with the Austrians in putting the Balkans on ice. Co-operation in preserving the status quo was the policy followed by Goluchowski and his Russian counterparts, for instance in the Mürzsteg agreement of 1903 on Macedonia.[108] The *entente* was always regarded by the Polish Goluchowski more as a way of preserving the Austrian position against Russian inroads, rather than the basis of a more positive alliance as Russophiles such as the ambassador to Russia, Baron Lexa von Aehrenthal, would have liked, yet it served Austrian interests pretty well, at least until 1906.[109]

Even while the *rapprochement* with Russia kept the Austrian external position in the Balkans fairly secure, the problem of the South Slavs within the Monarchy was taking a turn, or many turns, for the worse. The salient problem at this time was the Magyar mishandling of the Croats, which was exacerbated by the split of the Habsburg South Slavs between Cisleithanian provinces (such as Istria and Dalmatia) and the 'Hungarian' Kingdom of Croatia. The Croats had traditionally been among the most loyal of Francis Joseph's subjects. Despite their abandonment by the emperor-king in the 1867 Compromise the Croats retained a great fund of loyalty to the Habsburgs, if nothing else on the principle that my enemy's enemy is my friend. Francis Joseph did very little to repay this loyalty, leaving Croatia to the Magyars and their Magyarising tendencies, yet he remained a focus of loyalty. It was thus not surprising that in 1903 a deputation from Istria and Dalmatia should want to appeal to their monarch against the treatment of their national brethren in Croatia by the Hungarian authorities. Yet Francis Joseph refused even to hear them.

He had done something similar in 1892 when he refused to receive a deputation of Cisleithanian Rumanians protesting against Magyar policies, and he did so for the same reason: any appeal to him as Austrian emperor about Hungarian matters was prohibited, for that was the Hungarian king's responsibility. That he was himself both monarchs was to him beside the point: he refused absolutely to interfere in Hungarian (Magyar) affairs – if it was on behalf of his other peoples. He had more important, dynastic concerns in 1903: with the crisis over the Army Bill he did not want yet another major argument with the Magyars. Yet the effect of this crass rebuttal on Croatian politicians appears to have been decisive in making them look elsewhere than to the Habsburg monarch for help. Redlich was to call this refusal to see the South Slav deputation Francis Joseph's 'gravest political sin'.[110]

The outcome of the Croats' disappointment was the meeting of Croat deputies of the Croatian and Dalmatian diets at Fiume and their Resolution, on 2 October 1905, to support the union of Dalmatia with Croatia, and to lend the Magyar opposition to the king their support. This Croatian support for the Magyars against the Habsburg monarch was a shock to the Habsburg authorities, but almost worse was the meeting in Zara (Zadar) of Serb deputies from the same diets and their resolution of 16 October to support the Fiume Resolution. The almost unthinkable was taking place, of Serb and Croat leaders banding together, and, what is more, against the Habsburgs and with the Magyars. In 1906 the coming together of Serbs and Croats was taken a step further in Croatia proper when a large number of members of the Croatian Party of Right and Independent Serb Party formed the Croato-Serb Coalition, with a majority in the Croatian Diet (43 of 84), and allied with the Magyar nationalist opposition to Francis Joseph.

Such a configuration could not last long, and the Croato-Serb Coalition soon fell out with the Magyars over typically chauvinist impositions from the Magyars, concerning the railways in Croatia. Yet this split only irritated Croatian politics further, leading to the imposing of tantamount to absolutist rule in 1908, with Serbs and Croats still in alliance.[111]

Added to the crisis in Croatia, the situation in Bosnia–Herzegovina was far from satisfactory for the occupying Habsburg authorities. In many respects the occupation, administered by the Joint Ministry of Finance, had improved the province. There was some improvement of the standard of living (although Magyar demands that the occupation pay for itself severely limited efforts to encourage development).[112] Above all, order had been imposed and with it peace. Yet the lack of serious land reform (to mollify the largely Muslim landowning class) had left the peasant masses (largely Serb) disaffected, while the Muslim elite still looked to their Ottoman overlord. As so often in an imperial situation little gratitude was shown by the populace for the Austro-Hungarian authorities' efforts, and much resentment at their presence.[113]

It did not help when dealing with the discontents of the Bosnian Serbs that the sovereign nation-state of Serbia lay just across the border. Until 1900 this had not mattered much at all, for Serbia had either been in such a chaotic state that she offered no positive model for her Habsburg-ruled co-nationals, or she had been a client state of Austria–Hungary anyway. By 1900, however, the Serbian King Alexander and his kingdom had forsaken Austrian for Russian patronage.[114] The brutal coup of 1903, which replaced the Obrenovič with the Karageorgevič dynasty, elicited no military response from Francis Joseph or Goluchowski, for Serbia had already been discounted as an ally. There were even hopes that relations might now improve, but by the end of 1903 it was crystal clear that the reverse was the case, and that a stoutly Russophile Serbian government would pose a large, crucial problem for Austrian Balkan policy.

One of the great fears of the Austrians in their one remaining sphere of interest was of Turkey in Europe being replaced by a large Slav state, which would at once be a Russian satellite and a potential magnet to the Monarchy's South Slav population. As is the way with Austrian history, it was left to a Slav, the Polish Goluchowski, to express this fear in November 1903, when he recommended supporting an Albanian enclave in Macedonia: 'The Albanian nation after all forms a dam against the flood of the Porte's possessions in the Balkans by the Slav deluge.'[115] The union of Serbia and Bulgaria would effectively create just such a state; even a close alliance would certainly upset the Monarchy's 'timeworn' policy of playing one South Slav state off against the other. When, in late 1905, the Austrians learnt that the two Slav states had formed a secret customs union, alarm bells went off at the Ballhausplatz, the Austro-Hungarian Foreign Ministry.[116]

Austria had a good case in international law against Bulgaria, a not so good case against Serbia, but Goluchowski chose to retaliate against Serbia. He did so largely for domestic reasons, because there would never be an irredentist problem with Bulgaria, but there definitely was one with Serbia, 'which has been intriguing incessantly against the Monarchy for a few years now, stirring up the Serbo-Croat population and agitating against Austria–Hungary in Bosnia and the Herzegovina.'[117] The result was a hard-edged Austrian campaign against Serbian commercial interests, largely by the strict enforcement of veterinary regulations against Serbian pig imports. This conflict, complicated by arguments over where Serbia was to purchase its armaments (Bohemia or France), and exacerbated by Magyar landowning interest in cutting off Serbian competition in foodstuffs, produced the four-year long 'Pig War' (1906–10). This trade war had terrible short-term consequences for Serbia, which it however overcame, and equally bad long-term results for the Habsburg Monarchy, which it never did. Serbia was able to find other outlets for its produce, most notably in Germany, Austria's supposed ally, and the net effect for the Monarchy was the loss of its virtual stranglehold over the Serbian economy as well as a ratcheting of Serbian hatred to ever higher levels, and loss of face among the other great powers for bullying a small power, but even worse for failing to overawe her.[118]

When Goluchowski was replaced by Aehrenthal in October 1906 the broad outlines of policy remained much as they had been, but the new Foreign Minister, a supporter of closer ties to Russia and part of a wave of 'new men' which also included Conrad and Beck, brought a new air of forcefulness to Austrian diplomacy. He wanted to reclaim for Austria–Hungary her position as an independent force in great-power relations after too many years in which she had seemed merely passive, far too dependent on the Dual Alliance with Germany. His aim, as Roy Bridge has put it, was to provide a 'vigorous foreign policy to sharpen the patient's [the Monarchy's] self-confidence and interest in staying alive'. To him 'a strong, constructive foreign policy and a stable, healthy domestic situation were just two sides of the same coin.' In February 1907 he set down in a memorandum one way this equilibrium could be established. It suggested the annexation of Bosnia–Herzegovina, its integration into a new, South Slav territory amalgamated from Cisleithanian and Hungarian lands, under the suzerainty of the Crown of St Stephen. In this way an assertive foreign policy (annexation) could create a situation which would flatter the Magyars and, by a form of quasi-trialism, satisfy the South Slavs. Domestic problems would thus be solved by a dynamic foreign policy.[119]

The former British diplomat, Horace Rumbold, saw this domestic aspect to Aehrenthal's policy, and approved of it. In an account published in 1909 he blamed the constant national conflicts for destroying the 'imperial spirit' and dragging Austria–Hungary down as a great power, but thought he saw a remedy. Commenting on the turmoil left in the wake of the Badeni and Chlopy crises, Rumbold averred:

> With problems such as these facing them at every turn, it is not surprising that of late the Imperial Government should have resorted to a more decided policy in the Near East, in the hope that they may thereby awaken in both halves of the Monarchy a common sense of solidarity and a feeling of devotion to Imperial interests, irrespective of nationality, which have too long remained dormant in the polyglot empire.[120]

Rumbold's suggestion that the 'more decided policy' of the annexation of Bosnia–Herzegovina was motivated by domestic concerns was in other words a classic instance of Hans-Ulrich Wehler's 'social imperialism', accords with the prevailing view of Aehrenthal's understanding of the links between domestic and foreign policy.[121] If this was so, then it was indeed the domestic nationalities problem – and especially the dilemma posed by the South Slavs – which led Austria–Hungary into the annexation crisis of 1908, which almost all are agreed was disastrous for not only the Monarchy, but also the European balance of power.

Given that Aehrenthal wanted a more vigorous foreign policy, the only sphere in which he could display this vigour was in the Balkans. This led in 1907 to his plans for, and in early 1908 to his brash announcement of, a railway in the Habsburg-garrisoned Sanjak (the territory between Serbia and Montenegro) to directly link Habsburg and Ottoman territory. The result of this boldness, which was also a blow to Serbian and Montenegrin ambitions, was a severe crisis in Austro-Russian relations, already strained by differences over Macedonian reform. Yet the Bosnian annexation crisis, when it came, started with Russian attempts to revive and extend the *entente* with Austria, and progressed owing to a combination of Austria's essentially conservative wish to consolidate her position in Bosnia, and Aehrenthal's 'over-confidence' and the 'decidedly cavalier manner' with which he implemented the policy – as well as the usual unpredictability of the labyrinth of Balkan politics.[122]

The history of the Bosnian crisis is so full of secret deals, double-dealing, stabs in the back, misunderstandings and unfortunate coincidence, that it would be highly comic if its results had not been so terrible for the European diplomatic system. In brief, a deal between Aehrenthal and the Russian Foreign Minister Alexander Izvolsky, forged over the summer of 1908 and made final at Buchlau in September, to confirm the *entente* and use it to further both powers' interests in the light of the Young Turk revolution at Constantinople that summer, blew up in their faces and left Russia an irreconcilable enemy of the Monarchy.

The Monarchy had decided for annexation of Bosnia–Herzegovina as a way of masking its retreat from the Sanjak due to military considerations. Moreover the Young Turk revolution had left Bosnia, *de facto* part of the Habsburg Monarchy for three decades, as the only territory in Europe without a constitution. Yet this embarrassment could only be made good if Francis Joseph had the sovereign power to grant such a document: this was another reason for annexation. Another was the fear that elections would be held in Bosnia to send deputies to the new, *Turkish* parliament. Yet another was that Francis Joseph would finally have his one territorial gain for the dynasty fully confirmed.

Hence the actual annexation was made with Russian agreement and marked not an Austrian advance, but a retreat (from the Sanjak) in the Near East. What turned this move into a major crisis was partly Aehrenthal's fault. His haste in creating a *fait accompli* by announcing the annexation already on 5 October 1908, his neglect of consulting or even informing the other great powers beforehand, along with his letting Ferdinand of Bulgaria into the secret, so that Ferdinand announced his declaration of Bulgaria's full independence from Turkey two days *before* the annexation declaration, left the other powers outraged and suspecting an Austro-Bulgarian conspiracy to humiliate the new Turkish government. Yet events in Russia also were to blame. Not only was the Russian leadership furious at the speed of Aehrenthal's action and the apparent Austro-Bulgarian collusion, and further frustrated in its efforts to change the rules over the Straits, but it was also taken aback by the outrage of Russian public opinion at the prospective 'enslavement of Slav brothers in Bosnia' under the Habsburgs. Izvolsky was left entirely isolated. Instead of resigning he chose to blame Aehrenthal, claiming he had never agreed at Buchlau to the annexation as such, and that any claims to the contrary were just one more example of Aehrenthal's perfidy. (The records strongly suggest that there had indeed been a deal, and that Izvolsky lied to save his job.)[123]

The annexation thus led to a monumental crisis abroad and at home. The initial reaction of the great powers was uniformly negative. William II's first reaction was to talk of Aehrenthal's 'fearful stupidity'.[124] Britain and France stood behind Russia, and in Italy public opinion was strongly hostile to Austrian 'imperialism'. Serbia and Montenegro were humiliated and in high dudgeon at the frustration of their own ambitions in Bosnia–Herzegovina.

At home the annexation crisis also had very negative consequences for government relations with the South Slavs, as a rattled Hungarian government indicted leaders of the Croato-Serb Coalition, chief among them Francis Supilo, for treason. The Zagreb treason trial of 1909, with its appendage of the Friedjung libel trial later the same year, became a *cause celèbre* of Austrian Slav liberals such as the Czech, Thomas Masaryk, and Western liberal Slavophiles, such as R. W. Seton-Watson, when it became clear that the charges against the South Slav politicians were based on forged evidence.[125] What these trials showed of the workings of the supposed Austro-Hungarian 'state of law' greatly devalued the Monarchy's moral standing in the view of Western public opinion. They also saw a greater co-operation between 'Western' Slav (Czech) leaders and their South Slav brethren; further, they had a yet more alienating impact on South Slav opinion, in the Monarchy and outside.[126]

By this point Mile Starčevič, nephew of Ante Starčevič the former leader of the Party of Right in Croatia, could tell Seton-Watson: 'Austria is even worse than the Magyars, and has always betrayed Croatia ever since 1527 when the first Habsburg was elected.' Francis Joseph, he added, could put everything right if he wished, 'but he does not wish, he simply plays off the nationalities against each other.'[127] The Bosnian crisis saw a further drawing of the battle lines not between Magyars and Croats within the Hungarian half of the Monarchy, but between Francis Joseph and the Austrian imperial authorities on the one hand and the 'South Slavs', or even the 'Slavs' on the other.

There was also a hardening of the fronts on the international scene, reinforcing the antagonisms which had surfaced during the First Moroccan Crisis of 1906. Despite the awkward, even desperate situation in which Aehrenthal had found himself in the winter of 1908, the annexation crisis turned out to be a great success for Austrian diplomacy, in the short term. This was because, after their initial shock, the leadership in Berlin, fearful of the prospect of their one serious ally being humiliated, decided for once to stand by Austria–Hungary. With their German ally behind them, the Austrians could defy the other powers, who, in any case, proved far less united on this issue than they had at first appeared. Not only was the annexation recognised, but the crisis prompted the Germans to resume high level military talks with the Austrians for the first time in years, with Count Helmut von Moltke promising Conrad on 19 March 1909 German military assistance in the event of a Russian mobilisation in response to an Austrian attack on Serbia.[128] Moreover, the initial refusal of the Montenegrins and Serbians to recognise the annexation led to a diplomatic stand-off between Austria and the Serbians' patron Russia in March 1909, which almost led to war, but which resulted in Russia's diplomatic collapse, the humiliation of Serbia and Montenegro, and the apparent triumph of Aehrenthal's forceful diplomacy.

Aehrenthal clearly thought so. As he said a few months later, the episode offered a 'text-book example of how success is only certain if the strength is there to get one's way. . . . We are no *quantité négligeable.* We have reconquered again the place that belongs to us among the Powers.'[129] This was true, in the short term. In the longer term, though, the episode was more a text-book example of what happens when a power insists on 'punching above one's weight'. Russia, who had been a valuable counterweight to domination by the much more powerful German ally, was now lost beyond any recall. Thinking itself tricked, yet again, by the Habsburgs, and forced to climb down and abandon its Serbian protégé, Russia was now a clear enemy. The British, a traditional friend, had also been put out by Aehrenthal's actions. The result was that diplomatically Aehrenthal's policy of vigour, initially seen as making Austria–Hungary more independent of Germany, tied her even more closely to Berlin. As for the Balkan powers, Serbia and Montenegro had been humiliated, but not subdued. To extend the boxing metaphor, in Arthur May's words: 'Aehrenthal, in the Bosnian affair, had won the round, but the bout as a whole was to end with a knockout for the Austrian pugilist.'[130]

Austria–Hungary was simply not strong enough to follow the sort of muscular regimen Aehrenthal had prescribed. Economically, as we have seen, she was performing fairly creditably, more creditably than was once believed, but her economy continued to be vulnerable, especially when it came to her export trade, much of which was concentrated in the Balkans and was facing increasingly stiff competition, especially from her 'ally' Germany. In 1906 the Monarchy had its last balance of payments surplus. This economic vulnerability was coupled with continuing financial weakness. In 1907 came the Monarchy's last budget surplus (despite the extraordinarily low level of military expenditures).[131] The costs of military mobilisation during the crisis over Bosnia–Herzegovina in 1908–9 led to a very large deficit for 1909, and 1910 saw the imperial authorities *planning* for a budget shortfall. Any ideas about what Bridge calls 'costly adventures' were out.

Aehrenthal came to see much of this long-term weakness of the Austrian position and eventually drew the relevant conclusion. His policy from 1910 onwards was once again one of sticking to the status quo, as he demonstrated in disputes over Albania and Crete in that year. To bolster Austria–Hungary's position he followed a conciliatory policy towards both Italy and Britain. Yet the Balkan situation was far from pacified. Within the Monarchy, Croatia remained troubled, as another Friedjung Trial embarrassed the government again.[132] In Dalmatia in 1909 the authorities had been forced to allow Serbo-Croatian to become the internal language of the court system. In 1910 the Istrian Diet was dissolved, never to meet again in peacetime. Two years after the annexation of Bosnia–Herzegovina the province was still troubled, with only the shakiest beginnings of constitutional government.[133] Neighbouring Serbia meanwhile had emerged from the Pig War with expanded commercial contacts and no longer an Austrian economic puppet. Even in her own backyard the Austrian position was not strong. When the Germans asked for support in the Second Moroccan Crisis Aehrenthal did little to help. His justification was revealing of where the Monarchy stood in the great power system by 1911: 'What more can I do? We can pursue no *Weltpolitik.*'[134] This was meant sarcastically, but it still represented a sad fate for a dynastic power which had indeed once claimed to rule the world.

The combination of the Second Moroccan Crisis and the example of the Bosnian annexation prompted Italy to invade Libya in 1911 to get her piece of the Ottoman pie. Aehrenthal, unhappy with the Italian move, nevertheless stuck to his policy of containment. Italy was after all officially an ally. Conrad von Hötzendorf, in contrast, wanted to wage a preventive war against Italy while she was vulnerable. It is at this point, on 15 November 1911, that Conrad had his famous audience with Francis Joseph, who made it clear who, ultimately, ran Austrian foreign policy: 'These incessant attacks on Aehrenthal, these pinpricks, I forbid them . . . The ever-recurring reproaches regarding Italy and the Balkans are directed at me. Policy – it is I who make it! . . . My policy is a policy of peace . . .'[135] Soon after Conrad was dismissed, Aehrenthal's quietist policy, the emperor's policy, had triumphed.

But it was a quietist policy based on weakness not strength, and by the winter of 1912 one state above all, Serbia, was the focus of Habsburg fears, because of the threat it posed both inside the Monarchy and in the Monarchy's Balkan sphere of interest. Unfortunately it was Serbia who was to profit most from the dismantling of what remained of European Turkey precipitated by the Italian attack on Libya. When Aehrenthal died in February 1912, and was succeeded by Leopold Count Berchtold, the Balkan League, which was eventually to include Serbia, Bulgaria, Greece and Montenegro, was well on the way to being formed.

With Turkey prostrated by Italian invasion and Albanian revolts, it was too tempting a target for even Russian attempts at restraint, let alone Austrian protestations, to hold back the Balkan powers. On 8 October 1912, Montenegro led the league against the Turks. The First Balkan War saw the end of Turkey in Europe but the quick collapse of the Turkish forces also stunned the Austrians, who were left as military spectators while their foreign policy was dismantled before their eyes. Intervention was discussed in the Habsburg Crown Council on 14 September 1912, but there was not the money to pay for war, nor was the army in a sufficient state of readiness; help for Turkey would in any case have united the Christian Balkan states against the Monarchy and both Francis Joseph and Francis Ferdinand were against even modest intervention.[136] Yet the results of the war were disastrous. The Sanjak, once the Monarchy's strategic link to Turkey, was divided between Serbia and Montenegro, and the success of both powers threatened to undo even the minimum Austrian goals, of ensuring an independent Albanian state, and preventing Serbian access to the sea.

The crisis grew to such proportions that Conrad was recalled as Chief of the General Staff on 12 December 1912 and the Austrians were forced, nevertheless, to mobilise troops to back up their diplomatic threats against Serbian attempts to gain a seaport on the Adriatic. In the ensuing crisis Russia once again backed down, abandoning Serbia, and then Montenegro over the latter's occupation of Scutari. The Peace of London of 30 May 1913 was, owing it seemed to the unilateral threat of force on Austria–Hungary's part, not as bad as it might have been for the Monarchy, creating an independent Albania which prevented Serbian access to the sea. Yet it also saw Serbia now twice its previous size, without any Turkish 'counterweight', and deeply bitter at Austria's frustrating of its strategic interests.[137]

By now Serbia had become a veritable bogeyman for the makers of Habsburg foreign policy, and the conviction grew among many of them, Francis Joseph included, that war might be necessary to eliminate the perceived threat, even if it risked confrontation with Russia.[138] Yet Serbia was still only a poor, backward state, far smaller and less developed than the Monarchy. To explore why its prospering was held to be such a threat to the Habsburg realm that the denial of a seaport to it was worth a risk of war against Russia is to realise the extent of the interdependence of domestic and foreign policy in the Monarchy, especially as it concerns the thinking of the makers of that policy.

The short answer is that by 1913 Serbia was the most feared centre of South Slav irredentism: a Serbian-led South Slav state would effectively mean the end of the Monarchy. Yet in many ways it went against common sense to see Serbia attracting Habsburg South Slavs, rather than the other way around. Within the Dual Monarchy, including Bosnia–Herzegovina, there were over seven million South Slavs (roughly 1.4 million Slovenes, 2.9 million Croats, 2.1 million Serbs, 650,000 Muslim Slavs). In the whole of the rest of South-Eastern Europe there were only something over three million South Slavs (excluding Bulgars). Indeed the number of Serbs in Serbia, at 2.6 million, was not that much higher than the Habsburg Serb figure of 2.1 million. Logically, therefore, the Monarchy should have been the centre of attraction for South Slavs in Serbia and Montenegro, not the reverse.[139]

This was the numerical foundation to all those plans for trialism, which, as Aehrenthal had seen, and writers such as Joseph Baernreither expounded, would, by offering the South Slavs their own state within the Habsburg fold, have been a source of great diplomatic strength for the Monarchy as a whole.[140] Within such a scheme, Serbia and Montenegro would not have been threats but rather integral parts of an expanded Habsburg state dominating the Balkans. Given recent experiences of Balkan co-operation, one might well ask whether any such trialist federalism would have had much if any success, but then all such thought is completely speculative, for such a transformation of the Monarchy, as we have seen, was simply not possible as long as Francis Joseph was emperor. Therefore Serbia and Montenegro could only be perceived as threats to the Monarchy not only because of their being under the Russian wing but also because of their perceived threat as magnets for South Slavs within the Monarchy.

Then again the reason for this latter perception was a sense of a lack of loyalty among the South Slavs for the empire and its emperor. Had there been great confidence in their loyalty, the imperial policymakers could have viewed Serbia with equanimity, but there was not, and there seems circumstantial evidence at least to partially justify such doubts. In late December 1911 the dependable British vice-consul in Ragusa (Dubrovnik), Lucas-Shadwell, not unsympathetic to the Habsburg authorities, reported back to the Foreign Office on the political atmosphere in Dalmatia:

> The bulk of the population is anti-dynastic, because it looks upon the dynasty as being anti-Slav and as an essential part of the present regime. The feeling towards the Emperor is one of complete indifference; he is looked upon as a German with German sentiments and as being completely out of touch and sympathy with his Slav subjects. The Dalmatian Slavs feel that they are treated as an inferior race and they know too well that their country has been entirely neglected by the central government. It can hardly be expected that any affection can be felt for the Emperor who, in the mind of the peasant, is responsible for all this.[141]

With continuing troubles in Croatia, where the constitution had been suspended in 1912, and in Bosnia, where a working majority still could not be found in the new diet, the South Slav problem *within* the Monarchy was indeed of sufficient severity to make any increase of Serbia's power or prestige very alarming to the *imperial* Habsburg authorities.

It is only in this context that it makes any sense when Williamson claims that the outcome of the Second Balkan War, in 1913, sealed the Monarchy's fate. This second war began as a squabble between Bulgaria and Serbia over the spoils of the first war, was indeed started by Bulgaria in June 1913, but ended already in August with the Bulgarians' utter defeat at the hands not only of Serbia, but of Greece, Rumania and Turkey as well. The resulting Treaty of Bucharest of 10 August 1913 was yet another disaster for the Monarchy. Not only did it leave Serbia yet bigger, it also gave it yet more prestige and power among the Balkan states. Yet again the Austrians had sat out the actual war. Not only were they caught unawares by the speed of Bulgaria's collapse, but the expense of the mobilisation caused by the earlier Scutari crisis and the resulting economic downturn had led to apathy among the public, and also among the ruling circles, including both Francis Joseph and Francis Ferdinand. The fact that the Germans were supporting the anti-Bulgarian coalition made the Monarchy's position even more helpless.[142]

Yet again Austria could only salvage her minimum demands from the debacle, and again there was a stand-off with the Serbians, this time over the latter's occupation of large parts of Albania. Again the Austrians, much more directly this time, threatened force, issuing an ultimatum on 17 October 1913 to Serbia. By now the Austrians were prepared to countenance war with Serbia and hence Russia, because they perceived a strong Serbia not only as a threat to the *interests* of the Monarchy in the Balkans but also to her *prestige*, in the region and among her own South Slavs. If the Habsburg Monarchy could not even put down Serbia, then it no longer possessed the prestige of a Great Power, and if it was not a Great Power, it had lost its *raison d'être.*

The Serbians backed down yet again, because their Russian backers told them to, but this left the Balkans a tinderbox. Serbia felt yet more humiliated and frustrated by Austrian actions, Russia almost equally so at seeing her protégés so mistreated, and the Austrians felt desperation at the threat posed by Serbia externally and internally, and had come to the conclusion that the 'lessons of history' showed that the Serbians only understood force, or at least the real threat of it.[143] Moreover, William II's enthusiastic response to Austria's successful threat of force against Serbia would only have confirmed the imperial authorities and Francis Joseph in their ever more militant approach to Serbia.[144] The one figure in the Habsburg ruling circles who was for a more pacific policy was Francis Ferdinand.[145]

By early 1914 the Monarchy's relations with its Balkan neighbours were severely frayed, and a mood bordering on desperation had descended on Habsburg policymakers. While relations with a humbled Bulgaria were becoming ever friendlier, the two main victors of the Balkan wars, Serbia and Rumania, both centres of irredentism, were now viewing their irredenta within the

Habsburg Monarchy as their next areas of expansion. With Serbia this was clear and understandable: Austrian treatment of her, along with the immense prestige her victories had acquired for her among large swathes of Habsburg South Slavdom, meant that Pašić, the Serbian premier, had few qualms in preparing 'the second round against Austria', especially as by now he had Russian promises that the next time they would not back down to Austrian bullying. Rumania, though, was a secret ally of the Monarchy; yet her confidence-boosting victories in the Second Balkan War and the persisting Magyar mistreatment of her co-nationals in Transylvania left the Rumanian leadership less looking to Austria–Hungary for support than seeing her as a target for territorial acquisitions.[146]

Meanwhile the Entente powers were exploiting Austrian diplomatic and financial weakness in the Balkans, and Russia was rapidly expanding its armed forces with French capital barred from the Austrians. Conversely, Austria's relations with the other members of the Triple Alliance were not good. Italy was unhappy about Austrian actions concerning Albania, and Germany, after seemingly coming round to Austria's position on the Balkans once more was following policies quite at cross-purposes to Austrian interests, to the exasperation of the Ballhausplatz. It was to bring the Germans to a more 'reasonable' attitude that Berchtold, after discussions with Francis Ferdinand at Konopischt, had the Matscheko Memorandum drawn up in June 1914.

This was, in its original draft, a summary of the poor diplomatic situation in which the Monarchy found itself, and an argument for a diplomatic offensive. It emphasised the more assertive stance being taken by the Russians, the problems with Rumania, the threat of a new, encircling Balkan League under Entente auspices, and the threat a union of Montenegro with Serbia would pose, giving Serbia access to the sea and making her so great a threat that such a union could not be allowed, would be indeed a 'trip wire'. In this form, the memorandum was still a call for diplomatic action to prevent such awful contingencies (contingencies perhaps magnified to scare the Germans to more co-operative behaviour); but subsequent events changed all that.

Before the memorandum could be sent off, the news arrived in Vienna that the heir to the throne, Francis Ferdinand, and his wife had been assassinated – on 28 June 1914 in Sarajevo, the capital of Bosnia–Herzegovina, by a Bosnian Serb student, Gavrilo Princip. A South Slav, a Serb but a subject of the emperor, had killed the Habsburg heir in the capital of the dynasty's one territorial acquisition during Francis Joseph's reign. Given the recent experience of the Habsburg ruling circles, their fear of Serbia and the South Slav menace to Habsburg status and prestige, a forceful response of some sort was absolutely necessary, and this time the mere threat of force might not be enough. A month was to go by until the other foot finally followed, but the combination of the need to maintain Habsburg imperial pretensions with the complexities and turmoil of South Slav nationalism, both within the Monarchy and in the larger system of international relations, had made the eventual outcome all but inevitable.

In June 1912, with the Balkans shaping up for war, there had been an attempted assassination of the Ban of Croatia. Theodor von Sosnosky had described the shot by the would-be assassin as 'an early flash of lightning from heavy thunderclouds which are gathering menacingly in the southeastern part of the Monarchy'.[147] Two years later another assassin's shot announced that the 'thunder of heaven' had arrived. The 'peace emperor' was about to start a world war.

. . .

NOTES AND REFERENCES

1.   E.C. Corti and H. Sokol, *Der alte Kaiser: Franz Joseph I. vom Berliner Kongress bis zu seinem Tode*, Styria, Graz 1955, p. 234; A. Palmer, *Twilight of the Habsburgs: The Life and Times of Emperor Francis Joseph*, Weidenfeld & Nicolson, London 1955, p. 285.

2.   Palmer, *Twilight of the Habsburgs*, p. 314.

3.   S. Wank, 'Desperate Counsel in Vienna in July 1914: Berthold Molden's Unpublished Memorandum', *Central European History*, vol. 26 (3), p. 308; cf. E. Crankshaw, *The Fall of the House of Habsburg*, Viking Penguin, New York 1963, p. 140.

4.   On the nationalism problem see S. Wank, 'The Nationalities Question in the Habsburg Monarchy: Reflections on the Historical Record', *Working Papers in Austrian Studies*, vol. 93 (3), 1993.

5.   Cf. J. Kořalka and R.J. Crampton, 'Die Tschechen'. In A. Wandruszka and P. Urbanitsch (eds), *Die Habsburger Monarchie 1848–1918* (6+ vols). Österreichische Akademie der

Wissenschaften, Vienna 1980, vol. 3, pt. 1, *Die Völker der Monarchie*, p. 521.

6.   O. Jászi, *The Dissolution of the Habsburg Monarchy*, Chicago 1929, p. 311 (Studies in the Making of Citizens).

7.   A. Spitzmüller, *Memoirs*, trans. C. de Bussy, East European Monographs, Boulder 1987, p. 28.

8.   J.-P. Bled, *Franz Joseph*, trans. T. Bridgeman, Blackwell, Oxford 1992, pp. 467–8.

9.   J. Redlich, *Emperor Francis Joseph of Austria: A Biography*, Macmillan, New York 1929, p. 450.

10. L. Höbelt, *Kornblume und Kaiseradler: Die deutschfreiheitlichen Parteien Altösterreichs 1882–1918*, Geschichte und Politik, Vienna 1993, p. 199.

11. A.J. May, *The Habsburg Monarchy, 1867–1914*, Harvard, Cambridge 1951, p. 334.

12. Redlich, *Emperor Francis Joseph*, pp. 453–5; Höbelt, *Kornblume und Kaiseradler*, pp. 184–5.

13. Höbelt, *Kornblume und Kaiseradler*, pp. 197–9; Jászi, *The Dissolution of the Habsburg Monarchy*, p. 167.

14. C.A. Macartney, *The House of Austria: The Later Phase 1790–1918*, Edinburgh 1978, p. 211; Spitzmüller, *Memoirs*, pp. 31–2.

15. Redlich, *Emperor Francis Joseph*, p. 455.

16. Ibid., pp. 455–7.

17. Jászi, *The Dissolution of the Habsburg Monarchy*, p. 295.

18. G. Gudenus, 'Kaiser und Thronfolger'. In E. von Steinitz (ed.), *Erinnerungen an Franz Joseph I*, Kulturpolitik, Berlin 1931, p. 146.

19. Redlich, *Emperor Francis Joseph*, p. 452.

20. Höbelt, *Kornblume und Kaiseradler*, p. 182.

21. J. Kořalka, 'Deutschland und die Habsburgermonarchie'. In Wandruszka and Urbanitsch (eds), *Die Habsburger Monarchie 1848–1918*, Vienna 1993, vol. 6, pt. 2, *Aussenpolitik*, pp. 125–6.

22. J. Lukacs, *Budapest 1900: A Historical Portrait of a City and its Culture*, Weidenfeld & Nicolson, London 1989, esp. pp. 71–2.

23. Corti and Sokol, *Der alte Kaiser*, p. 237.

24. J.K. Hoensch, *A History of Modern Hungary, 1867–1986*, trans. K. Traynor, Longman, London 1988, p. 45; May, *The Habsburg Monarchy*, pp. 342–6.

25. Macartney, *The House of Austria*, p. 211; Spitzmüller, *Memoirs*, pp. 22–4, 31–2.

26. Spitzmüller, *Memoirs*, p. 24.

27. Macartney, *The House of Austria*, p. 235; May, *The Habsburg Monarchy*, pp. 348–52.
28. May, *The Habsburg Monarchy*, pp. 353–5; Macartney, *The House of Austria*, p. 235; Palmer, *Twilight of the Habsburgs*, p. 294.
29. Corti and Sokol, *Der alte Kaiser*, p. 289.
30. A.J.P. Taylor, *The Habsburg Monarchy 1809–1918*, Penguin, Harmondsworth 1948, p. 222; Hoensch, *A History of Modern Hungary*, p. 63.
31. Corti and Sokol, *Der alte Kaiser*, p. 295.
32. Hoensch, *A History of Modern Hungary*, p. 64; Macartney, *The House of Austria*, pp. 236–7.
33. G. Barany, 'Ungarns Verwaltung 1848–1918'. In Wandruszka and Urbanitsch (eds), *Die Habsburger Monarchie 1848–1918*, Vienna 1975, vol. 2, *Verwaltung und Rechtswesen*, pp. 421–7.
34. Ibid., p. 442.
35. Corti and Sokol, *Der alte Kaiser*, pp. 303–4; May, *The Habsburg Monarchy*, pp. 358–9; Macartney, *The House of Austria*, p. 237.
36. Cf. Jászi, *The Dissolution of the Habsburg Monarchy*, p. 362.
37. Ibid., pp. 362–3.
38. Corti and Sokol, *Der alte Kaiser*, pp. 302–3.
39. Redlich, *Emperor Francis Joseph*, p. 468.
40. May, *The Habsburg Monarchy*, pp. 337–8.
41. Höbelt, *Kornblume und Kaiseradler*, p. 252.
42. Redlich, *Emperor Francis Joseph*, p. 470.
43. May, *The Habsburg Monarchy*, p. 339.
44. Spitzmüller, *Memoirs*, p. 40.
45. May, *The Habsburg Monarchy*, pp. 341–2, 425.
46. P. Pulzer, *The Rise of Political Anti-Semitism in Germany and Austria*, Revised edn, Halban, London 1988, pp. 206–10; May, *The Habsburg Monarchy*, p. 428.
47. May, *The Habsburg Monarchy*, p. 434.
48. Macartney, *The House of Austria*, p. 239.
49. May, *The Habsburg Monarchy*, p. 440; Macartney, *The House of Austria*, p. 240.
50. Hoensch, *A History of Modern Hungary*, p. 67; May, *The Habsburg Monarchy*, p. 440.
51. D.F. Good, *The Economic Rise of the Habsburg Empire, 1750–1914*, University of California, Berkeley 1984, pp. 245–7.

52. Cf. S. Beller, *Vienna and the Jews, 1867–1938: A Cultural History*, Cambridge 1989; C.E. Schorske, *Fin-de-siècle Vienna: Politics and Culture*, Weidenfeld & Nicolson, London 1980.
53. J. Kořalka and R. J. Crampton, 'Die Tschechen', p. 510; G.B. Cohen, 'Education and Czech Social Structure in the Late Nineteenth Century'. In H. Lemberg *et al.*, *Bildungsgeschichte, Bevölkerungsgeschichte, Gesellschaftsgeschichte in den böhmischen Ländern und in Europa*, Oldenbourg, Munich 1988, pp. 38–9.
54. Jászi, *The Dissolution of the Habsburg Monarchy*, p. 329.
55. G. Barany, 'Ungarns Verwaltung', p. 461; E.C. Hellbling, 'Die Landesverwaltung in Cisleithanien'. In Wandruszka and Urbanitsch (eds), *Die Habsburger Monarchie 1848–1918*, Vienna 1975, vol. 2, *Verwaltung und Rechtswesen*, pp. 219, 239–42.
56. W. Goldinger, 'Die Zentralverwaltung in Cisleithanien – Die zivile gemeinsame Zentralverwaltung'. In Wandruszka and Urbanitsch (eds), *Die Habsburger Monarchie 1848–1918*, Vienna 1975, vol. 2, *Verwaltung und Rechtswesen*, p. 116.
57. S. Zweig, *Die Welt von Gestern: Erinnerungen eines Europäers*, Pbk. edn, Fischer, Frankfurt am Main 1970, p. 7.
58. See G. Stourzh, 'Die Gleichberechtigung der Volksstämme als Verfassungsprinzip 1848–1918'. In Wandruszka and Urbanitsch (eds), *Die Habsburger Monarchie 1848–1918*, Vienna 1980, vol. 3, pt. 2, *Die Völker des Reiches*, pp. 977–1206.
59. Stourzh, 'Die Gleichberichtigung der Volksstämme', pp. 1171–1200; A. Sked, *The Decline and Fall of the Habsburg Empire 1815–1918*, Longman, London 1989, p. 225; Wank, 'The Nationalities Question in the Habsburg Monarchy', pp. 12–13.
60. Crankshaw, *The Fall of the House of Habsburg*, pp. 305–6; Jászi, *The Dissolution of the Habsburg Monarchy*, pp. 295–6.
61. R.A. Kann, *A History of the Habsburg Empire, 1526–1918*, University of California, Berkeley 1977, p. 448; May, *The Habsburg Monarchy*, pp. 442–3.
62. Sked, *The Decline and Fall of the Habsburg Empire*, p. 264.
63. Ibid., p. 224.
64. Ibid., pp. 208–34.
65. H.W. Steed, *The Doom of the Habsburgs*, Arrowsmith, London 1937, p. 90.
66. Wank, 'The Nationalities Question in the Habsburg

Monarchy', p. 3; cf. Koralka and Crampton, 'Die Tschechen', p. 515.

67. I. Deák, *Beyond Nationalism: A Social and Political History of the Habsburg Officer Corps 1848–1918*, Oxford 1990, p. 77.

68. S.R. Williamson, Jr., *Austria–Hungary and the Origins of the First World War*, Macmillan, London 1991, p. 46; Deák, *Beyond Nationalism*, pp. 74–6.

69. F.R. Bridge, *The Habsburg Monarchy among the Great Powers, 1815–1918*, Berg, Oxford 1990, p. 255.

70. Crankshaw, *The Fall of the House of Habsburg*, p. 306.

71. Barany, 'Ungarns Verwaltung', pp. 423–42.

72. Goldinger, 'Die Zentralverwaltung in Cisleithanien', p. 175.

73. H.W. Steed, *The Habsburg Monarchy*, reprint 2nd edn 1914. Fertig, New York 1969, p. 59.

74. Ibid., p. 80.

75. W. Heindl, *Gehorsame Rebellen: Bürokratie und Beamte in Österreich, 1790–1848*, Böhlau, Vienna 1991, pp. 322–6 (Studien zu Politik und Verwaltung); W. Heindl, 'Was ist Reform? Überlegungen zum Verhältnis von Bürokratie, Staat und Gesellschaft in Österreich'. In H. Rumpler (ed.), *Innere Staatsbildung und gesellschaftliche Modernisierung in Österreich und Deutschland 1867/71 bis 1914*, Geschichte und Politik, Vienna 1991, pp. 171–4.

76. Steed, *The Habsburg Monarchy*, pp. 75–81.

77. Ibid., p. 88.

78. Goldinger, 'Die Zentralverwaltung in Cisleithanien', p. 114.

79. Barany, 'Ungarns Verwaltung', p. 415.

80. Steed, *The Habsburg Monarchy*, p. 78.

81. Ibid., pp. 136–7; cf. Jászi, *The Dissolution of the Habsburg Monarchy*, pp. 234–7.

82. Hellbling, 'Die Landesverwaltung in Cisleithanien', pp. 261–2.

83. Jászi, *The Dissolution of the Habsburg Monarchy*, p. 295; Goldinger, 'Die Zentralverwaltung in Cisleithanien', p. 111.

84. J. Klabouch, 'Die Lokalverwaltung in Cisleithanien'. In Wandruszka and Urbanitsch (eds), *Die Habsburger Monarchie 1848–1918*, Vienna 1975, vol. 2, *Verwaltung und Rechtswesen*, pp. 296–9.

85. J. Redlich, *Österreichische Regierung und Verwaltung im Weltkriege*, Hölder, Vienna 1925, pp. 19–20, 25–6, 73–5.

86. J.W. Boyer, *Culture and Political Crisis in Vienna: Christian Socialism in Power, 1897–1918*, University of Chicago 1995, pp. 1–110, esp. 38–9.

87. Hellbling, 'Die Landesverwaltung in Cisleithanien', pp. 259–61; Taylor, *The Habsburg Monarchy*, p. 171.

88. Redlich, *Österreichische Regierung und Verwaltung*, pp. 66–81; Jászi, *The Dissolution of the Habsburg Monarchy*, pp. 167–8; Steed, *The Habsburg Monarchy*, pp. 77–8.

89. Hellbling, 'Die Landesverwaltung in Cisleithanien', p. 259.

90. Steed, *The Habsburg Monarchy*, p. 75. In fact, Francis Joseph *had* perceived the threat posed to the Habsburg bureaucracy by the new language policy, but he had been prepared to sacrifice this to put down the German Liberal challenge to his dynastic prerogatives.

91. Kann, *A History of the Habsburg Empire*, p. 442.

92. Jászi, *The Dissolution of the Habsburg Monarchy*, pp. 111, 380–3.

93. Steed, *The Habsburg Monarchy*, p. 57.

94. Palmer, *Twilight of the Habsburgs*, p. 349.

95. Steed, *The Habsburg Monarchy*, p. 125; cf. Jászi, *The Dissolution of the Habsburg Monarchy*, p. 139.

96. Jászi, *The Dissolution of the Habsburg Monarchy*, pp. 291–2.

97. Redlich, *Emperor Francis Joseph*, pp. 485–93; Palmer, *Twilight of the Habsburgs*, pp. 295–7.

98. Redlich, *Emperor Francis Joseph*, p. 487; Palmer, *Twilight of the Habsburgs*, p. 297; Corti and Sokol, *Der alte Kaiser*, pp. 306–19.

99. Franz Joseph, *Meine liebe, gute Freundin! Die Briefe Kaiser Franz Josephs an Katharina Schratt*, ed. B. Hamann, Überreuter, Vienna 1992, p. 530.

100. A. Margutti, *The Emperor Francis Joseph and His Times*, Hutchinson, London 1921, p. 209.

101. Palmer, *Twilight of the Habsburgs*, p. 308.

102. Rudolf, *Majestät, ich warne Sie: Geheime und private Schriften*, ed. B. Hamann, Amalthea, Vienna 1979, p. 218.

103. W.A. Jenks, *Austria under the Iron Ring 1879–1893*, University Press of Virginia, Charlottesville 1965, p. 50.

104. E.g. Sked, *The Decline and Fall of the Habsburg Empire*, pp. 230–4.

105. Williamson, *Austria–Hungary and the Origins of the First World War*, p. 34.

106. Sked, *The Decline and Fall of the Habsburg Empire*, pp. 265–8.

107. Williamson, *Austria–Hungary and the Origins of the First World War*, p. 27.

108. Bridge, *The Habsburg Monarchy*, pp. 250–1.
109. Ibid., pp. 224–77.
110. Jászi, *The Dissolution of the Habsburg Monarchy*, pp. 323–4; Redlich, *Emperor Francis Joseph*, pp. 463–4.
111. H. & C. Seton-Watson, *The Making of a New Europe: R. W. Seton-Watson and the Last Years of Austria–Hungary*, University of Washington, Seattle 1981, p. 60.
112. Williamson, *Austria–Hungary and the Origins of the First World War*, pp. 63–4.
113. May, *The Habsburg Monarchy*, pp. 406–10; cf. Sked, *The Decline and Fall of the Habsburg Empire*, pp. 245–6.
114. Bridge, *The Habsburg Monarchy*, pp. 230–1.
115. Ibid., p. 251.
116. Ibid., pp. 261–2.
117. Ibid., pp. 261–2.
118. Jászi, *The Dissolution of the Habsburg Monarchy*, p. 417; Bridge, *The Habsburg Monarchy*, p. 262.
119. Bridge, *The Habsburg Monarchy*, pp. 268–70.
120. H. Rumbold, *The Austrian Court in the Nineteenth Century*, Methuen, London 1909, pp. 183, 330.
121. Cf. Williamson, *Austria–Hungary and the Origins of the First World War*, p. 42.
122. Bridge, *The Habsburg Monarchy*, pp. 276–81.
123. Ibid., pp. 280–4.
124. Ibid., p. 288.
125. Seton-Watson, *The Making of a New Europe*, pp. 68, 77.
126. Sked, *The Decline and Fall of the Habsburg Empire*, p. 216; Steed, *The Habsburg Monarchy*, pp. 100–4.
127. Seton-Watson, *The Making of a New Europe*, p. 69.
128. Bridge, *The Habsburg Monarchy*, pp. 292–3.
129. Ibid., p. 295.
130. May, *The Habsburg Monarchy*, p. 424.
131. Bridge, *The Habsburg Monarchy*, pp. 254, 298.
132. Seton-Watson, *The Making of a New Europe*, p. 69; Bridge, *The Habsburg Monarchy*, p. 296.
133. Stourzh, 'Die Gleichberichtigung der Volksstämme', pp. 1054, 1123; F.R. Bridge, 'British Official Opinion and the Domestic Situation in the Habsburg Monarchy, 1900–1914'. In B.J.C. McKercher and D.J. Moss (eds), *Shadow and Substance in British Foreign Policy 1895–1939*, University of Alberta, Edmonton 1984, p. 100.
134. Bridge, *The Habsburg Monarchy*, p. 306 quoted from diary

entry of 7/8/1911 in J. Redllich, *Schicksalsjahre Österreichs: Das politische Tagebuch Josef Redlichs*, ed. F. Fellner, Böhlau, Vienna 1953, vol. 1, p. 95.

135. Bridge, *The Habsburg Monarchy*, p. 308; Palmer, *Twilight of the Habsburgs*, pp. 311–12.
136. Williamson, *Austria–Hungary and the Origins of the First World War*, p. 124; Bridge, *The Habsburg Monarchy*, p. 316.
137. Williamson, *Austria–Hungary and the Origins of the First World War*, pp. 126–42.
138. R.A. Kann, *Dynasty, Politics and Culture: Selected Essays*, ed. S. Winters, Social Science Monographs, Boulder 1991, p. 300; Bridge, *The Habsburg Monarchy*, pp. 317–21.
139. Jászi, *The Dissolution of the Habsburg Monarchy*, p. 405.
140. May, *The Habsburg Monarchy*, p. 410.
141. Bridge, 'British Official Opinion', pp. 99–100.
142. Bridge, *The Habsburg Monarchy*, p. 322.
143. Williamson, *Austria–Hungary and the Origins of the First World War*, p. 155.
144. Bridge, *The Habsburg Monarchy*, p. 327.
145. Williamson, *Austria–Hungary and the Origins of the First World War*, p. 163.
146. Bridge, *The Habsburg Monarchy*, pp. 329–33.
147. Jászi, *The Dissolution of the Habsburg Monarchy*, p. 419.

Chapter 7

DEATH AND TRANSFIGURATION

. . .

GOING TO WAR

'Horrible! The Almighty does not allow Himself to be challenged with impunity . . . A higher power has restored the old order which I unfortunately was unable to uphold . . .'[1] These are reputedly the first words Francis Joseph uttered on hearing of the assassination of Francis Ferdinand and his wife. If so, they reveal a man whose first thought was to the standing of his dynasty with providence, who viewed the assassination of his heir as divine retribution for Francis Ferdinand's defiance of his dynastic duties by marrying a mere noblewoman. It was for this reason that, as Margutti reports, 'the Emperor – say what you will – could not restrain a feeling of relief.'[2] The emperor's first response was thus far from being one of such outrage as to immediately call for war against Serbia.

Soon enough, though, the implications of the assassination for Austrian prestige, and the opportunity it seemed to offer for 'settling' the Serbian threat once and for all, led to the same monarch who had felt 'relief' at his heir's demise going to war against Serbia to avenge the same man's murder. There were a great number of forces at work in the month which led up to the declaration of war on 28 July 1914, most of them for war, but the man who signed the declaration was Francis Joseph.[3] For the last, and most fatal time, the emperor played a crucial role on the world stage. Count Edward Paar, Francis Joseph's adjutant, reacted in disbelief when his master signed: 'men of eighty-four years of age don't sign war proclamations'.[4] Understanding why he nevertheless did would solve the last, and largest riddle of Francis Joseph's extraordinary career.

The standing of his dynasty with providence was his first reaction. His second reaction was one of being very shaken by the news.[5] When Berchtold met the emperor at Bad Ischl on 30 June he found him 'anxious to be reassured about the future of Habsburg rule'. So nervous was Francis Joseph that he offered Berchtold his hand and asked him to sit next to him, a most unusual honour, even for such a high aristocrat.[6] Berchtold himself had decided almost immediately after the assassination of Francis Ferdinand, who had been a close friend, that a tough response, including military action, was necessary. Failure to act decisively would be a 'renunciation of our Great Power position'.[7] It was Berchtold's advice, along with the mounting evidence of involvement in the assassination by elements within the Serbian government, which led Francis Joseph already on 2 July to write the letter to William II asking for German support in the event of Austrian military action against Serbia and consequent Russian intervention.[8] Yet it remains unclear just how decisively Francis Joseph supported the call for war, nor which war he envisaged starting.

There is evidence, much of it from his aide-de-camp Margutti, that Francis Joseph went extremely reluctantly to war, swept along by events and the hawkishness of his military and diplomatic advisers and German allies. At Christmas 1913, for instance, the emperor reportedly expressed second thoughts on policy to Serbia, admitting to Count Paar that he should have listened to Ferdinand of Bulgaria and allowed Serbia an Adriatic port, thus placating the Serbians and also reducing the Magyar stranglehold over Balkan trade policy.[9] In the July crisis, Margutti depicts the imperial entourage as viewing even the ultimatum to Serbia as merely a diplomatic bluff, and relates how shaken Francis Joseph was on realising the unacceptability of the Serbian reply. He quotes the emperor as saying: 'Even if diplomatic relations are broken off it doesn't necessarily mean war.' For Margutti a pacific emperor was pushed into war by circumstances and his advisers.[10]

That there was such pressure for war is clear. Berchtold, as we have seen, was immediately in favour of action, and he had previously been among the more dovish of the emperor's advisers. Among the most hawkish was the Chief of the General Staff, Conrad von Hötzendorf, who had been pleading for a preventive war for years, against either Italy or Serbia. To him it was not a question of whether Austria should go to war, but when; as he later put it: 'in 1909 the war would have been a game with open cards, in 1913 it would still have been a game with chances, in 1914 it had become a game of *va banque*, but there was no other alternative.'[11]

For Conrad, the assassination did not so much force Austrian action as offer an opportunity for war.

This seems also to have been the view of Berchtold's hawkish cabinet chief at the Ballhausplatz, Alexander Count Hoyos, who was sent to Berlin on 5 July with a rewritten, beefed up Matscheko Memorandum to seek German support. He received that support, the famous 'blank cheque', because, so the prevailing historiographical consensus maintains, the Germans were thinking along very much the same lines, if not on a Balkan but rather on a world scale. If the Austrians initiated the move to war in July 1914, the Germans were only too willing to back them up, for they had been seeking just such an opportunity for a pre-emptive strike, before, in the collective opinion of the German leadership, it was too late and the Entente's 'encirclement' strategy strangled Germany, in other words prevented her from claiming her 'place in the sun' as a world power.[12] The details of July 1914 are exceedingly complex, but in outline what appears to have happened is that Austria–Hungary, with its vision blinkered to the Balkans, started a war against Serbia, and possibly Russia, which their German allies, eyeing the four corners of the globe, successfully turned into a world war. As soon as the Monarchy had given Germany the opening of forcing Russia to mobilisation, it 'lost control of events – indeed, to a large degree, of its own destiny'.[13] The July crisis saw the Austrians as Germany's stooges, but willing stooges.

Against a combination of mostly hawkish advisers and enthusiastic support, for once, from the German ally there were few prepared to resist the move to war. The leader of the peace party, Francis Ferdinand, was of course absent. This left, ironically, one of the murdered heir's greatest adversaries, István Tisza, as the leading obstacle to war, indeed the only one at a Crown Council meeting of 7 July.[14] He was far from convinced of the sense of war. As a Magyar first and foremost, defeat would be catastrophic, but victory would probably mean a stronger dynastic power, more Serbs in the Monarchy, and even more pressure for the detested trialism. Yet he too came round by 14 July, owing to the fact of German support and arguments about the bad influence which no action against Serbia would have on other nationalities in Hungary, notably the Rumanians.[15] As he wrote to his daughter in justification of his agreeing to war: 'We must react seriously to the insolence of the Serbs; we cannot simply swallow it.'[16] Yet he also came round to the hawks' position because that is what Francis Joseph himself had approved.

Whatever the imperial entourage in Ischl might have thought, it appears that Francis Joseph, far from hoping against hope that war could be avoided was, from early on, convinced that strong action, up to and including war, was necessary. Indeed he seems to have been on the side of the hawks as early as the Scutari crisis of May 1913.[17] He was quite aware of the larger consequences of the ultimatum to Serbia. Leo von Bilinski, the Joint Finance Minister, pointed out to the emperor in an interview of 20 July that the ultimatum meant a European-wide war. Francis Joseph reportedly replied: 'Yes, I know, Russia cannot possibly tolerate such a note.'[18] Whatever the subsequent whistling in the dark of some of his advisers, and perhaps of himself as war drew near, Francis Joseph agreed to the actions which led to the ultimatum to Serbia, designed by Berchtold to be unacceptable, and it was his hand which signed the declaration of war, knowing full well that he was almost certainly starting a Europe-wide conflagration. He was, as Kann puts it, 'the source of the ultimate power of decision', and even a sympathiser such as Margutti has to acknowledge his emperor's responsibility: 'Francis Joseph, who had the last word, at any rate officially, let himself be drawn into a catastrophic situation without definite intentions, fixed aims or a clear appreciation of what might be expected to happen.'[19]

It seems the major reason he agreed to war was, as ever, to uphold the dignity and status of the dynasty. This was, after all, what the War Manifesto of 29 July, addressed 'to my peoples', stated. The war, for which providence was responsible, was to be fought: first, to protect the honour of 'my monarchy'; second, to protect its good name and position among the powers; third, to secure its possessions.[20] Berchtold confirmed this very dynastic version of the reasons for war in his later description of the emperor's foreign policy. The emperor's policy was a policy of peace, Berchtold wrote, but this policy had its limits: 'limits of decency and self-respect, but particularly of the concern for the continuation of the patrimonial legacy which he had inherited, with its family of nations entrusted to him.' He had to defend his Habsburg patrimony (which happened, be it noted, to come *with* a 'family of nations' attached).[21] It might well be, as has been ably argued, by Sked among others, that opting for war was an irrational response to Austria's problems within and outside the

Monarchy's borders. Clearly the 'irrational' motivation of preserving imperial honour, held to have been impugned by the Bosnian Serb terrorists (and their apparent Serbian government collaborators), was central to the decision for war, as Sked insists. Yet, as he also insists, the deeper cause of war in 1914 was 'the very nature of the Monarchy itself', for it existed in order to be a dynastic, great power, and it was this which, due to the previous mistakes and misfortunes of Habsburg foreign and domestic policy, appeared to be under threat in 1914.[22] As Williamson has stated, the main issue in 1914 was 'how Vienna conceived of itself as a great power. To uphold that status the policy-makers in the Dual Monarchy believed that they needed to demonstrate their strength to the Serbians – and to the Russians. A great power had to act like a great power, to show that it had the capacity to determine its own future.'[23]

It was thus the perception of the need for drastic action to preserve Austrian great-power status, especially on Francis Joseph's part, which was the direct cause of war. It is arguable that this was just perception, not reality. Indirectly, though, the failure of Francis Joseph and his ministers to achieve a workable arrangement within his empire, and the various deadlocks produced by dualism and the nationality strife, along with the crass mishandling of the South Slav problem had done a great deal to bring about not only the perception of being backed into a corner, but also the set of circumstances on which those perceptions were based.

Francis Joseph might never have been very sympathetic to his Slav subjects, and this might have added an irrational edge to his fear of Serbia, which should have been treated more sensibly.[24] He no doubt did retain German prejudices which tied him to the Dual Alliance and prevented a full recognition of the merits of federalism or trialism, which should have been tried. Perhaps he should never have wanted to acquire Bosnia–Herzegovina in the first place. Yet most of these options, if they were options, were options no longer available in July 1914, given the prevailing structure of power in the Monarchy. In any case, most went completely against Francis Joseph's understanding of the Habsburg Monarchy as a dynastic great power. This understanding and Francis Joseph's implementation of it over more than half a century, irrational and wrong-headed though they may have been, had created circumstances by the summer of 1914 which had *already* made Austria–Hungary in almost all respects a second-rate power. Often bullied and disregarded by its main ally,

Germany, informally hostile to two supposed allies, Italy and Rumania, and regarded as hopelessly enthralled to Germany by the Entente powers, defied by an upstart Serbia whose territorial ambitions in Bosnia–Herzegovina were real and not imaginary, Austria's decision for war really does not seem very irrational, for *not* doing anything would surely, as Berchtold claimed, have left Austria no longer regarded at all seriously as a great power. As the Foreign Minister was later to write: 'For Emperor Francis Joseph it was clear that our role in world history would be over if we feebly allowed fate to do what it willed.'[25]

For a multi-national state such a relegation might have been no bad thing, for it could have left Austria–Hungary out of the great-power race to settle her problems on her own, if the other powers had denied themselves and others the temptations of partition. But for the Habsburg Monarchy, for the power-base of the imperial dynasty, such a fate, of not being a great power, of indeed being a *'quantité négligeable'*, was unacceptable. It might have been reasonable, but it went entirely against the rationale of the empire, as Francis Joseph understood it. In this light the decision to go to war was not irrational at all, for it was reasonable to assume that this was the only way to maintain the Monarchy's prestige and status, which was its purpose for being.

Yet the consequences of war were understood by hardly anyone in Austrian ruling circles. They were only dimly aware of the global-level calculations with which the Germans were working, and even the implications of war for the Monarchy were only vaguely determined. No matter: given the desperate straits in which Francis Joseph and the Austrian leadership saw themselves, doing something to put the Serbians in their place seemed necessary, and as force seemed to be the only thing the Serbians understood, this meant war, regardless of the result. As Williamson writes: 'Contradictory to its dissolution, the Habsburg Monarchy went to war not for territory or glory but to save itself. How war would achieve that goal the policymakers never really examined. War was merely assumed to address the problem.'[26]

There was an air of fatalism about the Austrian decision for war in 1914. Conrad saw it as *va banque*. Francis Joseph saw things in even gloomier terms. In late July he told Conrad von Hötzendorf: 'If the Monarchy must perish it should at least perish with decency.' [27] On signing the declaration of war, the emperor parted from Alexander von Krobatin, the War Minister, with an even more fatalistic comment: 'Go, I can do nothing else.'[28] There are eerie echoes here of what a far younger Francis Joseph had said many decades before, at the nadir of his defeat at the hands of Prussia in 1866: 'When the whole world is against you and you have no friends, there is little chance of success, but you must go down doing what you can, fulfilling your duty and, in the end, going down with honour.'[29] Perhaps the deepest reason for Francis Joseph's signing of the proclamation of war was that, as someone who believed in a world where the assassination of his heir was a work of providential retribution; where maintaining one's honour, and the honour and standing of one's family and dynasty, were the prime duties; as a man who had survived terrible personal tragedy and endured awful political and military humiliations, he trusted once more in fate, in providence. He had done so all his long life, and, though chastened, had endured, as had his Monarchy. Perhaps, with this last gesture in defence of the old order in which he had been brought up to believe, he and his Monarchy would endure again? Might not the 'higher power' shine on them for once? If he thought so, he would be disappointed.

. . .

WAR AND DEATH

When war was proclaimed on 28 July 1914 one ironic result was that the man who had declared war, Francis Joseph, ceased to be the effective ruler of the Monarchy. All power was concentrated in the Army High Command, with Conrad von Hötzendorf at the helm, and the emperor, approaching his eighty-fourth birthday, was deemed too ancient to take an active part in the direction of the war.[30] Instead he now spent his time virtually interned at Schönbrunn, being fed information about the campaign by headquarters.[31]

If he had been in charge he could hardly have done worse than Conrad in the initial weeks of the war. Always one for taking the initiative, the now virtual dictator of the Monarchy managed by precipitate orders and counter-orders to completely confuse Austria's elaborate pre-war plans for mobilisation on either the Serbian or Russian fronts, 'Plan B' and 'Plan R' respectively. The resulting chaos, immortalised by Hašek in *The Good Soldier Švejk*, involved at one point troops being transported to one end of the empire in order to be immediately transported back to the other end. The confusion caused by Conrad's mismanagement only exacerbated Austria–Hungary's basic problem in the war: as in 1866, the Austrian forces found themselves stretched between two fronts. One of these might have been manageable, but not both.[32]

In the ensuing campaigns, in Serbia and in Poland, the Austrian Army, Francis Joseph's pride and joy, suffered surprisingly little from national divisions, with few instances of desertion or mutiny, but as a fighting force it performed abysmally. In Serbia an initial invasion had to be almost immediately abandoned as Serbian resistance proved stronger than expected; another invasion had captured Belgrade by December, but a Serbian counter-attack led to another Austrian retreat by the end of the year. In Poland much of the fault for the disastrous events of the Battle of Lemberg in September was the Germans', for their reneging on their pre-war promises of support on the Eastern Front, but the battle, which left the whole of Eastern Galicia in Russian hands by the end of the month, revealed an Austrian army which was simply not up to facing a real great power such as Russia. The long years when the army had been starved of funds and modern weaponry in the midst of the national and constitutional conflicts, combined with Conrad's obsession with offensive tactics, exacted a horrible toll on the imperial forces. The Russian advance into Galicia 'destroyed the Austro-Hungarian army as a first-class fighting force', and although the Austrians (with German help) managed to stop it outside of Cracow, and were even able to recapture Czernowitz, by the end of the year four-fifths of the army's trained infantry had been lost: dead, wounded or taken prisoner, as had half the original officer corps. By the end of 1914, 'the traditional Habsburg army' over which so much had been contested in the last decades of the Monarchy, had ceased to exist.[33] Francis Joseph, shut out of running the war, could only look on in near despair.[34]

He was able, however, to have a say on the diplomatic front, although it is very questionable whether he was of any help. Austria was faced here with a situation concerning Italy all too reminiscent of the events of 1866, with uncannily similar results. Italy declared her neutrality on 3 August, as she was not bound by the Triple Alliance to come to Austria's aid if Austria attacked Serbia. Instead, in a manner reminiscent of Napoleon III, she used Aehrenthal's 1911 reintepretation of Article VII of that alliance treaty to demand Austrian territory (the Italian irredenta) both as compensation for Austrian gains in Serbia and as payment for at least Italian neutrality. Under pressure from the Germans the Crown Council discussed ceding the Trentino as early as 8 August, yet from the start such a deal was highly unlikely. As Berchtold was to remark, the integrity of the Monarchy was one of the prime war aims: to lose possessions in order to win was against good sense.[35] Therefore the Austrian response was to make only the barest concession, of Valona, as the price of an active Italian alliance, but nothing else.[36]

This stand against Italian 'blackmail' was one which Francis Joseph, forgetting the lessons of 1866, heartily supported. Replying to a German request to accede to Italian demands, he made an extraordinary but typical statement: 'I prefer to lose everything and to go down with honour; rather than that I allow myself to enter into this commerce of thieves.'[37] Another German request, in 1915, elicited an even more poignant reply: 'I can understand, that after a defeat or even after merely a lost campaign one must cede territory. To do this, however, simply in order that the neighbour does not go over to our enemies, is inconceivable to me.'[38] Yet in 1866 he himself had ended up doing precisely that, with Venetia. He would not be moved on this idea of giving away 'ancient territories', and his refusal to allow even the cession of the Trentino led on 11 January 1915 to Berchtold's resignation.[39] His replacement, Stefan Count Burian, initially shared Francis Joseph's obstinacy, yet the discouragements of early 1915 and added German pressure led eventually, despite all Francis Joseph's talk of honour, to an offer of large tracts of Austrian territory to Italy in any case. By then, however, the offer was too little too late. Italy had signed the Treaty of London with the Entente on 26 April 1915, and declared war on the Monarchy on 23 May.[40]

If Italy was lost due to Austria and Francis Joseph standing on principle, it did not hurt the Central Powers' cause that much, initially. Indeed 1915 saw a string of victories for Austria. The joint Austro-German Gorlice-Tarnow offensive of May, led by the German General Falkenhayn, led to the greatest gains of territory in the whole war, sweeping the Russians entirely out of Poland. In October another joint offensive in the south, with the help of a new ally, Bulgaria, ended with the conquest of Serbia, the initial war aim.[41] Yet both of these great successes had only been won with German assistance. The one major independent Austrian campaign, Conrad's 'Black-yellow campaign' of Rowno in the autumn, was an inauspicious failure, resulting in even greater reliance on the Germans.[42] By 1915, in fact, the Central Powers might be winning the war, but Austria–Hungary was losing any independence within the alliance. The arguments over what to do with conquered Poland showed this only too well. While the plans for an 'Austro-Poland' were in any case compromised by Tisza's refusal to contemplate an Austro-Magyar-Polish 'trialism', any such ideas receded to the far background when it became clear what the Germans were demanding of the Monarchy for giving it control of Poland, which was nothing short of its effective subjugation to Germany. As Bridge says, 'by 1915 the control of Austria–Hungary as a satellite had become a German war aim.'[43] No wonder Conrad had called the Germans 'our underhanded enemy.'[44]

In 1916 this situation deteriorated markedly. Conrad, still determined to resist increasing German seniority, launched an offensive in May against Italy, ignoring General Erich von Falkenhayn's requests not to do so. With Austrian forces depleted on the Russian front, in June the Brusilov Offensive shattered the Austrian defensive lines, leading to huge losses yet again of men and territory.[45] To add insult to injury, Rumania, a former ally, entered the war on 2 August against the Monarchy and quickly overran Transylvania, to the shock of Austrian and Hungarian ruling circles. Yet again, German troops saved the day, halting the Russian advance in September and turning the Rumanian front around, so that General August von Mackensen was in Bucharest by December. The Monarchy had been rescued, but there was a huge price: on 3 August the Germans had taken over command of virtually the whole Eastern Front, and on 6 September 1916 the Austrians had to agree to a Joint High Command, headed by William II, Hindenburg and Ludendorff, taking control of both German and Habsburg forces.[46] The Habsburg Monarchy had lost its military independence to the German, Hohenzollern Empire.

By the autumn of 1916, while there was military success, the situation was not good for Francis Joseph and the Habsburg dynasty. In the Polish question what had been on paper a Habsburg territory had become by November an Austro-German condominium, effectively under German control.[47] German demands for ever closer co-operation between the two monarchies were bearing such fruit as the Salzburg agreement of September 1916 between German and Austrian German deputies. Within the Monarchy there were increasing signs of wear. Hungarian authorities had begun to close off food supplies to Cisleithania, and the economic distress of the home front was cause of and exacerbated by increasing labour unrest and a wave of strikes. The authorities' crackdown on any political opposition led to the hugely counter-productive arrest of Karel Kramař for treason, which merely encouraged Pan-Slavist sentiment among the Monarchy's Slavs.[48]

Francis Joseph, desperately frail as he now was, sensed his patrimony coming apart, and made one last effort to do something about it. Already in July, after a freak tornado touched down in Wiener Neustadt, he reportedly said to Margutti: 'Things are going badly with us, perhaps worse than we suspect. The starving people can't stand much more. It remains to be seen whether and how we shall get through the winter. I mean to end the war next spring whatever happens. I can't let my Empire go to hopeless ruin!'[49] By October even Burian was talking of the need to make peace. When Friedrich Adler, the son of the socialist leader Victor, assassinated Stürgkh, the Cisleithanian prime minister, Francis Joseph appointed none other than Ernest Koerber with the intention of once again trying to return to constitutional government.[50]

Whether or not Francis Joseph's change of heart on the foreign and domestic fronts would have had much effect; whether the moral authority he still possessed would have made him any more successful than his successor, Charles, in obtaining peace and constitutional government for the battered Monarchy; whether, ironically, Francis Joseph died too soon, is debatable. This, however, was to be the last 'might have been' of his long reign, for before anything could be done Francis Joseph, working at his desk almost to the last, died on 21 November 1916. He was buried in the Capuchin Crypt on 30 November, beside his wife and son.

. . .

TRANSFIGURATION

Francis Joseph's funeral procession was one of the last great displays of imperial Habsburg pomp which Vienna was to witness. Yet, in the midst of the catastrophe of the First World War, such pomp had lost much of its meaning and hence its authority. Manès Sperber, a young Jewish refugee from Galicia, had initially looked on astounded at the magnificence passing before him, but soon he became bored and started thinking of his own, Galician Jewish childhood:

While my tired eyes apathetically followed the progress of the Magyar nobles from Slovakia, I thought with pride of my great-grandfather, who had refused all honours, but who nevertheless had been respected by all, even the Ukrainians, and strangers as well. He had despised everything which was mere appearance and not authentic. And now I had seen the splendour of centuries go by, and it had in the end bored me. I now realised that this was not what was important, for it could only have a superficial meaning.[51]

As Redlich wrote, there was no great outpouring of grief, for the exigencies of war had caused too much apathy for that.[52] The passing of the old emperor was also felt as a passing of the era in which majesty had still had power of its own; the dynastic empire which had for centuries relied on such splendour, majesty and magnificence, the appearances of power, did not long survive him.

Francis Joseph's immediate legacy to his successor, Charles, did not at first glance seem hopeless. The Monarchy in late 1916 was still intact, as were the powers of the Austrian emperor and Hungarian king, which Francis Joseph had so doggedly defended. When Charles thus demanded István Tisza's resignation in May 1917 the man who had been Hungary's virtual dictator for years nevertheless obeyed his king's command.[53] The Habsburg Army also carried on, maintaining a surprisingly high level of loyalty among its various national contingents, as indeed did the population on the home front, despite increasing hardship. Yet these positive aspects were overshadowed by the steady deterioration both of the Dual Monarchy's ability to sustain the war and of its position within the Central Powers' alliance.

From the spring of 1917, with economic distress at home and revolution in Russia, Charles' Foreign Minister, Ottokar Count Czernin, was increasingly convinced of the need for peace to rescue the external and internal position of the Monarchy. This either meant negotiating with the Entente Powers, or depending on German victory. At first secret negotiations, behind Germany's back, were attempted with France through the dynastic links of the house of Bourbon-Parma, by the emperor's brother-in-law Prince Sixtus, but by May these had got nowhere. Meanwhile Czernin and the Monarchy were being forced to cede ever more power to the German ally, which admittedly did appear to be the winning side at the end of 1917. By March 1918 Czernin decided to give up all hope of a negotiated peace with the British and French, which led to the French revealing the previous year's Sixtus mission. This put the nail in the coffin of the Monarchy's independence, as the 'betrayed' German leadership exacted from Charles at the meeting at Spa on 12 May 1918 the effective subordination of Austria in a version of *Mitteleuropa* which was merely a mask for German domination.[54] As Bridge writes, even before the war's end, the Monarchy 'had in fact ceased to exist as an independent Great Power'.[55]

Francis Joseph's prediction about winning wars but losing provinces thus contained the most terrible of all counter-factual truths about the Monarchy. If the Central Powers had *won* the war, Austria–Hungary would still have ceased to be an independent Great Power, would in other words have relinquished that status which Francis Joseph had struggled his whole life to preserve. As it was, the Central Powers lost, and as it became clear over the summer and autumn of 1918 that the tide of battle had turned, with the reverses on the Western front and the collapse of Bulgaria in late September on the Balkan front, the Monarchy did what it had so often threatened to do before, and came apart at the seams.

Charles' manifesto promising federalism in Cisleithania (the Magyars still held out) of 16 October 1918 might have been a splendid action in 1912; by late 1918 no one much was listening. Already in May 1917 the return of the Reichsrat had 'opened a Pandora's Box which could not be shut'. Czech and South Slav leaders' demands for independent states (formally within a reformed Monarchy), though rebuffed, had simply grown in force and scope since then, so that even by the summer of 1918 plans were well developed for such separate states.[56] Far from the Monarchy being torn apart by the vindictive policies of the Western powers, the latter's embrace of the various national causes, and crucially the Czechoslovak cause, came very late in the day and in response to events on the ground.[57] As Mark Cornwall has nimbly put it: 'The Monarchy melted away through a combination of internal disintegration and external pressure.'[58] The Monarchy, which had gone to war for the sake of appearances, disappeared virtually overnight.

Some missed it after 1918, though initially they were not many. Of course there was the court society and the high nobility, whose titles soon became illegal in the Austrian Republic, and there were the former Habsburg officials who now flooded into Vienna, now the capital of 'German Austria', the prime successor to the 'Austrian' heritage. The German minority in Bohemia also soon missed the empire which had protected their position, and the Magyars, with their Hungarian state now a third its former size, no doubt regretted the turn of events. The vast majority of the Monarchy's former inhabitants were at first almost ecstatic at having the rule of the Habsburgs off their backs. Czechs, Slovaks, South Slavs, Rumanians, revelled in their new-found national freedom. Even the 'state-supporting' Austrian Germans, most of whom wanted union with Germany, and the Galician Poles, who finally had an independent Poland once again, harboured few regrets for the old empire and the old emperor. It was only later, when life in the successor states took a large turn for the worse, and the new 'nation-states' showed themselves hardly less problematic, and generally far more intolerant than the Monarchy had been, that the image of Francis Joseph became transfigured into the glowing portrait of elderly wisdom and tolerance which illumines the 'Habsburg myth' of inter-war Austrian literature, most famously, and most movingly in Joseph Roth's *Radetzkymarsch.*[59]

As Central Europe plunged into the abyss of first 1930s fascism, then 1940s Nazism and finally Cold-War communism, it is hardly surprising that the image of Francis Joseph as 'the good, old emperor' increasingly gained in currency, until today he is almost seen as the embodiment of the sort of tolerant and equitable Central Europe which so many would like to see come about, as a sort of revamped Habsburg Monarchy. Yet the currency in which this image is traded is the currency of nostalgia and masks the ways in which Francis Joseph's legacy was not so much an ideal of tolerance and national equity, as a major cause of the very problems which prompted such nostalgia.

It was largely due to his management of the Habsburg state, his absolutist convictions and his scepticism about and hostility to constitutionalism, that Austria–Hungary by 1914 had the hierarchical, bureaucratic – Kafkaesque – character, which was to be such a recurring theme of subsequent Central European history. The inter-war successor states thus inherited the lineaments of an authoritarian, bureaucratic state, indeed much of the personnel of that state, which they then developed in mostly not very positive ways.[60] When the communists instituted their 'big brother' states in Central Europe they did not seem that out of place, and there were bureaucrats with bureaucratic traditions which easily traced their origins back to the time before 1918.

Similarly, the way Francis Joseph had handled the nationalities' conflict was by putting dynastic advantage before questions of national justice let alone national co-operation. Despite what many, including his heir,[61] have said, he preferred centralism to federalism, because only the former could guarantee the monarch sufficient power and prestige to fulfil his role as Habsburg dynast. Yet this practising of the 'dynastic principle', amounting to dynastic selfishness, had been a large factor inspiring the sort of Machiavellian, dog-eat-dog political style which Austro-Hungarian politicians had adopted, and this too was a legacy to the inter-war successor states.[62] While some attempts were made, mainly in Czechoslovakia, to follow more equitable policies towards the various national 'minorities' the old temptation to do down the opponent too often won out; it was just that the shoe was now on the other foot. Even in Czechoslovakia Czech officials implemented the same rules which had set German above Czech, only now with the roles reversed.

Yet perhaps worst of all in Francis Joseph's legacy was the terrible 'civic education' which his Monarchy's peoples had received. The constant emphasis in Cisleithanian school text-books on the person of the monarch, on the way in which he was responsible for all the achievements of his reign, as the title of one, *What Emperor Francis Joseph did for his Peoples*, suggests, created little sense of *state* patriotism to counter nationalist loyalties, preferring to strengthen dynastic and not politico-constitutional ties.[63] This meant that the 'Austrian state idea' remained just that, an idea, rather than a conviction shared by the populace, and loyalties, when not nationalist, remained concentrated in the person of the monarch, the leader. It would be going too far to blame Francis Joseph for Adolf Hitler and the *Führerprinzip* – the two were in so many ways diametrical opposites – but his disdain for constitutionalism, his paternalist vision of 'his peoples' and his stress on dynastic and personal loyalty certainly did little to cultivate the political maturity which proved to be the best barrier to the fascist threat. In this sense A. J. P. Taylor was only partly unfair when he wrote that Hitler was 'Austria's greatest gift to the German people'.[64]

It is a large irony of history that one of Francis Joseph's worst legacies to Central Europe was the *lack* of a supra-national Habsburg Monarchy or Habsburg Monarchy surrogate after 1918. After all it has been my argument here that it was his stewardship of the Monarchy since 1848 and it was his agreeing to declare war in 1914, which were largely responsible for the collapse and disappearance of the Monarchy in 1918. Moreover, it was his adherence to the 'dynastic principle' which arguably was a decisive factor in creating the bad blood between the region's nationalities, and it was the experience of the Habsburg Monarchy under Francis Joseph which assured that few if any of the successor states were interested in reconstituting any form of 'Danubian Federation'. In this sense, Francis Joseph's legacy was also the compromising of any serious attempt at Central European co-operation between the wars.

Perhaps here is one answer to the riddle of the 'Habsburg Monarchy as European necessity'. If, as seems clear, the 'small nations' of Central Europe did benefit greatly, economically and diplomatically, by all being part of a large multi-national state, their ineluctable tragedy was, as subjects of Francis Joseph, to be part of a dynastic power structure, the Habsburg Monarchy, whose mishandling of the national problem and its unfortunate ordering of priorities ensured that what might have been a situation amenable to a workable multi-national arrangement was turned into its reverse, a dysfunctional political system which both exacerbated national conflicts and started a European, eventually world-wide war. As the embodiment of the imperial-dynastic tradition of the Habsburg Monarchy, Francis Joseph thus was a decisive contributor to the very problems of which he has so often been seen as the victim, or from which he has even been viewed as a symbol of salvation.

Admittedly, the nations of Central Europe would never have been united in a supra-national state if it had not been for the Habsburg Monarchy.[65] Nor is it at all clear that *any* system could have been devised to stabilise and make productive the national and ethnic diversity of the region. Consider the conclusion of Taylor's account of the *Habsburg Monarchy* in 1947:

'Democratic, federal Yugoslavia' translated into practice the great might-have-been of Habsburg history. Marshal Tito was the last of the Habsburgs: ruling over eight different nations, he offered them 'cultural autonomy' and reined in their national hostility. Old Yugoslavia had attempted to be a Serb national state; in new Yugoslavia the Serbs received only national equality and tended to think themselves oppressed. There was no longer a 'people of state'; the new rulers were men of any nationality who accepted the Communist idea. The Habsburgs had been urged for more than a century to follow this course: Metternich had been accused of communism in Galicia in 1846 and Bach of 'worse than communism' in 1850. No Habsburg since Joseph II had taken the risk; dynastic loyalty was too weak a force to enter such a partnership. More fortunate than the Habsburgs, Marshal Tito found an 'idea'. Only time will show whether social revolution and economic betterment can appease national conflicts and whether Marxism can do better than Counter-Revolution dynasticism in supplying central Europe with a common loyalty.[66]

Time has surely shown that Tito's was hardly any better than Francis Joseph's handling of the ethnic mélange of the South Slav lands. The horrors of Bosnia, the attitudes of the Bosnian Serbs and their Serbian counterparts in Belgrade, suggest perhaps that we view with somewhat less disdain Austrian 'delusions' that the only thing the Serbians understood (or understand) is force, or that the nationalities question is insoluble in general and only approachable *ad hoc.*

Yet the suspicion remains that many of Central Europe's existing problems can be traced back to the questions at the centre of this book: the power Francis Joseph possessed, how he understood it, what he did with it and what effects that had. In the end it is a question of a man whose understanding of his role was anachronistic. He himself spoke of being the last of the old school to one visiting American president, Theodore Roosevelt, but his reaction to another, Ulysses Grant in 1878 is more revealing of what this meant. At a military parade Grant, one of the most effective generals of the century, remarked to the emperor that by now he was sick of seeing military parades. Francis Joseph was so astounded that a general such as Grant might not consider military pomp and circumstance worthwhile that his only reaction was to laugh.[67] His and Grant's were simply two different worlds: past and future.

Francis Joseph's anachronism greatly influenced the state over which he reigned, because he not only reigned but ruled as well, for the first twenty years as an absolute monarch, for the remainder as a 'constitutional' monarch with varying, but always high, levels of actual power. He ruled, unfortunately, without much imagination, but with a dogged insistence on his prerogatives and those of his dynasty. He stuck by what he knew best, which was the world of prestige great-power politics and military manoeuvres and parades, but this was not good enough by 1900.

In many respects Francis Joseph does cut a sympathetic figure. For the most part he was fairly decent when his dynasty's interests could allow him to be, and in some respects he certainly improved with age. Although a devout Catholic, who resisted as much as he could the anti-clerical onslaught of liberalism, and initially spurned Jewish emancipation, he came after 1867 to respect the status of his Jewish subjects, and, with the rise of anti-Semitism, especially racial anti-Semitism, he came to be a staunch defender of their rights. If reports are to be believed, in 1914 he countered Christian Social threats to expel Jewish refugees from Vienna, by threatening to open Schönbrunn itself to the expellees.[68] His precious imperial army officer corps (especially the reserve) was, let it be noted, far more open to Jews than its Prussian equivalent.[69] At times he even showed signs of understanding the significance of his multi-national state.

Yet decency is not enough for *ruling* a multi-national empire. Perhaps the problems were, as the Yugoslav debacle suggests, insoluble, and even if they had not been, it would have taken a genius to figure them out, and one cannot blame Francis Joseph for not being a genius. Yet it was at his insistence that he remained at the helm of the Habsburg state, and it was his choice of men and policies which led to the collapse of 1918. If the problems were close to insoluble, Francis Joseph did not help in solving them.

It is sometimes claimed that Francis Joseph's tragedy was that he was too long on the Austrian imperial throne. His real tragedy was that he was emperor at all. Then again, he died in 1916, before the fate of all he had fought for was clear. Redlich wrote: 'Thus it seems that tragedy in the full sense belongs not so much to Francis Joseph as to the imperial idea, in the old Austrian sense, embodied in him.'[70] But the real tragedy lies with the countless thousands and millions who have been the victims this century of the failure of the Habsburg Monarchy and its monarchical embodiment to use the power at its disposal not only to ensure by transformation the continuance of itself, but to provide that 'homeland' where all could flourish together in peace and security. That the Monarchy never became that homeland, and that Francis Joseph was never the man to bring it about, is one of the harshest truths of modern Central European history, but it is true none the less.

. . .

NOTES AND REFERENCES

1. A. Margutti, *The Emperor Francis Joseph and His Times*, Hutchinson, London 1921, pp. 138–9.
2. Ibid., p. 139; cf. Marie Valerie's diary entry for 28–29 June 1914, in E.C. Corti and H. Sokol, *Der alte Kaiser: Franz Joseph I. vom Berliner Kongress bis zu seinem Tode*, Styria, Graz 1955, p. 412.
3. R.A. Kann, *Dynasty, Politics and Culture: Selected Essays*, ed. S. Winters. Social Science Monographs, Boulder 1991, p. 306.
4. Margutti, *The Emperor Francis Joseph*, p. 319.
5. Ibid., p. 139.
6. S.R. Williamson, Jr., *Austria–Hungary and the Origins of the First World War*, Macmillan, London 1991, p. 192.
7. F.R. Bridge, *The Habsburg Monarchy among the Great Powers, 1815–1918*, Berg, Oxford 1990, p. 335.
8. Bridge, *The Habsburg Monarchy*, pp. 336, 339; Williamson, *Austria–Hungary and the Origins of the First World War*, p. 193; L. Berchtold, 'Der Herrscher wie ich ihn bekannt'. In E. von Steinitz (ed.), *Erinnerungen an Franz Joseph I*, Kulturpolitik, Berlin 1991, p. 314.
9. Margutti, *The Emperor Francis Joseph*, p. 286.
10. Ibid., pp. 305–17.
11. O. Jászi, *The Dissolution of the Habsburg Monarchy*, Chicago, p. 424 (Studies in the Making of Citizens).
12. E.g. H. Pogge von Strandmann, 'Germany and the Coming of War'. In R.J.W. Evans and H. Pogge von Strandmann (eds), *The Coming of the First World War*, Clarendon, Oxford 1988, 114ff.
13. Bridge, *The Habsburg Monarchy*, p. 342; M. Rauchensteiner, *Der Tod des Doppeladlers: Österreich-Ungarn und der Erste Weltkrieg*, Styria, Graz 1993, p. 80.
14. Williamson, *Austria–Hungary and the Origins of the First World War*, p. 198.
15. Bridge, *The Habsburg Monarchy*, p. 340; Williamson, *Austria–Hungary and the Origins of the First World War*, pp. 197, 200.
16. Williamson, *Austria–Hungary and the Origins of the First World War*, p. 204.
17. Kann, *Dynasty, Politics and Culture*, p. 300.
18. Ibid., p. 294.

19. Ibid., p. 306; Margutti, *The Emperor Francis Joseph*, p. 317.
20. Corti and Sokol, *Der alte Kaiser*, p. 420.
21. Berchtold, 'Der Herrscher wie ich ihn bekannt', p. 313.
22. A. Sked, *The Decline and Fall of the Habsburg Empire 1815–1918*, Longman, London 1989, pp. 264–8.
23. Williamson, *Austria–Hungary and the Origins of the First World War*, p. 179.
24. Margutti, *The Emperor Francis Joseph*, p. 205.
25. Berchtold, 'Der Herrscher wie ich ihn bekannt', p. 314.
26. Williamson, *Austria–Hungary and the Origins of the First World War*, p. 211.
27. Corti and Sokol, *Der alte Kaiser*, p. 431; Jászi, *The Dissolution of the Habsburg Monarchy*, p. 424.
28. A. Krobatin, 'Aus meinen Erinnerungen an den Kaiser'. In E. von Steinitz (ed.), *Erinnerungen an Franz Joseph I.*, Kulturpolitik, Berlin 1931, p. 325; Corti and Sokol, *Der alte Kaiser*, p. 420.
29. A. Palmer, *Twilight of the Habsburgs: The Life and Times of Emperor Francis Joseph*, Weidenfeld & Nicolson, London 1994, p. 147.
30. Margutti, *The Emperor Francis Joseph*, p. 328.
31. Ibid., p. 330.
32. Williamson, *Austria–Hungary and the Origins of the First World War*, pp 206–7; Bridge, *The Habsburg Monarchy*, pp. 343–4; R. Jeřábek, 'The Eastern Front 1914–1918'. In M. Cornwall (ed.), *The Last Years of Austria–Hungary*, University of Exeter, Exeter 1990, p. 104.
33. Bridge, *The Habsburg Monarchy*, pp. 343–4; Palmer, *Twilight of the Habsburgs*, p. 334; I. Deák, *Beyond Nationalism: A Social and Political History of the Habsburg Officer Corps 1848–1918*, Oxford 1990, pp. 192–4; Jeřábek, 'The Eastern Front 1914–1918', pp. 106–7.
34. Palmer, *Twilight of the Habsburgs*, pp. 334–5.
35. Bridge, *The Habsburg Monarchy*, pp. 347–8.
36. Williamson, *Austria–Hungary and the Origins of the First World War*, p. 210.
37. Corti and Sokol, *Der alte Kaiser*, p. 437; cf. Margutti, *The Emperor Francis Joseph*, p. 343.
38. Krobatin, 'Aus meinen Errinerungen', p. 326.
39. Margutti, *The Emperor Francis Joseph*, p. 343; Bridge, *The Habsburg Monarchy*, p. 349.

40. Bridge, *The Habsburg Monarchy*, p. 350; Kann, *Dynasty, Politics and Culture*, p. 265.
41. Bridge, *The Habsburg Monarchy*, p. 354.
42. Jeřábek, 'The Eastern Front', pp. 108–9.
43. Bridge, *The Habsburg Monarchy*, p. 353.
44. Ibid., p. 346.
45. Ibid., p. 356; Corti and Sokol, *Der alte Kaiser*, p. 451.
46. Bridge, *The Habsburg Monarchy*, p. 356; Palmer, *Twilight of the Habsburgs*, pp. 338–9; Jeřábek, 'The Eastern Front', pp. 110–11.
47. Bridge, *The Habsburg Monarchy*, p. 355.
48. Corti and Sokol, *Der alte Kaiser*, p. 454.
49. Margutti, *The Emperor Francis Joseph*, p. 362.
50. Bridge, *The Habsburg Monarchy*, p. 358; Corti and Sokol, *Der alte Kaiser*, p. 460; Margutti, *The Emperor Francis Joseph*, p. 365.
51. M. Sperber, *Die Wasserträger Gottes*, Deutscher Taschenbuch, Munich 1978, p. 137.
52. J. Redlich, *Emperor Francis Joseph of Austria: A Biography*, Macmillan, New York 1929, p. 530.
53. Bridge, *The Habsburg Monarchy*, p. 358; I owe the recognition of the significance of this event to the information of Laszlo Péter.
54. Ibid., pp. 359–69.
55. Ibid., p. 380.
56. M. Cornwall, 'The Dissolution of Austria–Hungary'. In M. Cornwall (ed.), *The Last Years of Austria–Hungary*, University of Exeter, Exeter 1990, pp. 137–9.
57. Sked, *The Decline and Fall of the Habsburg Empire*, p. 264; Bridge, *The Habsburg Monarchy*, p. 370.
58. Cornwall, 'The Dissolution of Austria–Hungary', p. 140.
59. J. Roth, *Radetzkymarsch*, Deutscher Taschenbuch, Munich 1981.
60. Cf. J. Redlich, *Österreichische Regierung und Verwaltung im Weltkriege*, Hölder, Vienna 1925, pp. 286–7.
61. O. Habsburg, *Kaiser Franz Joseph*, Werner, Vienna 1966, pp. 8–9.
62. H.W. Steed, *The Habsburg Monarchy*, reprint 2nd edn 1914, Fertig, New York 1969, p. 295.
63. Jászi, *The Dissolution of the Habsburg Monarchy*, p. 436.
64. A.J.P. Taylor, *The Habsburg Monarchy 1809–1918*, Penguin, Harmondsworth 1948 (1964), p. 279.
65. Kann, *Dynasty, Politics and Culture*, pp. 65–7.

66. Taylor, *The Habsburg Monarchy*, p. 282.
67. E.C. Corti, *Mensch und Herrscher: Wege und Schicksale Kaiser Franz Josephs I. zwischen Thronbesteigung und Berliner Kongress*, Styria, Graz 1952, p. 537.
68. Corti and Sokol, *Der alte Kaiser*, p. 439.
69. Deák, *Beyond Nationalism*, pp. 172–8.
70. Redlich, *Emperor Francis Joseph*, p. 540.

FURTHER READING

The literature on Francis Joseph has recently been joined by two new biographies: J.-P. Bled, *Franz Joseph*, trans. T. Bridgeman, Blackwell, Oxford, 1992; and A. Palmer, *Twilight of the Habsburgs: The Life and Times of Emperor Francis Joseph*, Weidenfeld & Nicolson, London, 1994, both of which have their merits. Truly indispensable, however, are two older works. Corti's three volume biography: E. C. Corti, *Vom Kind zum Kaiser: Kindheit und erste Jugend Kaiser Franz Josephs I. und seiner Geschwister*, Pustet, Graz, 1950; E. C. Corti, *Mensch und Herrscher: Wege und Schicksale Kaiser Franz Josephs I. zwischen Thronbesteigung und Berliner Kongress*, Styria, Graz, 1952; and E. C. Corti and H. Sokol, *Der alte Kaiser: Franz Joseph I. vom Berliner Kongress bis zu seinem Tode*, Styria, Graz, 1955 (completed by Sokol after Corti's death), is a mine of detail about the emperor's life. J. Redlich, *Emperor Francis Joseph of Austria: A Biography*, Macmillan, New York, 1929, on the other hand, is a most insightful account of the man and the problems of his empire.

A. Margutti, *The Emperor Francis Joseph and His Times*, Hutchinson, London, 1921, provides an interesting picture of the emperor in his later years, as does E. Ketterl, *Der Alte Kaiser wie nur Einer ihn sah*, 2nd edn, Molden, Vienna, 1980. E. von Steinitz (ed.), *Erinnerungen an Franz Joseph I*, Kulturpolitik, Berlin, 1931, offers essays from many of the major figures in the Habsburg government, including Berchtold.

R. A. Kann, *Dynasty, Politics and Culture: Selected Essays*, ed. S. Winters, Social Science Monographs, Boulder, 1991, provides several essays discussing the place of Francis Joseph within his empire; on the same subject see W. A. Jenks, 'The Later Habsburg Concept of Statecraft', *Austrian History Yearbook* 2 (1966), and the interesting account by O. Habsburg, *Kaiser Franz Joseph*, Werner, Vienna, 1966. Comparative insight can be gained from

D. Lieven, *Nicholas II, Emperor of all the Russias*, Pimlico, London, 1993, and J. C. G. Röhl, *Kaiser, Hof und Staat: Wilhelm II und die deutsche Politik*, Beck, Munich, 1987.

The most recent general account of the Habsburg Monarchy's history during Francis Joseph's reign is A. Sked, *The Decline and Fall of the Habsburg Empire 1815–1918*, Longman, London, 1989. Sked's stimulating and provocative approach is in the tradition of A. J. P. Taylor, whose *The Habsburg Monarchy 1809–1918*, Penguin, Harmondsworth, 1948 (1964) is still most valuable. O. Jászi, *The Dissolution of the Habsburg Monarchy*, Chicago, 1929 (Studies in the Making of Citizens), is even older, yet remains a key work in the field. Standard histories to be consulted are R. A. Kann, *A History of the Habsburg Empire, 1526–1918*, University of California, Berkeley, 1977; C. A. Macartney, *The Habsburg Empire, 1790–1918*, Macmillan, London, 1969 (also in shortened form as C. A. Macartney, *The House of Austria: The Later Phase 1790–1918*, Edinburgh, 1978); and A. J. May, *The Habsburg Monarchy, 1867–1914*, Harvard, Cambridge, 1951. The widely available E. Crankshaw, *The Fall of the House of Habsburg*, Viking Penguin, New York, 1963, is entertaining but unreliable. The pro-Habsburg polemic, F. Fejtö, *Requiem pour un empire défunt: Histoire de la destruction de l'Autriche-Hongrie*, Lieu Commun, Paris, 1988, should be read, if at all, in comparison to the stimulating set of much less nostalgic essays in M. Cornwall (ed.), *The Last Years of Austria–Hungary*, University of Exeter, Exeter, 1990.

As a reference book of Habsburg history the now many volume series, A. Wandruszka and P. Urbanitsch (eds), *Die Habsburger Monarchie 1848–1918* (6+ vols), Österreichische Akademie der Wissenschaften, Vienna, 1973–, is to be strongly recommended. The *Austrian History Yearbook* (1965–) is to be similarly recommended as the main source of relevant scholarly articles*.

Francis Joseph's own written thoughts are largely available through the various collections of letters, especially to his mother and his wife, published in German. Of particular note are his letters to Katharina Schratt: Franz Joseph, *Meine liebe, gute Freundin! Die Briefe Kaiser Franz Josephs an Katharina Schratt*, ed. B. Hamann, Überreuter, Vienna, 1992. His son, Rudolf, was a more

---

*In subsequent references, *Die Habsburger Monarchie 1848–1918* is abbreviated to *HM*, while the *Austrian History Yearbook* is abbreviated to *AHY*.

lively and perceptive writer, as made evident in the revealing collection Rudolf, *Majestät, ich warne Sie: Geheime und private Schriften,* ed. B. Hamann, Amalthea, Vienna, 1979. The minutes of the equivalent of Francis Joseph's cabinet are in the process of being published. The minutes from 1848 to 1867 are being published by the Austrian Academy: H. Rumpler and W. Heindl (eds), *Die Protokolle des österreichischen Ministerrates 1848–1867,* Öst. Bundesverlag, Vienna, 1973–; the minutes of the joint Crown Council from 1867 to 1918 by the Hungarian Academy: I. Diószegi and E. Somogyi (eds), *Die Protokolle des gemeinsamen Ministerrates der österreichisch-ungarischen Monarchie, 1867–1918,* Budapest, 1991–.

There are several contemporary accounts in English to be recommended: Anonymous, *The Private Life of two Emperors: William II of Germany and Francis-Joseph of Austria* (2 vols). Nash, London, 1904; H. Rumbold, *Recollections of a Diplomatist* (2 vols), Arnold, London, 1902; and H. Rumbold, *The Austrian Court in the Nineteenth Century*, Methuen, London, 1909. The most significant pre-war account in English is H. W. Steed, *The Habsburg Monarchy*, reprint of the 1914 2nd edn., Fertig, New York, 1969. Comparison with Steed's post-war attitude, in H. W. Steed, *The Doom of the Habsburgs*, Arrowsmith, London, 1937, is instructive. Other contemporary accounts of note in German are P. Vasili, *Die Wiener Gesellschaft,* Leipzig, 1885, and Anonymous, *Kaiser Franz Joseph I und sein Hof,* ed. J. Schneider, Zsolnay, Vienna, 1984, as well as J. Redllich, *Schicksalsjahre Österreichs: Das politische Tagebuch Josef Redlichs,* ed. F.Fellner, 2 vols, Böhlau, Vienna, 1953.

For an understanding of Francis Joseph's rule an understanding of his dynastic precursors and the dynastic tradition is most important. R. J. W. Evans, *The Making of the Habsburg Monarchy, 1550–1700: An Interpretation*, Clarendon, Oxford, 1979, is a landmark work in this respect, and to be recommended strongly. M. Tanner, *The Last Descendant of Aeneas: The Habsburgs and the Mythic Image of the Emperor,* Yale, New Haven, 1993, provides an intriguing picture of the efforts of the Habsburgs at self-advertisement. The recently published book by Andrew Wheatcroft, *The Habsburgs: Embodying Empire,* Viking, London, 1995, also explores this theme. C. Ingrao, *The Habsburg Monarchy 1618–1815,* Cambridge, 1994 (New Approaches to European History), provides the most up-to-date account of the pre-nineteenth century Monarchy. The key figure of Joseph II receives a brilliant analysis in T. C. W. Blanning, *Joseph II*, Longman, London, 1994 (Profiles in Power). Only the first half of Derek Beales's definitive account of the same monarch has so far been published, D. Beales, *Joseph II*, Cambridge, 1987.

For the period immediately leading up to 1848 and Francis Joseph's ascension to the throne, there is W. L. Langer, *Political and Social Upheaval 1832–52*, Harper & Row, New York, 1969 (The Rise of Modern Europe); P. N. Stearns, *1848: The Revolutionary Tide in Europe*, Norton, New York, 1974 (Revolutions in the Modern World); and J. Sperber, *The European Revolutions, 1848–1951*, Cambridge, 1994 (New Approaches to European History). P. Jones, *The 1848 Revolutions*, Longman, London, 1981 (Seminar Studies in History) is a useful introduction. R. J. Rath, *The Viennese Revolution*, Greenwood, New York, 1969, and I. Deák, *The Lawful Revolution*, Columbia University Press, New York, 1979, are important more specific studies.

A key work for the Taaffe era is W. A. Jenks, *Austria under the Iron Ring 1879–1893*, University Press of Virginia, Charlottesville, 1965. L. Höbelt, *Kornblume und Kaiseradler: Die deutschfreiheitlichen Parteien Altösterreichs 1882–1918*, Geschichte und Politik, Vienna, 1993, provides an in-depth look at the crucial transition within the German bourgeois parties from a liberal to a national perspective. The work of P. Judson, especially '"Not another square foot": German Liberalism and the Rhetoric of National Ownership in Nineteenth-Century Austria', in *AHY*, vol. 26, is also to be recommended.

For the rise of the Christian Socials, J. W. Boyer, *Political Radicalism in Late Imperial Vienna: Origins of the Christian Social Movement 1848–1897*, University of Chicago, 1981, now joined by J. W. Boyer, *Culture and Political Crisis in Vienna: Christian Socialism in Power, 1897–1918*, University of Chicago, 1995, has become the standard work. R. S. Geehr, *Karl Lueger, Mayor of Fin de Siècle Vienna*, Wayne State, Detroit, 1990, is, however, a useful corrective to parts of Boyer's approach.

On Hungary, J. K. Hoensch, *A History of Modern Hungary, 1867–1986*, trans. K. Traynor, Longman, London, 1988, provides a good, concise account. L. Péter, 'The Dualist Character of the 1867 Hungarian Settlement', in G. Ránki (ed.), *Hungarian History – World History*, Indiana, Bloomington, 1984, provides an important insight into the functioning of the Hungarian constitution and Francis Joseph's role within it.

Francis Joseph's foreign policy is very well served by F. R. Bridge, *The Habsburg Monarchy among the Great Powers, 1815–1918*, Berg, Oxford, 1990. On the early period of his reign there is D. M.

Goldfrank, *The Origins of the Crimean War*, Longman, London, 1994 (Origins of Modern Wars). On relations with Germany, J. Kořalka, 'Deutschland und die Habsburgermonarchie'. In *HM*, 1993, vol. 6. pt. 2, *Aussenpolitik* is recommended, along with S. Wank, 'Foreign Policy and the Nationality Problem in Austria–Hungary 1867–1914', *AHY* 3 (1967); S. Wank, 'The Impact of the Dual Alliance on the Germans in Austria and Vice-Versa', *East Central Europe* 7 (2) (1980); and W. Wagner, 'Kaiser Franz Joseph und das deutsche Reich von 1871 bis 1914', unpublished Ph.D. dissertation, University of Vienna, 1951. On the period leading up to the First World War, the most recent work of note in English is S. R. Williamson Jr., *Austria–Hungary and the Origins of the First World War*, Macmillan, London, 1991. R. J. W. Evans and H. Pogge von Strandmann (eds), *The Coming of the First World War*, Clarendon, Oxford, 1988, has many insightful essays, as does the volume edited by Cornwall (see above). F. R. Bridge, 'British Official Opinion and the Domestic Situation in the Habsburg Monarchy, 1900–1914', in B. J. C. McKercher and D. J. Moss (eds), *Shadow and Substance in British Foreign Policy 1895–1939*, University of Alberta, Edmonton, 1984, provides interesting evidence from a British perspective.

On the war itself M. Rauchensteiner, *Der Tod des Doppeladlers: Österreich-Ungarn und der Erste Weltkrieg*, Styria, Graz, 1993, and N. Stone, *The Eastern Front 1914–1917*, Hodder & Stoughton, London, 1975, are recommended, as are the relevant essays in Cornwall's volume.

The army is well dealt with in G. E. Rothenberg, *The Army of Francis Joseph*, Purdue, West Lafayette, 1976. I. Deák, *Beyond Nationalism: A Social and Political History of the Habsburg Officer Corps 1848–1918*, Oxford, 1990, provides a somewhat nostalgic, but nevertheless fascinating picture of the Habsburg officer, and A. Sked, *The Survival of the Habsburg Empire: Radetzky, the Imperial Army and the Class War, 1848*, Longman, London, 1979, shows just how central the army was to the Monarchy's existence. The most recent work, showing the less romantic side of the Habsburg military establishment, and hinting at the reasons for its ultimate failure, is G. D. W. Wawro, *The Austro-Prussian War: Austria's War with Prussia and Italy in 1866*, Cambridge, 1996. See also Wawro, 'Inside the Whale: the Tangled Finances of the Austrian Army, 1848–66', in *War in History*, vol. 3 (February 1996), pp. 42–65, and Wawro, 'An Army of Pigs: the technical, social, and political bases of

Austrian Shock Tactics, 1859–66', in *The Journal of Military History*, vol. 59 (July 1995) pp.407–34.

On the Habsburg bureaucracy, W. Heindl, *Gehorsame Rebellen: Bürokratie und Beamte in Österreich, 1780–1848*, Böhlau, Vienna, 1991 (Studien zu Politik und Verwaltung) is very important, as are the various essays on the Austrian and Hungarian bureaucracies in *HM*, 1975, vol. 2, *Verwaltung und Rechtswesen*: W. Goldinger, E. C. Hellbling and J. Klabouch on the central, provincial and local Cisleithanian administrations respectively, and G. Barany on the Hungarian administration.

The constitutional and structural problems of the Monarchy are the subject of two classic accounts: L. Eisenmann, *Le Compromis Austro-Hongrois de 1867: Étude sur le dualisme* reprint of the 1904 edn, Academic International, Hattiesburg, 1971, and J. Redlich, *Das österreichische Staats- und Reichsproblem* (2 vols), Neue Geist, Leipzig, 1920. Also most valuable is J. Redlich, *Österreichische Regierung und Verwaltung im Weltkriege*, Hölder, Vienna, 1925.

Problems of reform and Francis Joseph's place within the system are discussed in R. A. Kann, *Dynasty, Politics and Culture: Selected Essays*, ed. S. Winters, Social Science Monographs, Boulder, 1991. A. Spitzmüller, *Memoirs*, trans. C. de Bussy, East European Monographs, Boulder, 1987, provides an insider's account of the problems within the officialdom.

The continuing influence of the aristocracy is discussed in S. Wank, 'Aristocrats and Politics in Austria 1867–1914: A Case of Historiographical Neglect', *East European Quarterly* 26 (2), 1992; S. Wank, 'Aristocrats and Nationalism in Bohemia 1861–1899', *History of European Ideas* 15 (4–6), 1992. The larger European context is discussed in A. J. Mayer, *The Persistence of the Old Regime: Europe to the Great War*, Pantheon, New York, 1981, and D. Lieven, *The Aristocracy in Europe, 1815–1914*, Columbia University Press, New York, 1992.

The standard work on the national question is R. A. Kann, *The Multinational Empire: Nationalism and National Reform in the Habsburg Monarchy, 1848–1918* (2 vols), Octagon, New York, 1977. R. A. Kann, *The Habsburg Empire: A Study in Integration and Disintegration*, Praeger, New York, 1957, is also useful. *HM*, vol.3, *Die Völker des Reiches*, provides essays on each nationality as well as thematic essays.

R. Robertson and E. Timms (eds), *The Habsburg Legacy: National Identity in Historical Perspective*, Austrian Studies 5, Edinburgh, 1994, contains many insightful essays, as does the more theoretical collection, R.L. Rudolph and D. F. Good (eds), *Nationalism and Empire*, St. Martin's, New York, 1992. A. S. Markovits, 'Empire and Province', in A. S. Markovits, F. E. Sysyn, *Nationbuilding and the Politics of Nationalism: Essays on Austrian Galicia*, Harvard, Cambridge, 1982; S. Wank, 'The Growth of Nationalism in the Habsburg Monarchy, 1848–1918', *East Central Europe* 10 (1–2), 1983; and especially S. Wank, 'The Nationalities Question in the Habsburg Monarchy: Reflections on the Historical Record', *Working Papers in Austrian Studies* 93 (3), 1993, are also recommended. G. Stourzh, 'Die Gleichberechtigung der Volksstämme als Verfassungsprinzip 1848–1918', in *HM*, 1980, vol. 3 pt. 2, *Die Völker des Reiches*, is the best account of the Habsburg authorities' efforts to deal with the national question. S. Wank, 'Desperate Counsel in Vienna in July 1914: Berthold Molden's Unpublished Memorandum', *Central European History* 26 (3), 1993, points to why they failed.

On the particular nationalities, the Germans have received the most thorough treatment: P. Urbanitsch, 'Die Deutschen in Österreich: Statistisch-deskriptiver Überblick'; B. Sutter, 'Die politische und rechtliche Stellung der Deutschen in Österreich 1848–1918', and G. Gottas, 'Die Deutschen in Ungarn', all in *HM*, 1980, vol. 3, pt. 1, *Die Völker des Reiches*, provide a good introduction. A. Whiteside, 'The Germans as an Integrative Force in Imperial Austria: the Dilemma of Dominance', *AHY* 3 (1), 1967; S. Beller, 'Germans and Jews as Central European and "Mitteleuropäisch" Elites', in P. Stirk (ed.), *Mitteleuropa: History and Prospects*, Edinburgh, 1994 (Studies in European Unity); and H-H. Brandt, 'The Revolution of 1848 and the Problem of Central European Nationalities', in H. Schulze (ed.), *Nation-Building in Central Europe*, Berg, Leamington Spa, 1987, are also recommended.

On the Slavic nationalities generally, Pan-Slavism is discussed in J. Erickson, *Panslavism*, Historical Association, London, 1964. On the Czechs there is J. Kořalka, R. J. Crampton, 'Die Tschechen', in *HM*, 1980, vol. 3, pt. 1, *Die Völker des Reiches*; and J. F. N. Bradley, *Czech Nationalism in the Nineteenth Century*, East European Monographs, Boulder, 1984. The South Slavs are discussed in H. & C. Seton-Watson, *The Making of a New Europe: R. W. Seton-Watson and the Last Years of Austria–Hungary*, University of Washington, Seattle, 1981; R. Okey, *Eastern Europe, 1740–1985: Feudalism to Communism*, 2nd edn, Hutchinson, London, 1986, is also useful here. On Bosnia, N. Malcolm, *Bosnia: A Short History*, Macmillan, London, 1994, is recommended.

The vexed topic of the Jews and anti-Semitism is masterfully handled in P. Pulzer, *The Rise of Political Anti-Semitism in Germany and Austria*, revised edn, Halban, London, 1988. W. O. McCagg, *A History of Habsburg Jews, 1670–1918*, Indiana University Press, Bloomington, 1989, has a great deal of interesting views and information. R. S. Wistrich, *The Jews of Vienna in the Age of Franz Joseph*, Oxford, 1989, contains a discussion of Austrian Jewry's relations with Francis Joseph; also of interest is J. S. Bloch, *Erinnerungen aus meinem Leben*, Rikola, Vienna, 1922.

The economic history of the Monarchy has of late been the subject to re-evaluation, most skilfully in D. F. Good, *The Economic Rise of the Habsburg Empire, 1750–1914*, University of California, Berkeley, 1984; N. T. Gross, 'The Habsburg Monarchy'. In C. M. Cipolla (ed.), *The Fontana Economic History of Europe* (5 vols), Fontana, Glasgow, 1973, vol. 4 pt. 1. is also of use.

For the cultural history of the Monarchy, W. M. Johnston, *The Austrian Mind: An Intellectual and Social History, 1848–1938*, University of California, Berkeley, 1972, provides a comprehensive introduction. A. Janik and S. Toulmin, *Wittgenstein' Vienna*, Simon & Schuster, New York, 1973; and C. E. Schorske, *Fin-de-siècle Vienna: Politics and Culture*, Weidenfeld & Nicolson, London, 1980, are key works on Vienna; J. Lukacs, *Budapest 1900: A Historical Portrait of a City and its Culture*, Weidenfeld & Nicolson, London, 1989, an entertaining introduction to Budapest. S. Beller, *Vienna and the Jews, 1867–1938: A Cultural History*, Cambridge, 1989, might also be consulted on the central role played by Austro-Hungarian Jewry in Viennese modern culture.

On the literature of the 'Habsburg myth', with its iconography of Francis Joseph, two examples are highly recommended: J. Roth, *The Radetzky March*, trans. E. Tucker, Overlook, Woodstock, 1974; and S. Zweig, *The World of Yesterday*, Viking, New York, 1943. M. Sperber, *God's Water Carriers*, trans. J. Neugroschel, Holmes and Meier, New York, 1987, should also be read, as a partial antidote.

CHRONOLOGY

1830	Born, 18 August.
1835	Death of Emperor Francis I of Austria; accession of Ferdinand.
1846	Galician Revolt.
1848	Tobacco Riots in Milan, January. Abdication of Louis Philippe of France, 24 February. Louis Kossuth's speech at the Hungarian Diet, 3 March. Revolution in Vienna, 13 March. Formation of separate Hungarian ministry, 17 March. Revolution in Berlin; revolt in Milan, 18 March. Radetzky's withdrawal from Milan, 22 March. Piedmont declares war on Austria, 23 March. Francis Joseph sees action at Santa Lucia, 6 May. Flight of the imperial family to Innsbruck, 17 May. Meeting of the Frankfurt Parliament, 18 May. Meeting of the Slav Congress in Prague, 2 June. Bombardment of Prague by Windischgrätz, 16 June. Austrian Parliament meets in Vienna, 22 July. Radetzky's army defeats Italians at Custozza, 25 July. Return of imperial family to Vienna, 9 August. Emancipation of the peasantry in Austria, 7 September. Jellačić's army invades Hungary, 11 September. Beginning of October revolution in Vienna, 6 October. Flight of the imperial family to Olmütz, 7 October.

243

Windischgrätz's army occupies Vienna, 31 October.
Formation of Schwarzenberg ministry, 21 November.
Austrian Parliament reconvenes at Kremsier,
22 November.
Ferdinand abdicates; Francis Joseph accedes,
2 December.

1849	Dissolution of Kremsier Parliament; 'grant' of Stadion Constitution, 6 March.
	Radetzky's army defeats Italians at Novara, 23 March.
	Frederick William IV of Prussia rejects Frankfurt Parliament's offer of German crown, 3 April.
	Russian intervention in Hungary, May.
	Hungarian surrender to Russians at Világos, 13 August.
1850	Erfurt Union established by Prussia, 9 February.
	Punktation of Olmütz, 29 November.
1851	Kübeck's *Reichsrat* established, March.
	Dresden Conference, April.
	Expert report advises rejection of breech-loading rifle for Austrian army, 15 November.
	Louis Napoleon's coup d'état in France, 2 December.
	Sylvesterpatent supercedes Stadion Constitution: re-establishment of abolutism in Austria, 31 December.
1852	Death of Schwarzenberg; Buol becomes Foreign Minister, 5 April.
	Tour of Hungary, May–June.
1853	Assassination attempt on Francis Joseph, 18 February.
	Commercial Treaty with states of the *Zollverein*.
	Russian occupation of the Danubian Principalities, July.
	Engagement to Elisabeth of Bavaria, 18 August.
1853/4–6	Crimean War
1854	Britain and France declare war on Russia, 27 March.
	Marriage to Elisabeth, 24 April.
	Austrian ultimatum to Russia, 3 June.
	Austrian alliance with Britain and France, 2 December.

1855	Founding of the Credit Anstalt.
	Francis Joseph signs Concordat with Rome, 18 August.
1856	Treaty of Paris, 30 May.
1856–7	Neuchâtel Affair
1857	Decision to raze city walls of Vienna, 20 December.
1858	Meeting of Napoleon III and Cavour at Plombières, 21–22 July.
	Birth of Crown Prince Rudolph, 21 August.
1859	*Gewerbeordnung* (Industrial Code) instituted.
	Franco-Austrian War, April–July.
	Austria declares war on Piedmont, 29 April.
	Buol resigns, 4 May.
	Rechberg becomes Foreign Minister, 13 May.
	Defeat at Magenta, 4 June.
	Death of Metternich, 11 June.
	Defeat at Solferino, 26 June.
	Armistice of Villafranca, 11 July.
	Peace of Zurich, 10 November.
1860	Dismissal and suicide of Bruck, 22 April.
	Meeting of expanded Reichsrat, 31 May.
	October Diploma, 20 October.
1861	February Patent, 28 February.
	Hungarian Diet rejects the February Patent, 8 April.
	Hungarian Diet dissolved, 22 August.
1862	*Gemeindegesetz* passed.
	Bismarck becomes Prussian prime minister, 29 September.
1863	Czechs boycott the Reichsrat, 17 June.
	Fürstentag at Frankfurt, 16 August–1 September.
1864	Intervention in Schleswig-Holstein, 1 February.
	Archduke Maximilian leaves for Mexico, 9 April.
	Rechberg replaced by Mensdorff-Pouilly, 27 October.
1865	Deák's Easter article, 11 April.
	Opening of the Ringstrasse, 1 May.
	Schmerling replaced by Belcredi as prime minister, July.

Suspension of February Patent, 20 September.
Hungarian Diet recalled, 14 December.

1866   Prusso-Italian alliance, 8 April.
Franco-Austrian treaty over Venetia, 12 June.
Austro-Prussian War, June–July.
Victory at Custozza, 24 June.
Defeat at Königgrätz (Sadowa), 3 July.
Armistice of Nikolsburg, 26 July.
Peace of Prague, 23 August.
Beust becomes Foreign Minister, 30 October.

1867   Francis Joseph decides for dualism, 1 February.
Andrássy becomes Hungarian prime minister,
17 February.
Secret *Punktation* with the Hungarian leadership,
March.
Czechs boycott Reichsrat again, April.
Hungarian Diet votes for the Compromise, 29 May.
Coronation as King of Hungary in Buda, 8 June.
Maximilian executed in Mexico, 19 June.
Reichsrat passes Fundamental Law, 21 December.
Cisleithanian 'Citizen's Ministry' formed with Carlos Auersperg as prime minister, 30 December.

1868   *Nagodba* (Hungarian-Croat Compromise) and
Nationality Law passed in Hungary; Army Laws passed
in Cisleithania and Hungary.
Anti-clerical 'May Laws' passed by *Reichsrat*, May.
Resignation of Carlos Auersperg, September.

1869   Establishment of *Reichsgericht.*
Travel to Suez Canal and Holy Land, October–
November.

1870   Potocki becomes Cisleithanian prime minister, 4 April.
Declaration of Papal Infallibility, 18 July.
France declares war on Prussia, 19 July.
Abrogation of the Concordat, 30 July.
Prussia defeats France at Sedan, 1 September.

1871   Declaration of German Empire at Versailles,
18 January.
Hohenwart Ministry formed, 7 February.
Beust's foreign policy memorandum, May.

Francis Joseph agrees to autonomy of Bohemian lands, 14 September.
Failure of Bohemian Compromise, 20–22 October.
Hohenwart Ministry dismissed, 27 October.
Beust sacked, 8 November.
Andrássy becomes Foreign Minister, 13 November.
Ministry of Adolph Auersperg formed, 26 November.

1872   Death of Archduchess Sophie, 28 May.

1873   New Criminal Law Code; direct elections for Reichsrat introduced.
Opening of the World Exhibition in Vienna, 1 May.
Crash at the Viennese stock exchange, 9 May.
Three Emperor's League formed, October.

1874   More anti-clerical 'May Laws', May.

1875   Establishment of *Verwaltungsgerichtshof.*
Tour of Dalmatia, April–May.
Bosnian Revolt, July.
Kálmán Tisza becomes Hungarian prime minister, 20 October.

1876   Serbia and Montenegro declare war on Turkey, 2 July.
Reichstadt Agreement (with Russia), 8 July.

1877   Russia intervenes in Balkan War, 12 April.

1878   Treaty of San Stefano (Russia and Turkey), 3 March.
Berlin Congress, June–July.
Occupation of Bosnia–Herzegovina, July–October.

1879   1st Hungarian Education Act.
Auersperg ministry replaced by Stremayr ministry, 15 February.
Reichsrat's ratification of Bosnian occupation, March.
Makart Procession in Vienna to celebrate silver wedding anniversary of Francis Joseph and Elisabeth, 27 April.
Reichsrat elections, June–July.
Formation of Taaffe ministry, 12 August.
Return of Czech deputies to Reichsrat, 16 September.
Dual Alliance of Austria–Hungary and Germany, 7 October.
Resignation of Andrássy, 8 October.
Defence Bill passed by Reichsrat, December.

1880	Stremayr Ordinances, April. Foundation of *Deutscher Schulverein*. Tour of Galicia and Bukovina, September.
1881	Beck becomes Chief of the General Staff. Packing of the *Herrenhaus* with conservatives, January. Assassination of Tsar Alexander II, 14 March. Three Emperors' Alliance, 18 June. Austro-Serbian Secret Treaty, 28 June. Kálnoky becomes Foreign Minister, 20 November. Ringtheater fire, 8 December.
1882	Linguistic division of Prague's Charles University. Electoral reform lowers tax qualification to 5 Gulden. Franchise reform of the Bohemian Diet's landed curia. Tiszaeszlar Affair in Hungary. Triple Alliance (with Germany and Italy), 20 May. Linz Programme, 1 November.
1883	Education Act (rolls back Liberal reforms). 2nd Hungarian Education Act (encourages 'Magyarisation'). Khuen-Héderváry becomes Ban of Croatia. Austro-Rumanian Secret Treaty, 30 October.
1884	Anti-Terror Law. Factory and Mines Act, May.
1884–5	Nordbahn Affair.
1885	Trades Law, March. Reichsrat elections, June–July.
1886	Anti-Socialist Law. Francis Joseph meets Katharina Schratt, 20 May.
1887	Accident Insurance Act. Formation of the Mediterranean Entente, March–May. Formation of the 'United Christians', 25 November.
1888	Sickness Insurance Act, February.
1889–90	Crisis in Hungary over the army budget.

1890   Bohemian Compromise (Old Czechs and German Liberals).

1889   Refounding of the Austrian Social Democrats, 1 January.
            Death of Rudolf at Mayerling, 29 January.
            Abdication of King Milan of Serbia, March.
            Tisza resigns as Hungarian prime minister, 13 March.
            Approval of change from 'k.k' to 'k.u.k.', 17 October.
            Imperial budget in surplus.

1891   Anti-Socialist Law lapses.
            3rd Hungarian Education Act.
            Franco-Russian rapprochement, July–August.

1892   Austria–Hungary adopts the Gold Standard.

1893   Martial law in Prague, September.
            Taaffe introduces Electoral Reform Bill, October.
            Windischgraetz replaces Taaffe as Cisleithanian prime minister, 11 November.

1894   Liberal Religion Act passed in Hungary, 10 December.

1895   Christian Social victory in Viennese elections, 1 April.
            Goluchowski replaces Kálnoky as Foreign Minister, 15 May.
            Resignation of Windischgraetz Ministry, 19 June.
            Badeni becomes Cisleithanian prime minister, 2 October.
            Lueger elected Mayor of Vienna, 29 October.
            Francis Joseph refuses to confirm Lueger as Mayor, 5 November.

1896   Hungarian Millenium.
            Hofburg reception of Lueger by Francis Joseph, 27 April.
            Electoral reform passed, May.
            Francis Ferdinand becomes official heir, 19 May.

1897   Reichsrat elections, March.
            Badeni Language Ordinances, 5 April.
            Francis Joseph confirms Lueger as Mayor, 16 April.
            Franco-Russian Alliance, August.
            German deputies' obstruction in Reichsrat to protest

language ordinances leads to street violence, November.
Attempt to pass the 'Lex Falkenhayn'.
Badeni sacked, 29 November.

1898 Thun becomes Cisleithanian prime minister, 7 March.
Assassination of Elisabeth, 10 September.

1899 Thun replaced by Clary-Aldringen as Cisleithanian prime minister, 23 September.
Repeal of the Badeni language ordinances, 17 October.

1900 Koerber becomes Cisleithanian prime minister, 18 January.
Francis Ferdinand's renunciation, 28 June.
Francis Ferdinand marries Sophie von Chotek, 1 July.

1901 Reichsrat elections, January.
Tour of Bohemia, June.

1902 New Compromise agreement reached, 31 December.

1903–4 Hungarian crisis.

1903 Francis Joseph refuses audience to Istro-Dalmatian deputation.
Assassination of Obrenovic dynasty in Serbia, 11 June.
Chlopy Order, 17 September.
Mürszteg Agreement with Russia, 3 October.
István Tisza becomes Hungarian prime minister, 3 November.

1904 Franco-British Entente, 8 April.
Resignation of Koerber Ministry, 31 December.

1905–6 Hungarian crisis.

1905 Moravian Compromise.
Gautsch becomes Cisleithanian prime minister, 1 January.
Elections in Hungary, January.
Fejérváry replaces Tisza as Hungarian prime minister, 18 June.
Francis Joseph approves Kristóffy's plan to expand the Hungarian franchise, September.
Francis Joseph decides for universal male suffrage in

Cisleithania, October.
Croats' Fiume Resolution, 2 October.
Serbs' Zara Resolution, 16 October.

1906–10   'Pig War' with Serbia.

1906   First Moroccan Crisis.
Last balance of payments surplus for Austria–Hungary.
Formation of the Croato-Serb Coalition in Croatia.
Clearing of the Hungarian Parliament,
19 February.
Wekerle's Coalition Ministry in Hungary, 8 April.
Hohenlohe replaces Gautsch as Cisleithanian prime minister, 30 April.
Max Beck replaces Hohenlohe as Cisleithanian prime minister, 2 June.
Elections in Hungary, May.
Aehrenthal becomes Foreign Minister, 24 October.
Conrad von Hötzendorf becomes Chief of the General Staff, 18 November.
Electoral Reform passes the Reichsrat, 20 December.

1907   Last budget surplus for Austria–Hungary.
Electoral Reform enacted in Cisleithania,
20 January.
First elections under new (universal male) franchise,
May.
New Compromise agreed, 8 October.

1908   Czech team at the Olympic Games.
Meeting of Neo-Slav Congress in Prague, July.
Buchlau meeting of Aehrenthal and Izvolsky,
15–16 September.
Announcement of Austrian annexation of
Bosnia–Herzegovina, 5 October.
Bienerth replaces Beck as Cisleithanian prime minister, November.

1909   Zagreb Treason Trial, followed by the Friedjung
Affair.
German offer of military assistance, 19 March.
Francis Joseph's last attendance at manoeuvres,
autumn.

1910	Breakaway Czech Social Democratic Party formed. Bukovinan Compromise. Dissolution of the Istrian Diet. Khuen-Héderváry replaces Wekerle as Hungarian prime minister, 17 January. Death of Lueger, 10 March. Elections in Hungary, May.
1911	Second Moroccan Crisis. Reichsrat elections, June. Stürgkh becomes Cisleithanian prime minister, 3 November. Italy annexes Libya, 5 November. Conrad's interview with Francis Joseph, 15 November. Conrad dismissed, 30 November.
1912	Military Bill passed by Reichsrat and Hungarian parliament. Suspension of Croatian constitution. Death of Aehrenthal; replaced by Berchtold as Foreign Minister, 17 February. Lukács replaces Khuen-Héderváry as Hungarian prime minister, April. 'Bloody Thursday' in Budapest, 23 May. Montenegro leads Balkan League against Turkey, 8 October – First Balkan War. Conrad recalled, 12 December. Tisza presents pre-sanctioned electoral reform bill to Hungarian parliament, 31 December.
1913	Tisza replaces Lukács as Hungarian prime minister, 10 June. Peace of London: end of First Balkan War, 30 May. Bulgaria starts Second Balkan War, 25 June. Bohemian Diet replaced by imperial commission, July. Treaty of Bucharest: end of Second Balkan War, 10 August. Ultimatum issued to Serbia, 17 October.
1914	Reichsrat prorogued, 16 March. Matscheko Memorandum drawn up, June. Assassination of Francis Ferdinand in Sarajevo, 28 June. Hoyos Mission to Berlin, 5 July.

Austro-Hungarian ultimatum issued to Serbia, 23 July.
War declared on Serbia, 28 July.
Russian general mobilization, 30 July.
Austro-Hungarian general mobilization. German
ultimatum to Russia and France, 31 July.
German declaration of war on Russia, 1 August.
German declaration of war on France; Italy declares
neutrality, 3 August.
British declaration of war on Germany, 4 August.
Austro-Hungarian declaration of war on Russia,
6 August.
British and French declaration of war on
Austria–Hungary, 12 August.
Failure of initial offensive against Serbia, late August.
'Battle of Lemberg' results in loss of Eastern
Galicia, 23 August–12 September.
Victory of Limanowa-Łapanów stops Russian advance,
3–12 December.
Failure of renewed offensive against Serbia, December.

1915   Berchtold resigns; replaced by Burian as Foreign
Minister, 11 January.
Italy signs Treaty of London with the Entente, 26 April.
Austro-German Gorlice-Tarnow offensive starts, May.
Italy declares war on Austria–Hungary, 23 May.
Reconquest of Lemberg, 22 June.
Austro-German offensive against Serbia starts,
6 October.
Failure of 'black-yellow' Rowno offensive,
26 August–14 October.
Serbia defeated, late November.

1916   Failure of the offensive against Italy, May–June.
Brusilov offensive starts, 4 June.
Burian replaced by Czernin as Foreign Minister,
22 July.
Rumania enters the war against Austria–Hungary,
2 August.
Germans take over command of Eastern front,
3 August.
Austro-German Joint High Command instituted,
6 September.
Salzburg agreement (of Austrian and German

deputies), September.
Assassination of Stürgkh by Friedrich Adler,
21 October.
Koerber becomes Cisleithanian prime minister,
28 October.
Death of Francis Joseph, 21 November.
Funeral of Francis Joseph, 30 November.

1917   Sixtus Mission, March–May.
        Resignation of Tisza, 15 June.

1918   Revelation of Sixtus mission, April.
        Spa meeting, 12 May.
        Charles' federalist Manifesto, 16 October.
        Ceasefire agreement with the Entente, 3 November.
        Charles renounces his imperial powers; end of the
        Habsburg Monarchy, 11 November.

MAPS

Key:
- Boundary of Habsburg Monarchy
- - - - Boundary of lost Italian territories
- Lands of the Crown of St Stephen
- Bosnia-Herzegovina (occupied 1878: annexed 1908)

Reichenberg

• Prague

BOHEMIA

MORAVIA

GERMANY

Br
(Br

R. Danube

Vienna

• Linz

Bregenz

Salzburg

UPPER AUSTRIA

LOWER AUSTRIA

Pressb
(Bratis

VORALBERG

Innsbruck

SALZBURG

STYRIA

Graz

CARINTHIA

Klagenfurt

TYROL

Laibach (Ljubljana)

Zagreb

LOMBARDY (lost 1859)

VENETIA (lost 1866)

CARNOLIA

CROATIA-SLAVO

• Milan

Venice

Trieste

ISTRIA

• Fiume

BOS

DALMATIA

ITALY

1. The Habsburg Monarchy, 1866–1914

256

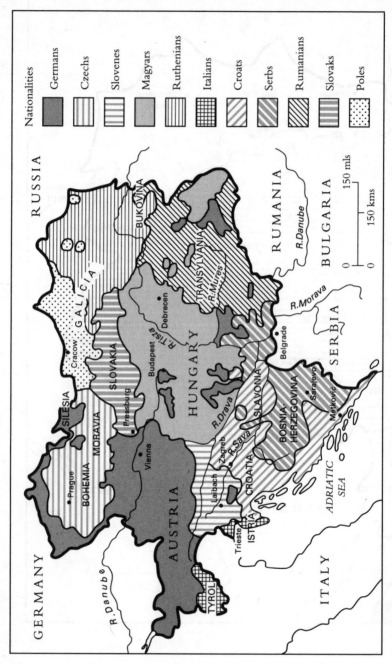

Nationalities

Germans
Czechs
Slovenes
Magyars
Ruthenians
Italians
Croats
Serbs
Rumanians
Slovaks
Poles

GERMANY

RUSSIA

R.Danube

TYROL

AUSTRIA

Vienna

SILESIA

BOHEMIA

Prague

MORAVIA

Pressburg

SLOVAKIA

GALICIA

Cracow

BUKOVINA

Debrecen

R.Tisza

HUNGARY

Budapest

TRANSYLVANIA

R.Mures

RUMANIA

R.Danube

Laibach

Zagreb

R.Drava

R.Sava

CROATIA

SLAVONIA

Belgrade

BOSNIA-
HERZEGOVINA

Sarajevo

Metkovic

R.Morava

SERBIA

BULGARIA

Trieste

ISTRIA

ADRIATIC
SEA

ITALY

150 mls

150 kms

0

0

2. Nationalities of the Habsburg Monarchy

258

Frontiers of independent
states

Frontiers between the
Dual Monarchy and
the occupied territories

Bulgarian-Ottoman
Frontier 1885-1908

Railways

Ottoman direct rule

3. The Balkans, 1878–1908

Frontiers in 1913

- - - - Frontiers in 1912

| 0 | | 150 mls |

| 0 | 150 kms |

4. The Balkans in 1914

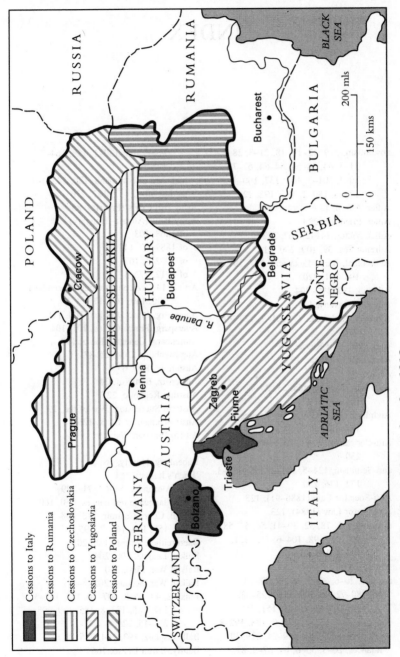

5. Breakup of the Habsburg Monarchy after 1918

Legend:
- Cessions to Italy
- Cessions to Rumania
- Cessions to Czechoslovakia
- Cessions to Yugoslavia
- Cessions to Poland

INDEX

INDEX

House of Lords, British, 174
Hoyos, Alexander Count, 215
Hübner, Count Alexander von, 72,
    109–10, 139, 145
Hungary, 2–4, 7–9, 13, 17, 20–2, 28, 32,
    35–40, 44–54, 58–65, 68, 71–3,
    80–7, 91–113, 118–19, 124–30,
    133–46, 150, 158–81, 185–204,
    215–27
Hungarian parties:
    Conservatives, 82
    Deákists, 124
    Independents, 126, 166
    Liberals, 111, 124–6, 167, 173
    Moderate Opposition, 126
    Party of Work, 173

Illyria, 41
Imperial Court, 31–2, 40, 44–5, 58, 104,
    126, 129, 133–6, 188
Independent Serb Party (see Croatian
    parties), 192
Infallibility, Papal Declaration of, 102
Innsbruck, 48
Ireland, 38, 174
'Iron Ring', 118, 121–6, 137, 183–4
irredentism, 109, 132–3, 137, 159, 178,
    190, 193, 201, 203
Ischl Clause, 166
Ischl, Bad, 214, 216
Istria, 132, 191, 199
Italians, 36, 39–40, 68, 88, 133, 146,
    177–8, 190
Italy, 2, 17–20, 25, 28, 32, 35–6, 39–40,
    42–8, 52–4, 60, 65, 68–70, 84–5,
    88, 92, 101, 107, 130–2, 146, 162,
    174, 197–200, 204, 214, 218,
    220–2
Izvolsky, Alexander, 196

Jagellon dynasty, 17
Jansenism, 21
Jászi, Oskar, 4, 6, 169, 177, 182, 185,
    186
Jellačić, Josip, 48, 62
Jesuits, 20
Jews, 4, 18, 21, 56, 64, 98–9, 102, 108,
    122, 124–5, 141–2, 162, 172,
    175–6, 223, 230
John, Archduke (Reichsverweser), 47

John, Archduke (Ott), 138
John, General Baron Franz, 103
Joint High Command (Austro-German),
    222
Joint Ministries, 95–7
Joint Ministry of Finance, 192
Joseph II, 21–2, 25–6, 34–5, 38, 40, 49,
    57, 59, 229
Josephism, 26, 35, 55–8

Kafka's Prague, 175
Kafka, Franz, 3, 175, 181
Kaizl, Josef, 166
Kállay, Benjamin, 139, 144
Kálnoky, Count Gustav, 119, 129–32,
    145–7
Kann, Robert A., 5–6, 52, 216
Karageorgević dynasty, 193
Kaunitz, Prince Wenzel, 20, 113
Kempen, Johann, von, 62, 71
Khuen-Héderváry, Count Károly, 124,
    144, 167, 172–3
Kjellén, Rudolf, 38
Koerber, Ernest von, 160–7, 183, 223
Kolowrat, Franz Anton Count, 34–5
Königgrätz (Sadowa), Battle of, 89–91
Konopischt, 204
Kossuth, Ferenc, 168
Kossuth, Louis, 5, 46–7, 61, 160
Kramář, Karel, 171, 177, 223
Kraus, Karl, 174
Kremsier (Kroměříž), 49–51, 55, 187
Kremsier constitution, 6, 51–2
Kremsier parliament, 49–51, 55
Kristóffy, Joseph, 168
Krobatin, Alexander von, 218
Kübeck, Karl von, 55–7, 82
Kuhnenfeld, General Baron Franz Kuhn
    von, 103
Kulturkampf, 57, 102

Landwehr, 97
Latin, 21, 40
League of Princes (1785), 23
legal system, 60, 102–3, 176, 197
legitimacy, principle of, 24–8, 37, 43,
    49–50, 58–9, 64, 68, 71–3
Leitha River, 95, 165
Lemberg (Lwow), 121, 220
Lemberg, (1914) Battle of, 220

267